Beautiful Oblivion

D1238411

ADDISON MOORE

Edited by: Sarah Freese
Cover Design and Photograph by: Regina Wamba of
www.MaeIDesign.com
Interior design and formatting by: Gaffey Media

Books by Addison Moore:

New Adult Romance

Someone to Love (Someone to Love 1)
Someone Like You (Someone to Love 2)
Someone For Me (Someone to Love 3)
3:AM Kisses (3:AM Kisses 1)
Winter Kisses (3:AM Kisses 2)
Sugar Kisses (3:AM Kisses 3)
Whiskey Kisses (3:AM Kisses 4)
Rock Candy Kisses (3:AM Kisses 5, 2014)
Beautiful Oblivion
Beautiful Illusions (Beautiful Oblivion 2, 2014)
The Solitude of Passion
Burning Through Gravity
Perfect Love (A Celestra Novella)
Celestra Forever After

Young Adult Romance

Ethereal (Celestra Series Book 1)
Tremble (Celestra Series Book 2)
Burn (Celestra Series Book 3)
Wicked (Celestra Series Book 4)
Vex (Celestra Series Book 5)
Expel (Celestra Series Book 6)
Toxic Part One (Celestra Series Book 7)
Toxic Part Two (Celestra Series Book 7.5)
Elysian (Celestra Series Book 8)

Ephemeral (The Countenance Trilogy 1)
Evanescent (The Countenance Trilogy 2)
Entropy (The Countenance Trilogy 3)
Ethereal Knights (Celestra Knights)

Prologue

My mother once wrote me a poem. It spanned many letters, some of which I've yet to receive. She wrote them on her deathbed, and I get one delivered each year on my birthday.

Sometimes, in the early morning hours, I think the world is still the same, and I'll find her in the room down the hall, cuddled in my father's arms. Then the callous sun magnifies the day, it startles my senses enough to let me know it was just a waking dream—that my mother is dead, and the cruel day has dawned without her.

When I was younger, hardly thirteen, I fell in love with an older boy with the biggest blue eyes—the exact shade of the night sky. Ace Waterman was a god that I venerated for as long as I can remember. His sister, Neva, and I would sneak into his bedroom, she out of spite and me out of sheer idol worship. An inexplicable joy speared through me as I bumped my fingers over his things, his books, his trophies, his glassy marbles stored neat in a jar.

"Hey, kid, whatcha doing?" His dimples invert, and my stomach sinks clear to my knees as if the rollercoaster of life just took a dip. Neva is in the bathroom, so here I am, caught red-handed, alone.

"They're so pretty." I run my fingers over the jar of marbles.

"So are you." He rumples my hair before dropping his book bag. A pinch of grief crosses his face as he reverts his attention back to me. "I'm really sorry about your mom, Reese." A moment thumps by with our eyes locked, immovable as stone as if they were having their own private conversation. Then he does the unthinkable. Ace pulls me in and wraps his arms around me tight, holding me like that a little longer than I could have hoped for.

It was in that moment I knew I would always want Ace Waterman to hold me—to never let me go.

People—relationships—scatter like birds, leaving you with dusty memories, empty beds, bones in a casket. We don't get to choose who stays and goes on the planet. We can't control who stays in our life and under what conditions. Seasons come and go—time presses on. It was this way the summer I was twenty, when I put my heart on a platter to see if the only boy I've ever loved would take it—but, first, it seemed logical, and perhaps a bit more safe, to offer up my body.

"What's the blanket for?" I step into Ace, my eyes never wavering from his immaculate features, his strong arms that might as well be hewn from granite.

"I thought you might get cold." He shrugs off his efforts like they were no big deal when we both know they were—candles, flowers, and bedding aren't things typical guys would remember to bring along on a date. Not that what we're doing is officially dating. Hell, I wish I knew exactly what we were doing.

I run my fingers through his hair in one clean sweep and take in how stunningly gorgeous he is. His chiseled face, those high cut cheeks, the dimples that don't know when to quit, and his demanding eyes that lay over me like hungry blue flames.

"Why would I get cold, Ace?" I bat my lashes into him, hoping he comes up with the right answer.

"Because tonight you're going to take off all your clothes."

Right answer indeed.

1

Leafless in Loveless

Reese

"Heads, we play Monopoly. Tails, we skinny dip." Ace gives a dirty grin that I wish I could bury the most intimate part of me in. He's been grazing over my body all night with those navy eyes, the exact shade of the deepest end of the ocean, and my insides have long since melted to cinder.

Skinny dip? I try to hide the smile threatening to bloom on my face.

I'm addicted to Ace. No really, I am. In fact I think they should have rehab and group therapy for girls like me who've spent far too long worshiping from afar. Of course, then I'd be forced to confess the constant pornographic reel I have streaming 24-7 about his rock hard body and that dimpled grin that steals a piece of my soul each time it ignites.

"I'm in," I say in spite of the fact I shouldn't be anywhere near Ace Waterman, let alone perched on a boulder overlooking the lake. His brand of handsome is dangerous for a girl like me who's just aching to be devoured.

The lights across the way at my father's house catch my attention. Kennedy, my stepsister, is hosting a let's-get-the-hell-wasted 'welcome to summer party,' and it seems like all of Yeats University showed up to get boozed and used. Warren is there—and he's the exact reason I'm not. It's actually an eighties theme party which would explain the gallon of Aqua Net holding my hair in a skyscraper position and my day-glow blue eye shadow. But I'm not too concerned about embarrassing myself in front of Ace. We've known each other forever, growing up on the lake you know just about everybody through all of their ages and stages no matter how embarrassing they might be.

Ace flips the quarter in the air. We watch as it rises to the sky and flirts with the stars pressed against the velvet expanse. It slams back to the boulder we're sitting on and rolls off unceremoniously, falling into a crevice. In the distance, the water glistens, black as an oil slick, while whispering its secrets into the night. I can feel my own secrets bubbling to my lips like a brook ready and willing to over flow. A part of me wants to blurt out my feelings for him, drop them at his feet like a shattered vase, and watch as he tries to pick up the pieces.

"Tails." Ace pushes out a killer grin before returning to his serious demeanor. He's got that come-hither look, those I'm-going-to-teach-you-a-lesson dark, thick brows that drive me insane, and his eyes are a shade that can only be described as an orgasm in blue. Ace has been extra playful all night. The banter between us is a little more sexual than I ever remember—sizzling and electric. Ace has my juices flowing in all the right places.

"Tails never fails." I can hardly believe the words as they come from my mouth, they float like a dream into the sky, all the way up to heaven, to my mother. I wonder how she would feel if she knew I was contemplating taking off all my clothes and jumping in the lake with a boy she dubbed the Lord of the Ladies.

I always think of my mother in the summer for two reasons: One, she died under a Cheshire cat moon much like this, and two, my father gifts me a letter from her each July on my birthday. She penned those notes during her final days on this spinning blue rock, and I treasure each one, even though I've just received five so far.

Ace cuts a glance across the lake at the flickering lights of the party.

"Reese." His lids hood over, and if I didn't know better, I'd think he were bedroom eyeing me. "You really want to do this?" He runs his tongue over his full lips, and I let out a breath at the masterpiece that Ace Waterman has become—the one he's always been. "You think Warren will mind?" He pulls his cheek back as if he were teasing, and I'm more than surprised he went there.

I give a little laugh. "Get real, you couldn't care less if Warren McCarthy told you to stay the hell away from me or he'd rip your balls off. I'm pretty sure you're not too worried what he might think of our midnight endeavors."

A smile cinches up his cheek, and his dimple digs in deep. "You would be wrong." He breaks out into a full-blown grin, and my stomach bottoms out. "I do care what he thinks because pissing him off is my new favorite hobby. He cut me off on the lake this morning. Only assholes do that."

Ace and Warren have rowed competitively ever since we were kids running rampant along the powder-white shores of Loveless. I miss those days when Ace was just like everybody else because we didn't hold everything to the light of the almighty dollar, especially not people.

"Well then"—I lean into him, inching my lips toward his—"Warren definitely fits the description."

"So, you dating him?" he asks, lower than a whisper. His shoulder bumps into mine, playfully, as if this were all a game. But, deep down, I wish he cared.

"He follows me wherever I go." I take the opportunity to rest my head over his rock hard chest. My body goes rigid a moment because, holy hell, I'm touching Ace in ways that I've never touched him before. This is huge. But I figure if I want to round out the bases with him, we'll have to start somewhere, and a face plant into the wall of concrete that is his chest is definitely a great place to do just that. "I guess we're sort of ambush dating." Stupid Warren. I hate that he's even a topic of conversation. Then again, maybe Ace just wants to make sure that my innocent lady parts and me are single and ready to mingle with his far more experienced extra-curricular bits and pieces. Not that I'm accusing him of housing something bitty in his boxers, far from it. I've glanced down at his Levis a time or two, and it's apparent he wields a nightstick. Nevertheless, Ace is a gentleman at heart, unlike Warren who's probably using beer pong as an excuse to hit on Kennedy's unsuspecting sorority sisters.

I curl into Ace as if I were snuggling up for the night, and I wish to God I were. Ace feels a thousand times better than I could have ever imagined. His soft breath tangles in my hair, enlivening my senses. His cologne holds a sweet layer that you need to be this close to truly appreciate. And, if I get my way, I'll be even closer before the night is through. If there were a Worshiping From Afar Anonymous I'm pretty sure every one of its stalker-like members would be cheering me on right now. Not every obsession leads to a life of crime on the streets. In fact, I'm sort of hoping for a life of *time* under the *sheets*.

The only crime around here is the fact Ace and I haven't explored a carnal connection as of yet. And that's exactly what I'm hoping this summer will be about, the summer of sexual rectification.

"Ambush dating." He rumbles beneath me with a silent laugh. "So are you blue-balling him?"

"Is that code for have we slept together?" I bite over a smile because the conversation just took a turn for the coital, and me and all of my Ace-worshiping girl parts completely approve. "If so, the answer is *no*." A tiny surge of hope spirals through me because if he cares about whether or not I've slept with Warren, it might mean something. "But I came close at Kristen Woodley's party last spring," it speeds out of me like some midnight confessional. "She was serving foot long hotdogs, and I had a sudden craving, but I chickened out last minute—left him naked in the bedroom and ran like hell all the way back to my dorm." Maybe this is a good time to mention the fact I have never seen nor imagined Warren's 'foot long,' in fact, I'm betting there are an entire medley of adjectives to describe his push pop, and *foot long* isn't one of them.

"Good deal." Ace holds up a hand, so I high five him. A spark ignites between us as soon as our skin connects, but we choose to ignore it—easy as ignoring a bonfire in a fireworks factory.

"How about we do some ambush swimming?" Ace peels off his T-shirt, nice and slow, and I watch as the moon illuminates him like a marble statue, nothing but skin over steel. His muscles ripple over his abs like a silent granite sea. His chest looks smooth like sheet rock, and I suddenly have the urge to map out the landscape of his body with my tongue—a task I could easily labor over for weeks. If Ace were willing to let me lap him up like a kitten with a bowl of cream, I wouldn't rush the effort. Ace is a dessert that's meant to be savored. If given the opportunity to leech over his abs with my lips, I'd languish for years, drag out the endeavor until the authorities stepped in, I'm sure my father would arrange for that. I can practically hear the theme music to *Cops* playing on a loop. Crap. For sure if Ace and I were together, I'd make it a point to keep my father in the dark. The last thing I'd want is him ruining my moment with the god of the G-spot. My dad can have Warren and his whole damn family. I just want *one* person, and that person just so happens to be off my father's short-list of suitors for his only biological daughter. Not to mention the fact Ace has probably never even seen the inside of the Loveless Country Club—a sin of the highest order when it comes to cold, hard cash contenders for my father's approval. Not that my father is all about money, he's just all about Warren McCarthy.

Ace jumps to his feet and starts tugging down his shorts, exposing a glowing line of skin highlighted low around his waist. "You'd better spin around, or you're about to see another foot long."

"A foot long, huh? Is that wishful thinking on your part? Are you sure it's not more of a centimeterpeter?" I tease as I turn toward the granite cliff side in the distance.

"You wish. We're talking yardstick, baby."

A splash of water rips through the air, followed by a short-lived howl.

"Get in, girl. It feels like a bath," he shouts from the lake below.

"I seriously doubt that." I turn back around and spot his slicked hair reflecting the moonlight like a mirror.

The night air blisters over my skin like an oven. I'm dying to fall into a body of water, but I'm iffy on the whole bearing more than my soul part of the equation. Ace has seen the body of a thousand girls, and not one pair of human eyes has laid eyes on mine.

A part of my mother's last letter comes back to me, *find the ecstasy where you can—catch it by the tail. It's in those moments you really live. All those other gaps in time are just filler until the next bout of delirium. You could as easily find ecstasy in the silence as you could in a scream, it could be locked in a beautiful flower, the scent of a fragrant spring morning. It could be in a kiss from a beautiful boy. All of those sweet moments make one hell of an adventure. And if life doesn't offer you an adventure—make one happen.*

I love that letter, but it's always the beautiful boy part that weirds me out a little. I used to cringe at the idea of my mother talking to me about sex at all, and, now, even with her gone, and with me just finishing my freshman year at Yeats, it still feels rigidly uncomfortable. And what boy is beautiful? I glance down at the lake and catch a glimpse of the only boy I have ever loved. His teeth illuminate as if his mouth were backlit with a flashlight, and the fire from that thousand watt grin sears over me like a nuclear heat wave.

Ace is clearly beautiful.

"You coming in?" he calls out. His ebony hair reflects in hues of blue as his face gets lost in the shadows. His chest is heavily glossed, annunciating his perfect-cut abs.

I cinch a smile in my cheek and wonder how the hell I got so lucky tonight.

"Damn straight, I'm coming in."

I race down to the waterline and duck behind the shadowy pines, plucking and pulling at my clothes until I'm as naked as the day I was born. My feet grind into the damp soil as I take in the scent of moist earth and the viral perfume of the evergreens. This is a night I want to remember in detail. I want to soak it into each of my senses and make them regurgitate it back to me with a clarity far beyond any memory, so I can live it again and again—Ace and me naked in that black, inky lake.

"Turn around," I command as I make my way into the open. Once I spot the back of his hair, I tiptoe my way in and seize, confirming the fact this was a piss-poor idea. If my feet are telling the truth, the lake has decided to do its best impression of an Arctic preserve, and we've picked a lousy time to reenact the bathing rituals from the Garden of Eden. "Oh God, oh God, oh God!" I whimper as I wade my way over to him.

"Just dive in. It's worse if you take it slow. Once it hits your middle, you're just torturing yourself."

"Says the boy who swore it's warm as a bath." I give a little scream as a wave skirts my ribcage.

"It's warm where I'm standing."

"That's because you probably relieved yourself once you got there."

"No one knows me like you." Ace glides backward, still facing the other direction. I give a private smile admiring his smooth skin, his shoulders as wide as a door. He starts to turn, and I splash a wall of water at him.

"Don't even think about it." A wave slaps me just beneath my shoulders, and I take in a sharp breath.

"Here I come, five, four, three"—he swoops in closer—"two, one."

I force myself to dip under until the water floats up to my neck, and my body gives a mean shiver, but then a burst of heat rinses over me, and I can breathe again.

"Hey"—I take a few steps out until my feet no longer touch the bottom—"it *is* kind of warm."

"That's because I had to take a mean piss." His dark brows rise as he swoops in closer. "Don't worry, sweetie"—he blinks a smile—"I only had your best interests at heart."

"You bastard." I flick my fingers, squirting him in the face. Ace shakes his head like a wet dog, peppering me with the residue.

"*Lying* bastard would be more accurate. I promise, Reese, I can find far more creative ways to keep you warm, and very few of them involve bodily fluids." Ace hoods his lids again. His dimples depress as he comes in ever so close. "I think this is the part where we hug it out—or maybe we should make out for the hell of it and call it a night." A smile tugs on his lips, and it only makes him look that much more achingly beautiful. Ace is a god among men, and he doesn't even know it.

I pinch my nose and dip under the waterline, relieving my hair of the gravity-defying pose I molded it into earlier.

"Big hair is officially out," I say, blinking into him.

"I think you just changed the topic."

"I didn't think you'd notice." I move in closer until his chest is within reach, and I wonder if he can see my body from this vantage point—if he wants to.

"I noticed a lot about you tonight." He swallows hard, taking in my features as if it's the first time he's seeing me.

"Like?" I push in an inch, anxious to steal a glance below the water and see his measuring rod for myself.

Ace winces.

We both know we're dancing a little too close to the flames, and I like it, I'm hoping he likes it too. Ace and I have been friends from the womb, never mind the fact I've been secretly crushing on him just as long, but we've never stepped outside the bounds of friendship. I hung out with a different crowd in high school, then went straight to Yeats while Ace has spent the last three years at the local junior college.

"Like the fact you're the only girl I know who can pull off big hair." His dimples reappear, mocking me with their superpowers. "Your neon leggings were pretty hot, too. I think you should bow to the eighties style gods and revamp your wardrobe."

"Please"—I hedge in ever so close—"I looked like an escapee from a John Hughes movie."

"A damn cute one."

My heart thumps just once when he says it.

"You think I'm cute?" I ask, moving in another few inches. It's a well-known fact Ace thinks of me more as a little sister than a contender for his endless supply of prophylactics. I should know about the never-ending supply, I've seen the testaments to anti-procreation he stashes openly in his bedroom. His sister Neva and I used to be friends until she ditched me for a group of stoner girls. Then, one day, out of the blue, she announced she's always hated me, and we haven't said two words since. Now she just gives me the finger in lieu of hello.

"Yeah, I think you're cute." He reaches over and messes up my hair, so I slip under again and come up slicked to perfection as only the lake can provide.

I spit a perfect stream of water into his face. "Yeah?" I pant out of breath. "Well, I think you're *beautiful*."

"What?" His head ticks back a notch. He's either genuinely amused or more-than-slightly pissed. Gone is the playful banter as his features soften, affording him a boyishness I've never seen in him before.

"You heard me. I think you're beautiful." A moment of silence whistles by with the breeze. "And, I think maybe we *should* make out for the hell of it." My heart races at the prospect of his mouth covering mine—his probing tongue having free roam inside me for hours. I'd give every pint of blood in my body to make this happen. Being dead by morning doesn't frighten me near as much as living a life in which I've never kissed Ace. I've wanted it, fantasized about it for years.

"Yeah, right." He squeezes his eyes tight for a moment as if trying to rouse himself from a dream. "You're all hopped up on moonlight and night magic and whatever else girls fill their heads with after midnight." He tips his chin up as he examines me. Water beads down his face. His stubble dusts over his cheeks like a shadow, and my gut cinches just taking him in like this.

The sweet scent of night jasmine perfumes the air and makes me heady for a special kiss that only Ace Waterman can masterfully deliver.

"I'm serious." I lean forward until I feel the warmth emanating from his chest. Every inch of me trembles with a new level of fear I didn't know existed. Who knew that deep down inside, Ace is the very thing I'm terrified of. "I want to have a crazy summer"—I reach out and touch my fingers over his glossy hair, soft and slick—"and the last person to give it to me is going to be Warren McCarthy. If I have to hang out with him and the banana republicans until I head back to Yeats, I'm going to fling myself off Wilson Bridge." I stick my finger down my throat and mock gag at the idea.

Ace ticks his head back a notch and looks at me with the slight air of reproach. Now that I think of it, I'm pretty sure mock gagging only made me look even more like a child in his eyes. The next thing you know, I'll be leading him into a sparkling conversation about late-night cartoons—maybe challenging him to a game of Candy Land to round out the evening. Just fuck. Way to kill a potential spit swap. I would have paid in solid gold Krugerrands to have his lips pressed against mine for even a brief moment in time.

"I see many flaws with your plan of action." He sinks until the water is up to his chin. Ace looks up at me as the stars reflect in his eyes, and I marvel at this small miracle. "Not only is Wilson a *covered* bridge, but the water in the stream is a shallow four feet." His lips twitch. "Blame it on the lousy rainfall we had last year."

Ace floats back a few inches, but the gap he's building may as well have an entire continent between us. A part of me wonders if he finds me too repulsive for that ever-elusive kiss. I might be leaning toward the dramatic, but I'm probably not too far off base. Rumor has it he's slept his way through the entire state of Connecticut, and, yet, I've never garnered so much as a second look from him. Not that I've put out any signals that I was interested before, at least not like I am now. I think he's right, I'm drunk off night magic, and it has me fearlessly asking for the very thing I've always wanted—Ace himself.

"And what about that kiss?" It comes from me barely audible, broken—because if he doesn't deliver I might raise the water levels of this lake with tears.

"Reese," he presses my name out in a broken whisper. "You're going to regret it in the morning. You'll probably realize Warren is the exact person you're going to marry one day, and you'll hate me for taking advantage of you like this."

"I'm not marrying Warren." I huff an incredulous breath. "God—you sound just like my dad." Warren's father and Dad are golf buddies who have not so secretly been working out the finer details of our prenuptials while they walk the green all day. They own a law firm together, Westfield and McCarthy. They've been fostering a budding bromance ever since law school, and now they're ready to take the next logical step in their relationship by marrying their children off to one another. The scary thing is, Warren would probably go along with it because a wife is just another thing you acquire on your way to prison for orchestrating a Ponzi scheme. But I'm not going along with this prearranged marriage of inconvenience. Not now, not ever.

A devilish grin takes over as I swim over to him and boldly wrap my arms around his neck.

My bare chest brushes over his, and I die a little as an electrical current travels from his skin to mine. A heated breath gets locked in my throat as I try to stave off a groan. My heart thumps in my ears, my vocal cords go into lockdown.

Dear God. I'm holding Ace Waterman in the nude—his naked everything just inches away from mine, while the lower half of my body roars out an invitation for him to come inside.

"Whoa." His chest rattles a dull laugh, but his eyes grow serious, his dimples wink in and out like a warning. "You sure you want to do this?" His warm breath rakes over my cheeks as his chest pumps with an adrenaline all its own.

Ace and I are straddling the platonic line that's carefully kept us on the opposite side of the sexual divide, and tonight, our feet, every square inch of our bare flesh, is ready to cross it.

Ace doesn't move, which begs the question maybe he wants this, too. Maybe he's *not* repulsed by the sight of me. Maybe he does think of me as something more than his sister's friend—a girlfriend, someone to wrinkle the sheets with. And, at the moment, I'm feeling every bit the contender.

"Hell, yes, I want to do this," it comes from me breathy. "The only thing I'll regret in the morning is if I don't."

A laugh rumbles deep in his chest, but he doesn't let it cross his vocal cords. "Well, if you feel that strongly," he says it low, seductive. His dimples quiver with the trace of a smile. Ace pulls me in by the small of my back and caresses my curves as his hands glide up my body, warming me, electrifying me to heaven and back in the process. "But, for the record, it's going to be *me* kissing *you*." He presses out a slow-spreading smile before his expression melts to something all too serious. "Get ready, Reese, because I'm about to blow every kiss you've ever shared with that banana republican right out of the fucking water."

My insides pinch with heat. Every ounce of my being shakes because Ace Waterman just threatened me with an expletive in the most erotic way. Hot damn. His mouth is coming for mine, and now all of my dreams, my fantasies, are about to come to fruition.

Ace pulls me in gently by the cheeks and lands his mouth over mine. His lips brush over me, softer than air, far softer than I would have ever pegged them to be. My legs circle around his as I give an involuntary moan. He secures me by the back of the neck and glides his tongue over mine, sending a quiver between my thighs until it creates its own beautiful spasm. The entire night sky breaks out in a hallelujah choir because Ace Waterman is loving me with his mouth in ways that I had truthfully never expected.

I cinch my legs up around his waist, tight as a coil, landing the most intimate part of me against his heated skin. Here I am, spread wide and vulnerable as a series of climactic seizures rocket off in my sweet spot, straight up to my belly. I'm not sure this is the response Ace wanted—me dry humping him, having a string of orgasms right off his body while his mouth explodes in mine like a series of shooting stars.

I clamp my arms over him like an anchor, securing me right where I was destined to be as I wash myself in moonbeams, making magic in the night with the only boy I've ever really cared about.

Ace gives a groan that thunders from his chest, primal and urgent. His kisses intensify and methodically blow each vanilla exchange I've ever shared with Warren right out of the fucking water just like he predicted.

I wonder if my mother would be disappointed to know that I'm kissing a boy in the lake after midnight with his hard-on rising to greet my bare bottom. But I'm merely doing exactly as she requested. This is the summer I'm going to chase my ecstasy—create my own adventure. And I'm starting right here under a firefly moon, kissing a beautiful boy.

Ace

For the better part of my life I've had a hard-on for Reese Westfield, but never in my wildest wet dreams did it ever play out like this with her feasting on my tongue while my erection does its best to impale her.

Her soft skin presses hard against mine, the weight of her tits against my chest is about all I can take, not to mention the fact her hips are tucked against my stomach with her hot slick buried in my abs. It takes everything in me not to perseverate on that one sensation because if I do I'll lose it.

"Nice." I pull back an inch and inspect her in this dismal light, the cool of the lake rinsing over our shoulders every now and again. That kiss was a hell of a lot better than *nice,* but I'm not ready to verbalize how whipped I am for her just yet. Not that my dick is doing anything to hide the way it feels.

First, I didn't think for a minute she'd shed the stitches and hop into the lake with me. And, second, that kiss was enough to fuel every wet dream I'll ever have until I'm nothing but a bag of bones, one step away from a casket, and, at that, I'll probably die with a hard-on from the memory of it.

"It *was* nice." She gives an impish grin. "We should do this more often." She presses in another kiss, and this time she lingers, no tongue. "Like every single night."

"You didn't hit your head earlier, did you?" I'm only half-teasing. Reese and I go way back, and I have no memory of her ever coming on to me. I mean, sure, we've stolen glances, I've caught her looking in places that would happily salute her efforts for even acknowledging their existence but nothing like this, tonight blows doors off stolen glances.

"Nope. Didn't hit it." She licks her lips as if she's hungry for more. "Who are you again?"

"Very funny." I run my hands along the underbelly of her thighs, and she cinches herself around my waist. Her tits are pressed over my chest so tight, I'm about to come without much more effort on her part. "You know, the sun is going to come up, and you might want to reprise the amnesia." I swallow hard. "And, if you do, I promise I won't hold it against you." It feels like an odd thing to say since I'm holding just about everything else against her. "I won't kiss and tell if you won't." I give a playful wink. Really, I just wanted to give her the out. A long time ago my father suggested I point my boner the hell away from Reese Westfield. He said that people that came from money feel like they're better than the rest of us— that mixing with someone like Reese would never work out in the end. Of course that was days after Reese's father refused to bail him out on a DUI. That sort of killed their friendship, and it was right about the time Neva and Reese axed theirs. Although I doubt one had anything to do with the other. I'm still not sure what the fallout was there, never could get my sister to open up about it.

"There's not a chance in hell I'll forget this." Reese runs her tongue over her lips, glossing them a deep shade of crimson even in this dull light. "You probably will." She splashes water in my face, and I hold back from retaliating like I normally would. "I bet I'm second rate compared to the girls you've let defile you with their body parts." Her face pinches with grief a moment before that playful smile bounces back to her lips.

She couldn't be further from the truth. Reese detonated in my mouth like a powder keg, twisting my guts like a pretzel in every good way.

"There's nothing second rate about you." I try to sink her hips off me in an effort to defuse the real bomb ticking away, the one between my legs. "I think we'd better get you home. Kennedy is going to have every P.I. in Connecticut on the hunt for you in just a few minutes."

"Let them look." She tilts into me, stroking her fingers through the back of my hair. "I'm right where I want to be."

A dull smile rides on my lips. "I'd better get some clothes on you, and then I probably should throw myself in a cold shower." I leave out the fact I'll be alleviating the tension brewing in my balls while I'm in there, and it wouldn't be the first time she's put me in that position.

"Throw me in there with you." Her cheeks darken, and I'm ready to call her bluff.

"There's nothing we can do in there that we can't do right here."

The whites of her eyes expand like stars as she fumbles for words.

"Knew it." My chest rumbles over hers with a quiet laugh. "I call bullshit." I sink out of her grasp and start swimming toward shore.

"Hey, *wait*." She glides up alongside me and latches onto my arm. "I'm not playing games." She glances down at the water and takes a measured breath. "I thought maybe, you know, we could have some fun."

"Yeah, well, I'll beat you at basketball in the morning. I'll make sure you have lots of fun trying to steal the ball from me."

She wrinkles her nose, and I do my best to hide a smile. Reese is cuter than hell when she's pissed.

"Do you think I'm pretty?" She bats those amazing lashes at me, but there's a hint of sadness layered just beneath the surface.

"What?" Reese is a masterpiece in and out of her blue jeans, and if she doesn't know it, she's got some serious self-esteem issues. "I think you're a beautiful goddess." There. That should cure her.

Her mouth curves with a slow smile. She seals her hips to mine once again, and my gut flinches because it's torture having her so close and not being able to touch her the way I want, the ways I've meditated over for so many years.

"I want you to be my first, Ace." The smile melts off her face as her lips come in close again. "I want to know the things you know, do the things you do—*with* you."

"Reese," I let it out in a heated whisper. "You need to do those things with someone who means something to you—someone special. Don't waste your time with a guy like me." I came within an inch of calling myself a loser which I don't believe for a second, but, in a way, I think my dad has been right all along, Reese doesn't belong with someone like me.

"*You* mean something to me." She takes a hiccupping breath as if she's about to cry. "I think you're someone special, Ace."

"I think we're great friends"—I force a weak smile—"who just shared something amazing. But you need something bigger like love. You need flowers and candles—everything that comes with it."

Her eyes narrow over mine, and, for a second, I think she might clock me.

"Yeah, well, I've already made up my mind that I'm going to have a wild time this summer." She pushes off my thighs until she's floating on her back. Her tits roll back just under her neck, solid and round as if someone shoved oranges under her skin, and suddenly I'm very fucking hungry for oranges. She glides backward, fanning her arms around her like an angel. "I'm so tired of my boring life," she whispers the words to the sky, and suddenly I feel like an intruder. "I'm ready to move onto the next. Dive into the ecstasy of it all and see what the rest of the world keeps talking about."

I swim up beside her and pull her in until her body is upright and pressed against mine once again. Reese gives a pouting smile and takes my breath away with her beauty.

"Promise me you won't have a wild summer." I touch my forehead to hers for a second. "Just because I'm not going to have you, doesn't mean I want some other asshole to cash in on your brain malfunction."

"You've had a wild summer every year since you were sixteen." A laugh bubbles from her throat, and her skin vibrates in tune.

"I'm a guy—wild summer's are practically a rite of passage." All of the blood in my body rushes to my dick, and I might pass out and drown if I don't do something about it soon.

"Trust me, this is far from a brain malfunction. This is happening."

She lifts her knees to my hips, and I gently push them back down.

"Reese"—I close my eyes a moment—"what made you decide to have a wild summer? Hell, *when* did you decide?"

"*You* and about fifteen minutes ago." A sly smile plays on her lips. Hot damn. Reese Westfield is hotter than a wildfire and is threatening to get out of control like one, too. Nope, I'm not going to let that happen. I think what we need here is a controlled burn under the watchful supervision of someone who cares—someone like me.

"Okay." I take a quick breath. "I'm in."

"You're in?" She marvels. Her mouth parts as if she were ready and willing to start tonight.

"Yes." I shake my head, disbelieving. "I'll be your wild summer—your fling, whatever you want to call it." Now it's my face filling with heat.

"My summer fling," she says it slow like a very sad poem. "Thank you, Ace." Her eyes sweep over mine as her hand smooths over my features.

Reese falls into me, landing her hot mouth over mine. I run my hands along her thighs, and it takes all my strength not to venture a little further north, but I hold out. We stay in the lake with our bodies twisted around one another like rope, our lips fused together as we try to put out the inferno going off in one another's mouths.

Reese has already turned this into the best season on record.

I have a feeling I just dove into the best damn summer of my life.

2

The Summer of Ecstasy

Reese

The following day, in the late afternoon, I rouse to an empty, yet, appropriately disheveled house. I wade my way downstairs through a sea of red Solo cups. I'm not too surprised, considering half my stepsister's sorority showed up last night, including their matchups, Kappa Pi, which I've nicknamed get-the-clapa-pie—and appropriately so since Kennedy's "sisters" have been known to frequent the school clinic in order to disinfect themselves of crabs.

I catch my reflection in the mirror with my hair wound up like a bird's nest and make a face. My eyes are bloodshot from tossing and turning. I was lost in a violent sea of kisses all night long, and it was Ace delivering them, both in and out of my dreams.

"Well, look who's up?" Kennedy takes a careful sip of her coffee. She has the same long, dark hair as me, same light grey eyes, and, yet, we're only related by law. "What turned you into a walking turd?"

"Play nice," I chide as I fall into the seat beside her.

She pushes her steaming mug over, and I take a careful sip.

"Bleh." I slide it back. "I hate coffee. It tastes like someone put out a cigarette in my milk."

"Nobody hates coffee, Reese. For the sake of your social standing, fake it when you're in public."

"Sure, why not. Rumor has it you do exactly that in bed," I tease. Truthfully I have no knowledge of what Kennedy and her boy toy do in or out of the bedroom. Kennedy and Keith have been together forever, or at least as long as she's been my stepsister for the last four years.

"You're not funny." She spins her mug, eyeing me like a snake. "You missed my eighties party."

"I'm sorry. Did you dance in the purple rain?"

"No we walked like an Egyptian." She assumes the position with her hands. "There were tons of boys, and you missed every one of them. It was practically raining men."

"Maybe I like being the *owner of a lonely heart*."

"Really?" She snorts into our eighties laden gab session. "Did it hurt so good?"

"No, it cut like a knife."

"Warren was asking about you all night." Her pale eyes widen. "I told him you were watching a movie with friends. Were you?"

"Sort of." My favorite movie—a love story starring Ace and me. But, I suppose after that arrangement I made with him last night, it's panning out to be more of a porn flick.

I give a little wink over at her.

"Don't do that. People who wink give me the creeps. Now, onto the details of said movie." She raps her knuckles over the table, and the sound echoes in my skull long after she's through. "Spill."

"You wish." I give her a light kick. "I'm not one of your sorority sister wives. I don't have to submit to your special brand of torture." I glance out the large series of windows that stretch up to the second floor, and take in the glory of the lake as it expands in every direction, a thick, clear blue. Across the way I spot a line of colorful umbrellas spiked in the sand. The sun has already sealed the day with a kiss, and it feels stuffy in here which lets me know I should turn on the AC. It's usually me who runs the house while our parents are away. The only upkeep Kennedy partakes in is strictly relegated to her own body. "Okay." I give in without any real prompting. "I went skinny dipping last night with Ace Waterman." He poured kisses into my mouth like wine straight from the throne of God, but I leave that part out.

"*Ace?*" Her features contort. Her mouth opens and closes. "Did he kiss you?"

"Only after I begged." Apparently I'm all about the truth this morning, and I'm not sure I like it. I smooth my hand over the table. It's the last decorator touch of my mother's in this oversized house. My mother had an affinity for all things Victorian—and Beverly, my stepmother, prefers art deco.

"You did not." Kennedy sucks in a breath as if I had just confessed to sleeping with an entire boat full of homeless men.

"No really." My finger glides over the rim of her mug like an afterthought. "Then I convinced him to be my summer fling. The end." I give a simple shrug as if what just flew from my lips had a thread of sanity attached. Kennedy would sooner have her fingernails plucked off than ever consider Ace Waterman as her plus one. She's a trust fund baby who needs a good millionaire to wrap around herself like a coat for the long haul.

"You're not serious." Her eyes grow wild, a lewd grin buds on her lips because she knows I am. "Holy shit, Reese. This will never work."

"It doesn't have to. Come move in day at Yeats, it'll all be over." I bite down on my lip at the thought of walking away from the only boy I've ever dreamed about, hell, wet my panties over, for that matter.

"Just something quick and dirty, huh?" She meditates over the idea. "Reese and Ace..." She makes a face. "You don't even sound like a couple." She strums her fingers over the table a moment. "Your couple's name would be *Race,* as in moving too fast."

"Race." I nod into the idea. "I like it. It's better than nothing. Warren and I never had a couple's name," I'm quick to point out. "Nothing ever made sense, sort of the way we didn't make sense. But Ace and me..." I let my words hang in the air like a love song. "We've known each other forever."

"You're getting way ahead of yourself, little sister. Who cares if you've known Ace forever? He's just some guy you grew up with. Nowhere does it say you have to give him your virginity in order to occupy your precious summer vacay. Keith and I took six full months before we went there, and, believe me—the sex was amazing because we took it slow. You should totally put this off and find a real guy to dive into bed with, not some boy who happened to grow up next door. God, does he even have a job?"

"Yes, he has a big net and goes around catching crazy bitches all day long. So, I guess you'd better watch your back." I raise a brow. It's easy for Kennedy to dismiss Ace. By the time she came into the family picture, Ace and I were already socially world's apart, then came college.

"You're funny, you know that?" She narrows her silver eyes over mine. "I think the heat is getting to you," she hisses it out like a threat. "I told you not to lay out so long in the sun yesterday. Wear a hat when you go out. You're on reserves with those brain cells of yours."

"Now who's the funny one? Besides, Ace is amazing."

"You're not serious, are you?" Kennedy takes a breath when I don't answer. "Reese." Her eyes close as if she's come to the end of me. "Warren isn't going to like this."

"He'll never know. Ace and I don't plan on advertising our little fuck-fest. I'm not selling tickets to my deflowering session, so you don't have to worry about Warren's little heart getting splattered all over the wall. And, by the way, it's made out of rusted iron, so I hardly think I could do any damage to begin with." Last year when I cried on my mother's birthday, he had the balls to ask if it was really necessary. I should have eviscerated him with my fingernails. Every now and again I still consider it.

"Warren's a good guy." She averts her eyes like she knows he's not. "You just have to give him a chance."

"No can do because I'm already giving more than a chance to Ace." I stretch my arms high over my head. "I'm hoping to *race* to that special place with *Ace* post haste."

"Dear God." She moans, taking back her coffee. "If you go Dr. Suess on me again, I might be moved to twist your head off." She gets up and makes her way out of the room. "Get yourself laid already, would you?"

"That's the plan," I shout back.

Race. I shake my head while a smile blooms on my face.

That's exactly what he's made my heart do all these years.

❧❦

The phone rings before I can finish downing Kennedy's cigarette-laced coffee, and I pick it up just so I don't have to listen to Beverly's annoying voice on the answering machine, but, just as my crappy luck would have it, it's Beverly herself. She spends a half-hour straight bitching about the rain in Italy. Beverly could never see the beauty in things like rain. Everything is a chore to her highness. Life is nothing more than one, long monotonous task. I swear, even with all my father's money that woman will never be happy. I try to imagine Ace and me on some Italian gondola adrift in the Adriatic just as a light rain begins to mist. I'd kiss him right then. If a downpour followed I'm pretty sure the urgency in our kisses would only kick up a notch. I imagine peeling his sopping clothes off and taking him right there. Only, I suppose there's an actual gondola driver who commandeers the vessel, and things could get uncomfortable for him, but in my fantasy it's just the two of us, making wild love in the driving rain. And, now, I've added that very impractical thing to my ever-growing carnal bucket list.

I spot Ace across the lake in his bright-orange canoe, his oars moving at record pace as he glides across the water in one smooth track. I make up some lame excuse about burning toast and hang up on Beverly. I'm sure she called hoping to talk to Kennedy, but their relationship has been frigid these past few months ever since Beverly confessed to the fact she didn't approve of Keith because of his mother's questionable social standing. I doubt she'd care too much for Ace either since his mother ran out on his family when he was in junior high. His father barely makes ends meet working as the lake patrol. Then, again, Beverly couldn't care less about my future.

I watch riveted as Ace wages a war over the water, his biceps popping in turn, his chest bronzed and slicked with heat.

That's it. His perfect body is all the motivation I need as I run barefoot all the way to the edge of the lake. I give a wild wave until Ace finally lifts an oar out of the water.

A laugh bubbles from me as I slick my hair back into a messy bun.

From behind him, a pale, blue canoe appears, and my smile dissipates as Warren speeds his way over.

Ace cuts him off and maneuvers past him as if he weren't putting in a real effort. I watch as his muscles twitch in tandem, his chest broadens, his abs cut in detail, and my mouth waters just looking at him. Ace is perfectly tanned and toned under the smoldering summer sun. He glides up on shore with Warren just a few seconds behind him.

"I win," Ace pants through a smile. "That means I get the girl, right?" He gives a sly grin in my direction, and my stomach pinches tight. He's so gorgeous with his dark hair, that body of chiseled steel. I'd have him right here on the sand if he let me.

"No one's taking my girl." Warren jumps out of his canoe and tosses his oar high on the grass just beyond the sand. He turns to Ace. "Let's get some coffee. My treat." He slaps me on the shoulder. "She's a real bitch if I don't put some caffeine in her."

I choose to ignore Warren and his stupid remark. Normally I'd say something, but with Ace around it's like Warren ceases to exist. Ace has the power to dissolve lesser men with simply the flash of his killer smile.

Ace raises his dark brows. His eyes bear into mine, and the memory of our bodies fusing together last night sends a chill racing up my spine. I don't ever remember feeling so electrified with Warren.

We walk just past Ace's family cabin, over to the Loveless General Store. Inside it smells like sundries and burnt coffee. The owner turned it into a quasi cafe a few years back, and it's been a hit with both tourist and locals ever since.

Ace's sister Neva sits behind the counter, and I spot Brylee Peters in the back hunched over her laptop. We were best friends growing up, along with Neva.

"Morning," I say it loud and clear, but Neva doesn't look up from her phone. Her hair is freshly died jet black with a tint of purple running through it like lightning pressed against a stormy night sky. I'd tell her it looks good, but she'll probably think I'm mocking her, so I don't bother. We were best friends up until after my mom died, then, out of the blue, Neva told me off, the end. All I know is she's at the community college with her brother. Ace took two years off after high school and saved up just to attend.

"Just an iced mocha for me." I give a shy smile, and Neva proceeds to ignore me. I glance over at Ace and catch him eyeing Warren's arm still latched around my waist. Funny, I didn't even notice he was holding me. "I think I'm going to say hi to Brylee." I ditch the boys and head toward the back. I give a quick wave to Bry. It's only then I notice she's sitting with Gavin Jackson, Ace's buddy that he chops wood with. It's Gavin's side business that helps put Ace through school.

"Look who's here?" He springs up and pulls me in. Gavin smells good, clean like soap. He's a blond god that has most of the girls in Loveless dropping to their knees, but Ace is the only one I'd ever engage in idol worship for.

"Girl!" Brylee springs to her feet and tackle hugs me until I stumble backward into a rock hard body. "I have missed you so damn much!"

"Whoa." Ace raises our drinks out of the way before setting them on the table.

"Nice save." I pat the seat next to me, and Ace complies without hesitating. "I almost knocked us both right over."

"You couldn't knock me over if you tried. Besides, I'll always catch you, girl." His dimples depress, and, for a moment, it's just Ace and me with my heart palpitating in honor of his glory.

"So how was school?" I glance around.

Gavin shakes his head. "The school of hard knocks suits me just fine." He opted out of the scholastic route and opened his own business instead. Outside of firewood, he carves oversized bears and eagles that the residents buy to adorn their yards. Gavin is pretty amazing in his own right.

"I have lots to tell you." Brylee pierces me with a hard stare. Her stony-green eyes drill into mine. Brylee is cute and bubbly with her long, blonde hair, her body that most girls pay for, and she happens to get away with murder due to the aforementioned attributes.

"You choose a major this year?" I ask, taking a quick sip of my mocha freeze.

"Business." She rolls her eyes as if she regrets it already. "Guess where I'm headed in the fall?"

"No way!" It comes from me a little louder than necessary. I turn back for a moment and catch Warren talking to Neva. His hand brushes over hers, and I ignore it. "Do you know what dorm you'll be staying in?"

"Beuller Hall."

"That's where I am! I'll see if I can get our roommates to switch. I'd die to have you with me."

Ace and Gavin hold their own conversation about woodcutting, something about cords being stacked later this afternoon. I never did understand the woodcutting lingo, so I wait for a lull in their conversation before interjecting.

"How's school for you?" I say it quieter to Ace, hoping he knows my question is still layered with heat from last night's kisses.

"Good." His dimples flex, setting off a set of mini tremors between my thighs. "Still rowing. I declared business as my major. The year flew by. And you?"

Warren comes back before I can answer and drops a kiss on the top of my head. He smacks Ace to scoot over, and he does without hesitating.

Warren can be a good guy when he's not busy being an asshole. He's tall, a little lanky but clean cut and for the most part attentive—to his own needs.

"I'm headed to Collingsworth in an hour." He pushes into me with his shoulder until I nearly fall off the bench. "You in?" Warren has a scar that jags up his left cheek from an accident he had when he was a kid. He fell from a horse onto a barbed fence and slit his face open. His caramel-colored hair is a little longer than it's been, but he keeps his face clean-shaven as a baby's bottom.

"What are you going there for?" Brylee asks while sipping her creamy Frappuccino and suddenly I wish I would have ordered that instead. I have a tendency to want things that aren't mine, like Ace.

"My dad needs me to run some briefs to his buddy down the hill." He slinks his arm around my waist again and gives my ribs a squeeze. I forgot Warren is doing an internship with his father this summer. "You up for a quick run? We'll make a day out of it. I'll let you beat me on the golf course later."

My mouth opens as I look to Ace, and he quickly deflects my gaze.

"I was thinking about laying out. You know, catching up on a book, maybe." Laying out? He just offered to treat me to an entire day, and I cancel because I have to work on my tan? Nice. Maybe Warren pegged me right. Maybe I'm a bitch with or without caffeine coursing through my veins. On the other hand, I'm not in a hurry to send him anymore mixed signals. I'd rather endure a third degree sun burn than listen to Warren drone on about all things legal, let alone ride shotgun in a golf cart for three hours straight.

"I'll go." Brylee volunteers. "But only if we can stop at Costco. The refrigerator's on empty, and my parents are out of town for the next few weeks."

"Deal." Warren glances at me as his lips twist with disappointment. "Catch you in the p.m.? Dinner at the Blue Crab?"

"Sounds great." I shrug. There I go again, getting sucked into Warren's special brand of ambush dating. But I had already turned him down once. I'd hate to cut him off at the balls in front of everyone at the table. Maybe I'll tell him at dinner that I want to see other people. Obviously he thinks we're exclusive even though I'd sit on an entire stack of Bibles to testify the fact we're not.

Ace nods over to Gavin. "Ready to go?" His face is peppered with stubble, and it gives him that sexier-than-hell look I ingrained into my memory last summer before leaving.

"Where you off to?" I ask, trying not to sound so desperately interested. But, dear God, am I ever desperately interested. I've taken a mental inventory of our every exchange for as long as I can remember. I'm so thirsty for Ace in the worst way, and last night he offered a sip, but I'm greedy. I want to fall into his ocean and drink him down to the last drop if he'll let me.

"Emerald Forest." Gavin answers for him. "We've got a quarter acre of nobles just begging for us to hack 'em to pieces."

"There's also a grove of walnuts back there." Ace holds my gaze with his deep-sea eyes a moment too long, and I can't look away. "We need to dry them out—season them."

"Dude." Gavin shakes his head. "Like anyone cares." He hops up and slaps Warren on the back as he heads for the door.

"I care." I bite down over my lip as everyone starts to disband. Warren and Brylee discuss their departure as I slide into Ace. "You think I can see you tonight?" My voice warbles like a frightened child, and I don't know why.

"Sounds like you're busy." He shoots a quick glance to Warren. A smile plays on his lips, but he won't give it. He's teasing me, and, secretly, I'm loving it. "Reese"—he leans in hard, his heated breath licks against my neck—"forget about what happened last night." His lips brush against my temple, and a wild jolt moves from his body to mine. "I did."

Ace presses out a sad smile before heading for the exit. I watch as he piles into Gavin's truck, and they speed off in a plume of dust.

There's no way in hell Ace forgot about our heated exchange. And I'll be damned if we don't share even more than that tonight.

Ace

The sun magnifies through the windshield and blinds me until we make our way west, past Pleasure Point and up into the woods. If I didn't break my back this morning trying to add an extra hour to my routine, I'll be sure to finish it off in the woods.

"So where were you last night?" Gavin's cheek twitches. That usually signals bullshit like maybe he's lying, but in this case I'm betting he knows exactly where I was. "Did you do that whole eighties thing at Kennedy's?"

"She invited me." My chest bounces with a silent laugh. The last thing on the agenda was hanging out with a bunch of stoned preppies, unless, of course, Reese was there, then I would have gone. "I wasn't up to it, so I stayed home, chilled out. And you?"

"I was at the party." He shakes his head. "I thought maybe you had some chick in the back. Rumor has it, those sorority girls are hot and wet in all the right places." He blinks a smile.

"You can always get your ass back in school if you want. Lots of girls roaming those halls down in Collingsworth." It's been a sore spot with him recently especially since I announced I'm transferring to Yeats in the fall. Gavin has pretty much taken care of himself after his parents died in a car accident his junior year of high school.

"Nice try, but let's stay on topic. I saw your shiny white ass crawl out of the lake on my way home. And whose beautiful ass did I spy crawling out with you? And is she free tonight? Because if you're done, send her my way, bro. She looked like she had a serious rack to contend with."

Shit. I let out a breath.

Gavin's not a player. He's just enjoying the hell out of himself while he breaks my balls.

"It was Reese."

I watch as his eyes widen then retract before he straightens out the wheel.

"And, no," I continue, "I'm not sending her your way." I let him in on the arrangement she tried to haul me into.

"Are you shitting me?" He swerves for a moment.

"Nope, I'm not shitting anyone."

"So, are you in?" He slows the truck down as he parks in the clearing.

"Hell, no. She's got Warren. She was probably pissed at him for not getting her latte right, or, who knows, maybe it's some game to get him worked up." That kiss we shared pulses through my mind, and the hairs on the back of my neck stand on end. I didn't think it was possible to feel that way with just a simple kiss, but nothing about that kiss was simple.

"Maybe she doesn't want Warren." He swings open his door and pauses. "Maybe she's into you. You ever tell her how you feel?"

"Not going there." I shake my head at the thought. I've made the mistake of mentioning my emotional hard-on for Reese one too many times before.

Gavin tugs on his ball cap. "If I were you, I'd tell her how I felt. But, if you're too big of a pussy to own up, I'd take her up on the offer anyway. Might be the last chance you get to hook up with the girl of your dreams. And for the entire summer?" He shakes his head while staring at the trees. "Something is definitely up. I'm betting she's feeling it for you, too."

"No way." Even if she were, I'd never be enough for her.

"I think you're wrong." He tosses out a knuckle bump. "Let's go hack down a forest."

"Let's do it."

I step out and secure my baseball cap over my head.

That final exchange with Reese at the coffee shop runs through my mind. I tried to put out the signal that I wasn't interested—that she shouldn't venture in my direction, but if she does make an effort to find me tonight maybe I will take her up on her offer.

Hell—I know I will.

∞∞∞

In the evening, after hours spent decimating an entire forest with Gavin, I sit my ass on the front porch of the cabin and nurse a cold one. I pretend not to notice the fact Warren's Beamer is still missing from his driveway, even though it's a quarter to ten. I know for a fact they left around six because I passed them on my way down to the dock to help tie my dad into his slip.

The heat of the day still radiates from the boulders like a furnace. Loveless is socked in with hillsides in all directions, so the heat tends to settle and pretty much turns the lake into an inferno from May to September.

A beat up Chevy Impala pulls in front of the cabin like it belongs here, and A.J. Goodman, my sister's boyfriend, hops out clad in black with his combat boots laced to his shins. He's got at least a dozen piercings I can see and probably a dozen more I don't care to know about.

"If you're going to wear those things, maybe you should enlist?" I say as he jets past me. He's sporting his Saturday night Mohawk, his thick guy liner—a requisite to scaring the crap out of old ladies at the mall. I wish he'd scare Neva. She's been dating him on and off since Christmas and neither my dad nor me are too happy about it.

"*You* should enlist." He twitches his bottom lip. He's got a double loop woven through it and a tongue piercing that still hasn't healed right. Any day now I'm expecting to hear a report that its fallen off, sort of the way I wish his dick would fall off. Just because my sister and I aren't that close, doesn't mean I want anybody fucking her.

"You enroll in college for fall?" I don't mind breaking his balls a little. It's no secret he's been leaching off Neva the past few months. I know for a fact she shells out her hard-earned cash each time they go out.

"Fuck you." He heads inside and slams the screen.

"Nice seeing you, too."

Dad comes out onto the porch and lights up a cigarette. His hair is still plastered down from the hat he wears all day, and he's got his Loveless patrol jacket on even though it's a balmy eighty degrees out tonight.

"Where you off to, all spit shined?" I tease and kick the rocker next to me for him to take a seat, but he doesn't.

"Down the mountain for a while." He blows a white tornado from his lips while staring back into the house from the screen. "Remember Darnell Potter?"

"Redhead with neck gear. Warren McCarthy used to sock him in the arm on the way to school just for the heck of it." Junior high. I remember those years. It was before dollars really meant anything, and all the Loveless kids used to hang out.

"Ran into his mom, Charlene." He taps his cigarette over the railing, and the ash lights up the night with its orange tail. "She invited me over to catch a flick."

Right. More like catch his *dick* but I'm not going there with my dad, not now or ever.

"I'll be back in the morning. Watch the kid for me, would you?" He pats me on the shoulder and heads down to his truck.

"Will do." She's twenty and doesn't listen to a damn thing I say, so it's mostly lip service, but I know he needs to hear it.

In the distance, a car takes the turn a little too quick and zips into the McCarthy's estate. It's Warren. I'd know that erratic driving anywhere. They're home.

I don't even notice as Dad pulls out and Gavin pulls in, hopping up to the porch and planting his ass next to mine until his cologne clots up the air like its about to strangle me.

"Dude, did you bathe in that shit?" I fan the air a moment.

"You know it turns you on, princess." He slaps my back. "You want to hit Kooks?"

Kooks is a bar on the other side of the ridge where their motto is, *it's easy to find love in Loveless*.

"No thanks."

A car door slams in the distance, and I try to gauge which direction Reese might be headed next. I can see her from here, small as my thumb. Reese has on a miniskirt or shorts, either way I can appreciate her long, bronzed legs, and I'm not objecting one bit.

"I see how it goes." He nods across the lake. "Why don't you call her in an hour? See if she's up for another dip? Wet your wick for real this time and put the both of you out of your misery."

"It's not like that." In fact, I want to smack him for thinking it is. "She's never been with anyone. I'm not doing her in the lake." I bite down on the inside of my cheek. "At least not the first time."

Gavin shakes his head and takes a quick sip of my beer. "I'm out of here. Kennedy's having a private party tonight—just a few chicks and dicks. She call you?"

"Nope." I go to shake my head and pause. "Looks like Reese's social calendar is double booked for the night. Speaking of dicks, I doubt mine is getting the company it was hoping for. Maybe I shouldn't have been so quick to turn her down."

"What the hell did you turn her down for?"

"Look at me." I hold out my hands. "I'm living at my dad's." I tap my hand over the armrest. "Neva is a fucking mess. Where would I take someone like Reese? The back seat of the Cougar?" Dad gifted me a '67 Mercury for my sixteenth birthday. It was my first and last birthday gift, but it was well worth the wait.

"So that's the dilemma. And I take it nature's a little too raw. I get it."

"I'm not hitting the bushes with her, dude." I blow the frustration through my lips. "McCarthy's got a million bucks to take her to any place he wants. His parents are gone half the time. He's got the house to himself, plus he's got an apartment at Yeats."

"Slow down, Ace. You stalking him?" He pushes out a laugh. "You should tell Reese you got in. You'll have a dorm on campus, right?"

48

"Maybe. The scholarship details are still in the air. The coach is trying to get me a room, if not, I'm on my own." Which translates into an hour and a half commute both ways. The gas alone will kill me. I'll have to take out a loan just to fill the tank three times a week.

"All right." He digs his palm into his eye. "Here's what I'm going to do. I've got the shop in order—"

"I'm not sleeping with her in the shop." I can see it now, an air mattress among the wood chips—Carl, his three-fingered assistant, showing up at sunrise and kicking us out.

"Relax, genius." Gavin narrows into me. "Geez, you really have it bad, don't you?" He folds his hands a moment. "I was going to say I gutted the boathouse. I had it renovated a few weeks back when my sister threatened to pop into town."

Gavin and his sister, Zoey, don't always get along so I get why he'd fix up the boathouse.

"Is Zoey coming back?" A noise rustles in the bushes, and my heart thumps as I spot a pale shadow moving in this direction. I try not to get my hopes up in the event it's not Reese.

"Nope. She said maybe in the winter." He digs into his pocket and snaps a key off his chain. "It's yours, dude." He hops off the porch before I can say anything and heads toward his truck. "What's up, girl?" He nods into someone just outside my line of vision, and I hear them making small talk for a moment.

A beautiful face illuminates the shadows like a pearl in the night, as the most gorgeous girl in the world bounces her way up the stairs. Her dark hair is wound in long, perfect waves. Her silver eyes reflect the light like a cat's.

"You up for some company?" Reese flashes that million-dollar smile.

"With you? Anytime."

ⓈⓄⒸⒼ

Reese yanks me up by the hand and pulls me into a nice, long hug. The scent from her perfume hypnotizes me for a moment, grapefruit and vanilla—a perfect combo of sexy and sweet just like Reese.

The truth is, I've been under Reese Westfield's spell for as long as I can remember. I take in a nice, slow breath, soaking in her sweet scent. It's the same perfume she's worn since she was a teenager.

"How was your date?" I nod for her to take a seat, and she does. Reese looks amazing tonight with her hair spiraling out in long, dark plumes like the feathers of some exotic bird. It takes all my self-control not to run my fingers through it.

"It wasn't a date, believe me." She wrinkles her nose as she rocks back and forth in the glider. "He had the bisque, and I had the lobster. End of story." She skims her bottom lip with her pearly whites, and my dick perks to life as if she were throwing out an invitation.

"Lobster." I nod. God knows I can't afford to keep her in crustaceans. "So what's McCarthy up to?" Really I want to know if she said anything of value to him—if he did to her.

"He's keeping busy, helping out his dad this summer." She reaches over and picks up my hand, her eyes drilling into mine. "I really don't care what he does."

"Does he care what you do?" If I make a move on Reese, I might find myself inhaling large amounts of lake water before the summer is through. Although, if the exchange rate for sleeping with Reese is something as meager as my life, I might consider the tradeoff. Reese is worth pushing up a daisy or two, but knowing Neva, I wouldn't be lucky enough to go the casket route. She'd toss me into the fire and warm herself while I melted to ashes. When we were younger, Dad gave us strict orders not to die because funerals were expensive as shit.

"Warren always seems to care what I do." A cheeky smile plays on her lips. "But he's hitting the sheets early tonight. He's his daddy's lackey, bright and early."

"I know how that goes." I've pinch hit for my father on the lake more times than I care to remember, mostly just giving people warnings for fishing without a license. Not that I care.

"So"—she digs in her pocket and pulls out a quarter that winks like a silver eye as she tosses it in her hand—"heads, we go skinny dipping." Reese runs her pink tongue over her lips. "Tails, we find somewhere new to hang out." She throws it high, and I catch it before it ever has a chance to fall. I flip it onto her bare thigh, and my fingers linger over her velvet soft skin.

"Tails." I blink a smile up at her, and my heart takes off like a greyhound down the track. "I know just the place to take you." I hop up. "Wait right here." I run into my bedroom and eye the box of condoms sitting on my desk. For a moment I envision Reese on top of me with her hair raining down over my face as she rides me. My dick perks up as if it were casting its vote, but I swipe the Monopoly game off the dresser and get the hell out of Dodge.

Reese and I drive down the road about a quarter of a mile, taking that last stretch nice and slow no thanks to the rocks strewn about, threatening to take out a tire. It's dark as hell, but that's the best time to look at the stars. I park square in front of Gavin's boathouse and eye the tiny structure.

"The G-man's love shack?" Her dark hair falls like a curtain as she leans in hard to get a better look. "I'm impressed."

"You shouldn't be."

We get out, and I let us in. It's clean, mostly. The light scent of pine lies thick in the air, but it smells more antiseptic than it does anything derived from nature.

Reese circles my waist from behind, and I spin into her.

"Whoa, girl." I give a satisfied groan as she melts her fingers across my chest. "Let's get some lights on." I flip the switch and am pleasantly surprised to find a double bed tucked in the corner, a red, white, and blue quilt of the American flag lying neat over the center. There's a small braided rug, a table, and a couple of chairs—a mini-fridge in the corner.

"Wow." She steps in past me. "This place is so cute. I've always wondered what it was like inside. For some reason I pictured it loaded from floor to ceiling with little aluminum boats." She eyes the box in my hand. "What's that, Waterman?" She takes a bold step into me and bats her lashes as if trying to seduce me. And lucky for me because I'm pretty damn sure she is.

I hold up the game for a second, and she gives a long blink. "What'd you think we we're going to do?" A shit-eating grin waits to break out on my face, but I hold back.

"I thought"—she flattens her hands over my chest and drips them down slow and even—"maybe we could do more of what we did last night."

A dry laugh pumps through me.

"Let's get to work." I'm quick to set up the board. Reese calls "bank" and sorts the cash in front of her like a seasoned teller.

"Just try to steal, and I'll make sure you're punished to the fullest extent of the law," I say it dry like I mean it, and I do.

"Will you do the punishing?" Her lips part as if she were wagering just how much she should take.

"That depends. Would you want me to?" I shuffle the tiny cards in my hands for no good reason.

"Yes, Ace. You have my full permission to severely punish me." Her eyes press into mine like she's serious just before she jolts back to game. "So, did you think about what we said last night?" She rolls the dice. Her eyes cut up to mine, and I'm about to flip the board over and take her right here on the floor—punish her with my tongue in all the right places.

"Yup. I thought long and hard about how I should invest in hairspray because I'm confident you're about to single handedly bring back big hair."

"Very funny." She glides her fingers over the board, and I move my hand before she can catch it. "So you don't want me," she says it low just this side of a whisper and breaks my heart in the process.

"Yes, I want you. In fact I *need* you because it's downright impossible to play this game by myself." My chest rumbles with a silent laugh, but she's not coming along for the ride. Her features soften, any residue of a smile she might have been sporting dissipates faster than snow in June.

She gives a hard sniff and locks her gaze over mine.

"Warren wants you, too," I say it plain and simple before rolling the dice. "You go first." I scoot them over to her, but she doesn't budge.

"You sound like my dad." She shakes her head. "I guess it really doesn't matter what I want. Does it?" She leans back on her hands and stares off at the wall behind me.

"Of course, it matters what you want. In the event you haven't noticed, you're the only person who should care who you're with. If you're not into Warren, I'm sure you'll find some other nice kid at Yeats." Not that I want her to. I reach over and pick up her hand, massaging her palm with my thumb. "Fall in love, Reese. Get so head over heels you can't see straight. It'll be magic. I promise, you'll want to write me a thank you note because when you finally have that moment, it's going to be incredible."

"Have you ever been in love?" It comes out raspy, sexy as hell. "So head over heels you can't think straight?"

Right fucking now, but I don't say it.

Reese gets up, never letting go of my hand, and slips her legs on either side of me until she's sitting right in my lap, straddling me with her warm, soft body. Right about now I'm regretting the metric distance between my dick and that box of condoms sitting in my bedroom.

"Last night you said you'd be my someone special this summer." She pulls off my shirt and runs her hands across my chest. Her eyes latch onto mine, and I'm dying to pluck off her T-shirt and return the favor.

"Last night was an illusion." I replace her hands into her lap. "You're just hopped up on hormones. It's the heat." I could list a thousand different things it could be, but I'm hoping not one of them is true.

"It's the heat—my hormones," she mocks. "You've got me all figured out, haven't you, Waterman?" She leans in and takes a soft bite of my bottom lip before stretching it out, painfully slow, agonizingly perfect.

"Reese," I whisper her name with my eyes sealed tight. One more glance at that lust-driven look she's giving, and I might lose it. "Fuck."

"Now we're on the same page." She sinks her hands down to my hips, and I catch her before she strikes a jackpot. "Ace," she blows my name out in a sigh. "Be honest with me." Reese pulls back, and we square off, eye to eye. "Am I like a little sister to you?" Her eyes swell with tears. Her lips turn a bright shade of crimson.

Here it is, my official out. I can say yes. I can tell her that I think of her like I do Neva and blow this entire bad idea out of the water before it ever takes flight, but I don't.

"Reese." I pump a quick smile. Who the hell am I to turn down Reese Westfield?

I crash my lips over hers and run my hands up and down her back like I'm putting out a fire.

Screw Warren McCarthy. Screw the man who Reese is destined to marry one day. I'm already head over heels. I can't see straight—all I think about, see, hear or feel from eyelids open in the morning is Reese Westfield.

This is our summer.

I'm all in.

3

All The Dirty Details

Reese

Ace runs his tongue over mine, achingly slow, and I pull him in by the back of the neck, forcing him into me, deeper, harder. Ace Waterman has melted me for the better half of the last decade, and seeing that I'm just shy of my twenty-first birthday, that's a pretty impressive streak.

Ace pulls back slightly and takes me in. "Okay." He flexes those dimples that drive me wild, and my insides reduce to cinder. "Let's set some ground rules."

"The last time I checked, a fling didn't have any rules. Besides, I don't like the word *fling*, it sounds ridiculous." True story. I find it weird, right up there with affair and rendezvous. I prefer the more colloquial terms of my people, fuck buddies, friends with benefits, booty call. And believe you me I can't wait to dial into Ace's rock hard booty. Well, mostly I want to dial into his heart. I'm hoping he wants that, too.

"All right." He dots my lips with a kiss and pulls away with a smoldering look in his eye. "Let's start with what we're going to call it." He shakes his head just barely. "Say something nice."

"I take it *fuck buddies* is off the short-list?"

He pushes out a quiet laugh. "Never want to hear you say it." He pulls a kiss off my neck, and a groan escapes my throat. "This is going to be special," he whispers.

"Okay, let's go with that. You're my someone special." I press my lips together tight because I mean every damn word. "I want you to take me places that only you know how. I trust you, Ace. I trust you with every part of me." And certain parts of me are dying to show him just how much they trust him more than others. I clench my legs for a moment because, honest to God, I half expect a mutiny. My lower half is aching to pole vault onto something long and hard, and it damn well knows Ace is housing the hardware in his Levis. I'm not sure why I'm so worked up. I'm usually a lot more reserved, but I've waited all year, and now the prospect of being with Ace is dangling in front of me like a carrot. I'm not going to lie, I want it. I want *him* in the worst way.

"What's your goal?" His eyes bear down over mine and my soul liquefies as it boils from the heat.

"My goal?" To be his someday, but I leave that off the table for now. I glide my hand over his bare chest and hold my breath, far longer than meaning to.

"What do you want from me, Reese?" He looks resigned to the fact he's going to give in no matter what my demands might be. He simply wants an outline of things to come—a syllabus, a checklist so he'll know when he's through.

My mood sinks like lead at the thought that's all this might be to him, just someone helping out a friend.

"When I go back in the fall, I don't want to feel like an outcast." That's not entirely true. The truth is, I've thought of Ace every damn day we were apart, and I couldn't bear not being near him. We're not close enough to talk every day. Once in a while I'd send him a text, but I can count on one hand how many times that happened, and most of those were holidays. There was that one time I visited Kennedy's sorority and got ripped. I was all hot and bothered and tried to take a braless selfie and send it to him, but thankfully I dropped my phone into the toilet while I was trying to dislodge myself from my bra. Thank God for small porcelain mercies. Anyway, I have no clue how to tell him that I want more of him in my life. That I want him saturating my days and nights in ways that other people could never do. That I've seriously considered dropping out of Yeats just to sit on this mountain with him, not that I would really drop out, but still, if he wanted me to I'd drive home every weekend just to have him hold me.

"Reese Westfield an outcast?" His chest bumps with a quiet laugh. "Not likely."

"Okay, then I want to have an amazing time all summer long and who better to join me in the endeavor than my best friend? Who better to share my body with?" I bite down hard on the inside of my cheek to deflect the tears that threaten to spring to my eyes. I said the words I've wanted to say all night and now they're out there, swimming around us, dangerous, like a bunch of hormonal piranhas.

His head ticks back a notch. "Am I your best friend?"

"When it comes to guys." I give a circular nod as I nestle in his lap. "And, you happen to be my most gorgeous male friend, who also happens to be the nicest guy on the planet." I run my finger just under his jaw, and his chest expands with a breath. "You're amazing." I glance down a moment. "I missed you. Did you miss me?" I hate how desperate I sound. How broken and fragile I'm coming across. I wish I were like Brylee. She would have shoved him over the mattress the first three seconds of their arrival, and, here I am, helping to set up a board game.

"Yes, I missed you." He glides his finger down my cheek, and I tremble at his touch. "And, you happen to be the sweetest girl *I* know. You're *my* best friend, Reese. You know you've always been that."

"So we're best friends." I latch onto his eyes and hold his warm gaze. My girl parts sigh, and my panties start to slide down on their own volition. It's becoming obvious that I will never survive this summer.

"And I want to keep it that way," he says it firm. His eyes never waver from mine. "God, if you hate me at the end of all this, I'll never forgive myself."

A string of laughter ripples from my throat as I take in his sweet cologne. "There's nothing you could ever do to make me hate you, Ace. I swear on all that is holy, at the end of this summer, we will still be friends." And, if I'm lucky, we'll be something more, forever.

"Best friends." He gives a curt nod. The light shines down over his thick, dark hair, and I twist my fingers through it like I've wanted to do so many times before, like I've dreamed of all those lonely nights in my dorm.

"Best friends," I parrot back to him while feathering my fingers down his chest in a giant letter S.

"So let's get this mapped out, plain and simple. I'm a guy"—his left dimple plays peek-a-boo—"I need a roadmap." His hands float down to my waist, and my body is ready to start a riot and take over. "You want to have sex."

I give a quick nod, a little too overeager, and he rumbles with a soft laugh. I wonder what Ace would think if he knew I've already had him a dozen ways in my mind just tonight alone.

"You want to stay friends." He ticks into me with his forehead.

"Yes," it comes from me emphatic. "Friends forever." Maybe something more, but my heart breaks at the thought that he might not agree, so I don't bother going there. Why argue with the price of the future when I already have the prize right here in the present.

"So this is strictly platonic." He seems almost amused.

"Platonic—but not vanilla. I don't want to bore you." An image of him wielding a whip comes to mind, and I quickly usher it away. We're far from the exploratory kink phase of our relationship. Besides, that's not what this is about. This is going to be sweet, beautiful. If I come across as a freak, he'll gladly give me the boot long before the end of the summer. "But, I don't know jack, so that's where you come in." I lean in and press my lips directly into his ear. "Make this exciting for me—for the both of us." And I go right back to kink. There's that.

His abs twitch, and I run my hands over them in the shape of a rainbow.

"Trust me"—he swallows hard with his eyes closed, his neck slowly arching back—"this just might be the most exciting summer of your entire life."

"And what about you?" My cheeks burn with heat as the question sails from my lips. "I mean, I'd love to return the favor." And I very well plan to once I figure out how.

"Oh, sweetie"—he gives a dark laugh—"you already have."

He presses out a smile as my insides cinch.

Maybe Ace has feelings for me after all. Maybe molding them into something meaningful will chase the shadow of all other girls right out of his head.

"Great." I lean back and take him in. "Let's start right now." My legs tighten around his waist. God knows I've already saturated my panties just hoping tonight was the night. When I dreamed up the idea of a summer fling, I never thought in a million years, he'd be so easy to sway. I thought vats of hard liquor would be involved, a pistol at point blank range, and here I am, on his lap without a drop of alcohol or a 45 in the vicinity.

"We *will* start tonight." He brushes the hair from my face as his gaze wanders over me openly. I feel exposed like this with Ace—as if I'm being seen for the very first time, and I glow under his watchful supervision. Ever since we were teenagers, I've felt a blistering heat whenever Ace laid eyes on me. And, tonight, his open gaze feels like a blowtorch over my skin. "We'll start with kissing." His Adam's apple rises and falls. A patina of wanting washes over his features, and it empowers me.

"I think we've got that down." I feather my fingers over his stomach, and it cinches. "Let's move the lesson along." Slow just might kill me. I tuck my hand into the waistband of his boxers, and he plucks me right back out again.

"I want to kiss you"—he brings my hand to his lips—"on the bed."

"Yes, master," it comes from me guttural and throaty as I glide my leg across him nice and slow, my fingers dripping down to his. I pull Ace over to the mattress with me and lie down for him.

Ace lies over me and leans up on his elbows—his hungry mouth just inches from mine.

"Sex is just an act, Reese." He dusts my features with his lips. "If there's no meaning behind it, it's just some mechanical event, a timed session, a chore."

"It'll never be like that with us." I try to hold back the laugh begging to bubble out of me. I have a bad habit of giggling at inappropriate times, and while proclaiming my true feelings for the only boy I've ever cared about would definitely be one of them. *God*—what if I laugh my ass off the first time I see the pride and joy he keeps tucked in his boxers? I cringe a little because a small part of me knows this is a very real possibility. I'm guessing laughing at man parts is cause for disqualification of said summer fling and will warrant a serious reevaluation of our newly minted best friend status. Crap. Is it too early for me to strut around with a muzzle? I think we're back to the kink.

"Maybe it won't be a chore, but if it is—if I overstay my welcome"—his dimples dig in a moment—"I want you to tell me. Summer can be an eternity if you're not happy, and I'd rather die than make you feel that way."

"*Ace.*" I give into the joy percolating in my chest. "You will never overstay your welcome." I touch my hand to the back of his neck. "I promise you this. I swear on a thousand Bibles. I'll want you near me every single day." There is no greater truth.

"Good." He gives a slight grin, but it melts away just as fast as it came. "We're going to take things slow, Reese. It's one thing to think you want it and another to *really* want it. We need to build momentum." He rakes his lips over my neck and pants into my mouth. "That's what we're doing tonight—building momentum."

"Momentum," it chokes from me. "But, for the record"—I trace out his lips with my finger, and he gives a playful bite—"I'm not into slow. In fact, it just gained four-letter word status because it just so happens to be one."

Ace offers the hint of a smile before landing his scorching mouth over the hollow of my neck and moving down just shy of my cleavage.

"It's not happening tonight." He strings a trail of kisses down lower into the soft skin of my breast and buries his face in one for a moment.

I let out a groan far louder than expected. God, if this simple act elicits my vocal cords to strangle out a cry, I'll be screaming my lungs off when things get viral. But I hope not. The last thing I'm in the market for is turning him off while doing my best impersonation of a werewolf.

His breathing picks up. A growing protrusion stiffens against my thigh, and I give a dull smile. Ace Waterman is mine, whether it's tonight or tomorrow—I can't wait to have him.

Ace glides back up, landing his lips on mine. He crashes over me with a wave of fury that spells out right here, right now far more than it ever does slow and serious. I dance my tongue over his, and my toes curl as his hands glide up my shirt. Ace cups my breasts, giving a gentle squeeze. He rolls his thumbs over my nipples until they're firm under his command. Ace has an unusual definition of slow, but I'm not complaining. Maybe he meant slow motion. I can live with that.

I dive my hands toward his jeans, and he catches me.

"Just kisses," he says as he flexes my hands up high over my head.

"And what happens tomorrow?" I wet my lips in anticipation.

"Exploratory kisses." He gives a crooked grin. "I get to kiss you everywhere."

"And what do I get to do?" I purr the words out like a dream.

"You get to enjoy it."

I'm already enjoying the hell out of it, but I don't say it.

"So"—I nestle my head into the pillow and soak in this moment while the boy of my dreams lies over me—"I guess I'll be losing my virginity to you." Every part of me quivers as I say it.

Ace gives a sad smile. "I guess you will."

∞〇⅗

After a marathon kissing session that spanned hours, and potentially dehydrated the both of us to deliriously dangerous levels, Ace drops me off at home. I let myself in, trying to ignore the familiar voices coming from the family room. I thread through the kitchen and peek from the hall, affirming the fact an entire roll call of Kennedy's sorority sisters are present and accounted for. There are a smattering of guys here, although Warren and Gavin are the only two I recognize. The rest look like refugees from a local prep school with their matching khakis, their brand name Polos with the collars turned up to their ears. I make a face at the collar poppers. I bet they've got something in their chinos just waiting to pop once they divvy up the girls. My eyes run along the border of the coffee table and spy a stack of pizza boxes, enough red Solo cups to outfit the US military, and two six packs still untouched. Kennedy has systematically turned Beverly's museum room into a bar and a brothel, and I clearly see all ten of my stepmother's uptight commandments breaking simultaneously.

"Reesie?" Kennedy calls me from the across the room, and I startle. She has a habit of calling me Reesie when she's shit-faced, and, now, I regret ever telling her about my special summer plans with Ace. "Come here for a minute. We're debating something very important, and you know I value your opinion." She slurs that last bit out so bad, it sounded more like *I vacuumed your opium.*

I huff a little laugh. Ace is the only form of opium I need. I'm still high as kite off our encounter.

"Here we go," I mutter under my breath as I make my way over.

Warren pats a seat beside him, and I take it like an obedient child. His hair is slightly rumpled. His eyes are glazed over. The scent of whiskey permeates the air and it becomes clear that pretty much everyone here is wasted. Maybe Kennedy wants me to bitch slap them all and then take away their keys? I'd be up for a quick smack down before bedtime, with the exception of Gavin, of course. He's sweet down deep where it counts like Ace. He's just looking to get laid like the rest of the people here tonight, Warren included.

"So"—Kennedy holds up a finger and leans in until she falls into the lap of Charlie, her favorite protégé—"we're coming up with unconventional ways to torment new recruits. We can't just let anyone into Alpha Kappa."

"Right," I say. But judging by the bevy of skanks in the vicinity, they *so* do.

Warren pushes his red Solo toward my lips, but I'm quick to bat him away. Warren smells like a bad combination of rubbing alcohol and nail polish remover. I won't be revoking his keys since he lives within walking distance, or in his case, stumbling distance.

"What's the lowest level of shame you think someone would be willing to stoop just to fit in?" Kennedy suddenly comes to long enough to string together a coherent sentence.

"Lowest level?" Like begging their best friend to unleash his body on theirs for the summer? Wait, that's not low, that's genius. I give a private smile.

Warren slips his hand between my thighs, and I graciously pluck him the hell right off.

"I guess the lowest low is being with someone you don't really want to be with." I shoot Warren a look, but he's too busy checking out Charlie's boobs to notice. Her left nipple has escaped captivity and is quivering at us like a frightened Chihuahua. Not that I'm surprised. A red Solo explosion like this one practically merits a clothing malfunction or two. It's nights like this that unwanted pregnancies are made of. Hey, I wonder if the good people over at Solo headquarters have ever considered that as a company slogan?

"Like in a sexual sense?" Charlie's mouth drops open at the salacious implications. And, for a minute, I have to rewind my Solo commentary just to remember the topic at hand. Oh, that's right, the lowest of lows—being with someone you don't want to be with.

"Yes, in a sexual sense." I glance over at Warren as his hand migrates to the back of my shorts. "Nobody wants anyone's sticky fingers on them unless they're one hundred percent into them." I slap his hand off my ass. Case in point.

"Rush is going to be brilliant." Kennedy nods as if a life-changing event were on the horizon. "We'll have each girl that makes it to the final phase pick a boy from Kappa Pi, and she'll have to make out with him."

"That's disgusting." Crap. Why do I get the feeling I've just contributed to her future sexual harassment lawsuit?

Kennedy has been steadily propagating all kinds of quasi-inappropriate behavior with her cult-like group. Last year, there were talks of blowjobs being instated as a punishment. But I was quick to talk Kennedy out of it by inundating her with the plagues of prison life that would soon be upon her if she kept up the oral offensive.

I can see she's busy clawing her way back to prison. "Do not, I repeat, do *not* require your pledges to do anything that remotely involves a bodily fluid. Maybe just have them do something you would find ultra humiliating like show up to class without red lipstick and pearls." You can spot a girl from Alpha Kappa a mile away with those identifying accouterments.

Kennedy and her sorority sisters ashen at the thought of being seen without their signature look. Clearly my work here is done. I evict myself from the couch and head upstairs. It's only when I reach the top do I notice that Warren has followed me, stealth as a ninja.

"There's a bathroom downstairs." I'm half tempted to push him down one flight to help him get to it a little quicker. Obviously he trotted up here in hopes to continue that thigh-warming action he was initiating in the living room.

His lips curl as he gurgles in my direction. Warren looks as if he could be a Ralph Lauren model. He's gorgeous, and has his future mapped out like a constellation, but for whatever reason I've never really connected with him on a romantic level. God knows I've tried for my father's sake.

"I'm just walking you to your room," the words stream from his mouth like toxins. "Making sure you get to bed safe." He walks me down the hall and opens the door to my room. "After you."

"Well, aren't you the perfect gentleman?" Not really. I can taste the liquor on his breath from a three-foot clearance. "Thank you and goodnight." I slip in and start to close the door, but he sticks his foot into the room before I can shut it.

"Let me tuck you in." Warren hedges into my dark room and wraps his arms around my waist. I hear the door shut as he inches me toward the bed.

"Let go. This isn't funny." He lands me backward onto the mattress, and the wind gets knocked out of me for a second.

Warren dives down a sloppy kiss over my cheek, and I squirm trying to break free from his powerhouse embrace.

"You know you want this," he moans as he flops down over me, taking the breath from my lungs in the process.

"I don't want this. Warren get *off*." I struggle as he jams his tongue down my throat, polluting the sweetness Ace left there earlier. I twist my face into the bed until it feels like my neck is about to snap off.

"Come on, baby." His breath reeks as he presses in with his full weight.

"Warren, I can't breathe."

He shoves his hand down the front of my shorts, and his fingers brush against the most private part of me.

"Damn, you're wet," he pants hard in my ear.

That's it. Every cell in my body is officially pissed.

I reach down and give his balls a hard squeeze, and he screams like hell right into my ear. It takes all of my strength to push him off, landing him on the floor with a thud.

"Get *out!*" I turn on my desk lamp and the room explodes with far too much light. I kick him in the ribs until he rolls over to the door, and I open it for him. "I will take a baseball bat to your nuts if you don't crawl your ass out of here in the next two seconds."

"I'm out," he barks, holding up his hands. He scoots over the threshold and shakes his head up at me. "Fuck, Reese. Grow up and stop being such a bitch. You know you want it."

I slam the door in his face to make it clear just how much I want him.

Ace

In the heat of the next afternoon, I wax my paddleboard before taking it out on the lake. There's nothing like standing over the surface of the water to make me feel like I don't have a worry in the world. That I don't miss my mom or think my dad is going to go on another bender because Neva is fucking her boyfriend at the top of her lungs in the next room. Sometimes I wonder if I'll ever have a decent family of my own one day or if I'll just drag the curse that's plagued us for so long right into the next one and screw up everyone else's lives, too.

My mind wanders back to Reese and those hotter-than-hell kisses. After I dropped her off last night, I hit the shower and released a little pent up frustration, hell, a lot of pent up frustration. I'm not sure why I didn't take her right then and there. Who the hell opened my brain and dropped morals in while I wasn't looking? The last thing I want to do is take anything slow with Reese. Never once in my wildest fantasies did I ever take things slow with her. But this isn't a fantasy, this is real, and if I play my cards right all of my wildest dreams are about to come true. This isn't some barfly I picked up at Kooks, not some girl from one of my classes that's ready and willing for a quickie in some deserted supply closet. This is Reese, and I want to make it extra special for her. In two weeks it's the Fourth of July. That sounds like a good target date to actually doing the deed, but I'm not entirely sure how I'll keep sane until then.

"Douchebag." A voice booms from behind.

I turn to find Gavin strutting in my direction.

"Takes one to know one." I get back to the fine art of waxing down my board, so I don't slip off like the last time and almost knock myself unconscious. "What's up? Who was the unlucky girl last night?"

"Some chick named Charlie. Never did get her last name. And, believe me, she considered herself very, very lucky." He takes a step in and kicks the wax from my hand. "How about you? You get lucky last night?"

"Hell, yes. Every moment I spend with Reese feels pretty damn lucky."

"Whoa, keep it down, Romeo. Voices carry." He nods over toward the McCarthy house. "Before I left last night, I saw Warren head up to her room."

My chest pinches. I cut a quick glance over to the Westfield estate before smoothing my hand over the board.

"And? So what. We're just having a platonic thing, nothing serious. If she wants to be with McCarthy on the side then who am I to stop her?" But according to Reese she doesn't want to, and I know for a fact she wouldn't lie to me.

"Don't get all bent out of shape." He cracks open a soda and hands it to me. "He wasn't up there long. He stumbled downstairs nursing his balls. I had to help him out to the driveway."

A spike of adrenaline shoots through me, and a smile breaks loose on my face.

"She kneed him?" I'm suddenly proud as hell.

"Something like that." Gavin glances over my shoulder and nods. I turn in time to catch a glimpse of a pair of long, luscious legs, both attached to the girl I'm losing my sanity over.

"Morning." I straighten.

"Afternoon," she counters. Reese is wearing a pair of cutoffs and a skimpy red bikini top that ties in the back, and, holy shit, if my hard-on doesn't want to pop out to greet her.

"I need to split." Gavin slaps me on the back. "Catch you later, Reese."

"See you." She never takes her eyes off me. "Whatcha doing?" She leans in seductively, inspecting my paddleboard like it had the potential to play out in one of her fantasies.

"Have you ever been on one of these?" I try not to dip my gaze to her cleavage like I want to. Why do I feel like the wolf luring an unsuspecting girl into the woods?

"Never have. You think I can come along for the ride?" Her silver eyes widen. Her hair swoops forward and frames her face. Reese Westfield is a work of art. I've never taken pencil to paper, but looking at her perfect curves, her face that could launch an entire fleet of paddleboards—it makes me want to try just about anything.

"Get on, girl." I push the board out onto the lake until the water is up to my hips.

I turn back in time to catch her slipping out of her shorts, and my dick wags like a tail. And to think I almost missed the show.

Reese gives a satisfied smile as if she were hoping to seduce me all along.

I might have to bump up the timeline of our conjugal union. That red bathing suit is calling my name in so many fantastic ways.

"So I just get on?" She wades out and tries to hop on the board but glides right off.

"Here." I pick her up by the waist and set her dead center over it. "Lay down toward the nose on your belly, and I'll paddle us out."

Reese lays out flat and maneuvers her way to the front.

"That's perfect." As in perfect view. I stand over her, careful not to get any water on her as I paddle us past the buoys. Normally I would make a giant clockwise circle until I grew bored as shit before heading back, but considering that might put us beneath Warren's front window in less than three minutes, I take a hard left and head into a forest of reeds. It's no place for a paddleboard but who cares? As soon as we clear the first round of hedges, I know for a fact no one will be able to see us unless they're lurking in the marsh, and as far as I can tell, it's just Reese and me—the way I like it. The way I hope she likes it, too.

I get down and dangle my legs on either side of the board.

Crap.

Reese's perfect ass is in my face, and it takes everything in me to keep a hard situation from cropping up between my legs. I try to think of all the time we've spent on the lake. The times we raced out to Boulder Island, and I let her win—the times she genuinely beat me. It's hard to believe the way things, are shifting for us this summer. Taking it a step further is going to change things, and I know damn well things will never be the same once we cross that line. It breaks my heart to think this might be it for us—going out in one spectacular fit of glory. I doubt she'll want much to do with me after the summer. I can't stand the thought of it, so I push it out of my head for now. If Reese is on board with our special summer, so am I.

She turns briefly before spinning around.

"Hey, what are you doing?" She gives one of her signature grins, and my gut pinches. "I thought you were supposed to be paddling us around? You're my paddle boy for the afternoon, remember?" She thumps her foot over my leg.

"Your paddle boy is slacking off. I'm too busy enjoying the view."

"Funny—that's exactly what I'm about to do." She scoots in close, placing her thighs over mine until she's just about sitting on my lap. A groan works its way up in my throat, but I won't give it.

"So what happened last night?" I brush my thumb over her soft cheek, her pillowy lips. "I heard Warren took a hit to the boys. Rumor has it the blow might have been delivered by someone I know." I had to go there. I'm dying to hear if she broke things off with him for good. I've sort of declared the boathouse a Warren-free zone, so I didn't bother bringing it up last night. Not that I want to discuss their relationship, but a part of me demands to know.

"Gavin told you." She shrugs as if she doesn't really care. "And, yes, the not-so fatal blow was delivered by yours truly." A twinge of pride glimmers in her eye, but there's a sadness layered just beneath. "Warren followed me up to my room and tried to 'tuck me in.'" She looks down and runs her finger through the water.

"And you kicked him in the nads?" I tweak her ribs, playfully. "Remind me to never attempt to 'tuck you in.'"

"No, actually"—her expression dims as she gazes out at the forest just beyond the boulders—"he grew into this monster. Before I knew it, his tongue was down my throat, and his hand flew into my pants. It was a disaster sponsored by malt liquor. Anyway, I kicked his ass all the way out of my room." She shudders reliving the memory. Her dark hair falls like a sheet, hiding her face from me.

Fuck. My blood boils faster than I can catch my next breath, and I fight the urge to swim back and kick his ass all the way back to Yeats.

I pull her in and tighten my arms around her cool waist. "I'm going to kill him." It comes from me controlled, almost tongue-in-cheek, but it's the furthest thing from it.

"Relax." Reese presses her chest to mine, and the sweet scent of sugar expels from her. "He's not worth the felony. Besides, I can take care of myself." She takes up my hand, gliding it over her stomach, all the way to her perfect round tit and keeps it there. Her eyes meet with mine, and the smile slides off her face. "The only person on the planet I want touching me is you."

"Yes, ma'am," I whisper as if she just gave an order, and our lips find one another. For the next ten solid minutes, she pours a fire into my mouth with a passion I have never felt before. Reese lashes her tongue over mine like she's trying to teach me a lesson. Her top twists in ten different directions as my fingers indulge in how fucking soft she is in my hand. I roll her nipples over my fingers until they're rock hard and pull back to take her in like this.

"Ace," she trembles my name from her lips, and I lock eyes with her, forcing her to look at me.

"I'm going to run my tongue all over your body tonight," I say it plain like a fact—like it wasn't killing me on the inside to show this much restraint to tell her how I really feel instead. "I'm going to kiss you in places you've only dreamed about." I twist my thumbs over her nipples, so she knows precisely where. The truth is, I want to push Reese to the limit—make her squirm, uncomfortable even, to see if she'll back out of our deal. "I'm going to put parts of you in my mouth that are guaranteed to make you insane." I give a brief smile, but she doesn't seem to flinch. Instead, her eyes flutter briefly as if she's already about to lose it. My heart thumps wild at the thought of Reese wanting this. I won't deny there is definitely something strange about this whole thing, but I'd be lying if I didn't say I was glad it was me she chose to have a special summer with.

She gives a quick nod. "We can start right now—that is, if you want to." She tries to sound calm, as if it were no big deal, but the heavy wobble in her voice lets me know she'd more than like to speed up the process.

"Tell me something"—I lean in and whisper just over her lips—"have you ever had an orgasm?" This is it. If she doesn't flinch, I'll know she's serious. I can't imagine anything more uncomfortable than contemplating orgasms in the middle of the afternoon.

Her chest palpitates. Her breathing grows erratic. Reese takes in a heated breath as if she's about to have one now.

"Not with anyone else in the room." She bats her lashes at me.

Shit. She knows she got me going with that one.

I try to hang onto my poker face as long as I can. "I might like to see you in action some time. If you ever feel the need to reenact the deed, I won't stop you."

"Why would I pleasure myself when I have you to do that for me?" Her hands float over my shoulders as she pulls me in by the neck.

"You got me there." I push out a breath. It looks like she wants this. Tonight will be the real test. "Prepare to be pleasured."

Reese wraps her arms around me, and her lips expand in a toothy grin. Reese has the face of an angel, and she knows it.

"What the hell are we doing?" I shake my head. "You deserve everything, Reese."

"Then give me everything you've got." Her eyes widen at what exactly that might be.

"I will."

I've already given her my heart.

She just doesn't know it.

4

The Build Up

Reese

The sky darkens a shade, wrapping itself with a blanket of white flannel clouds, thick and soft. I head home after my paddle boarding session with Ace, and I can't wipe the silly grin off my face.

Brylee waves at me from the porch with a towel draped over her shoulders. She's still dripping wet from the lake, but I don't care. I race up the steps and take her by the hand all the way to my bedroom, laughing as if it were junior high and the cutest boy in school just asked me to the dance—which he sort of did. A very erotic, sexually pleasurable dance for two, usually performed horizontally, or, until tonight, only in my dreams.

"What?" Brylee shuts the door behind us. "Did you set a bag of crap on fire outside Neva's door?" She gets that gleam in her eye as if she just gave birth to a very wicked idea. The three of us used to be inseparable. After Neva kicked me out of her life, Brylee decided not to take sides. Somehow she still manages to maintain a genuine friendship with the both of us.

"*No*," I correct. "But her brother took me out on the lake and set *me* on fire. I'm damn lucky my bathing suit didn't melt right off." I glance down to verify the fact it's still firmly in place. It's wet in all the right places, and I think that in and of itself is a testament to Ace.

"Really? Right on the lake?" She glances out the window in disbelief. "God—Ace Waterman is an animal. Warren is *so* going to kick his ass when he finds out." Her brows rise and fall as if this were all some amusing prank I'm pulling.

"He's not going to find out." But if I had it my way, I'd want the world to know. "Me and Ace are keeping things low key since it's just a summer thing." I pick up my brush and rake it through my hair. "Ace wants to stay friends." I stare at my reflection in the mirror and wonder if deep down maybe that's what I want, too. Having Ace in my life would rearrange things for my dad more than it would me, not to mention there's a sour feeling in my gut when I think of breaking the news to him. I push the thought out of my mind. For sure this is nothing I have to worry about right now. If my father thinks I'm with Warren for the summer. So what? My mind just wants to turn this thing with Ace into something it's not, so does my heart.

Brylee presses her lips together until they're white as paper and reverts her eyes to the ceiling.

"I saw that." I spin around. "You're not buying it, are you?"

"Are you buying it?" Her powder blue eyes blink at me as if I'd be an idiot to think Ace and I could get away with still being friends after the fact. "He's too nice of a guy to do you a favor like that. Don't you think he might be genuinely interested?"

"The thought crossed my mind. Or, more to the point I was hoping." I plop on my bed, and she follows. "But he hasn't expressed any feelings to me outside of the friend zone. If he doesn't give me those kinds of signals, I'll have to gauge our relationship by the one's he does give me. And, for now, that would be friends." I pull the brush through my hair again, smooth, like running it through satin. "Best of friends, by the way. He pushed you right off the pedestal."

Brylee knocks into my shoulder to protest the idea.

"You only like him better because he's got a power line hanging between his legs."

"Power line?" I suppose this is the part where I tell her I can't wait for him to electrocute me, but I hold back. "You're right." I lie back on my pillow and think about what tonight is going to be like. "He said we're going to take it slow."

"As in?" She glides up beside me.

"We've been kissing." I shrug. "Tonight, he says he's moving his mouth to more interesting places." I press my lips together tight. "He promised me a happy ending."

"Get the hell out." She sticks her face in my pillow and laughs up a storm before emerging.

"Swear to God if you pee in my bed, you're boiling the sheets."

Brylee hacks out an air laugh before coming to. "Too late," she whispers, wiping her eyes with my comforter.

"So...is there anything I should know, or do in preparation for the big event?" I'm only asking because Brylee's had her fair share of earth-shattering moments. Brylee has never been too shy in the kiss and tell department.

She nods, considering this for a moment. "Shave everything from the neck down."

"What?" I balk at her razor-sharp advice. "Oh wait, the only thing I don't shave is my—"

"Exactly. Boys are more likely to explore the fun zone if it looks less like a jungle they might need a roadmap to get out of alive."

"Oh really," I say it curt. "Do you think he's going to shave his *fun zone* using the same brand of logic? I think not. It's totally sexist to suggest I lose the bush. By the way, nary a sharpened blade will get near my sweet spot."

"Suit yourself." She slaps her thighs as she sits up. "But when he pulls out a weed whacker to maneuver his way around your not-so-fun zone, don't say I didn't warn you."

"Anything else you feel the need to warn me about?" I sit up beside her. "Any other hair styling solutions my man might find pleasing and navigationally friendly?"

Brylee pushes her shoulder into mine. "You just called him your man."

I take a breath at the thought. "I did, didn't I?" I can feel my cheeks filling in with heat. "Hey, Bry—what do you think my dad would say if he knew Ace and I were dating?"

"I don't know. He's sort of gunning for Warren, I think we both know that."

"True story." And it breaks my heart.

"You know who else is gunning for Warren?" She slips a blonde curl behind her ear.

"Who?" My cheek rises on one side disapprovingly. "If you say it's you, I'll hurl all over your feet. I have higher standards for you."

"*Warren.*" She taps my foot with hers. "He talked on and on this morning about how he felt like an ass and wanted to make it up to you."

"Did he tell you what he did?" God, if he's blabbing about our mattress mishap to anyone who'll listen, I'll die. It's bad enough I confessed to Ace what happened.

"He mentioned something about coming on too strong. And, before you freak out it was just Neva and me."

"Lovely." I don't like the thought of Warren letting Neva and Brylee in on what happened last night. "Did you guys have a pillow fight afterward? I mean, that's what besties do, right?"

Brylee shakes her head at me. "Just go shape your hairy sweet spot into a heart, would you?" She hops off the bed. "I'll be back in the morning for the dirty deets." She heads out the door and pauses. "Oh, and happy endings!"

ༀ)(ༀ

After what felt like hours of plucking, and shaving, and shaping—my entire body is hygienically clean enough to eat a meal off. Of course, I'm hoping to be the meal. My insides throb at the idea of what Ace and I might be doing later. I have a feeling it won't take long to achieve that happy ending. I'm just hoping I can hold out long enough to make it worth his while.

I change into a sheer lace dress that stretches over each of my curves in the event Ace forgets where to land his special kisses, but before I bolt out the door, I hop on my bed a moment and do the unthinkable. I reach under my mattress and pull out the letters from my mother. I suppose there's more than a brain malfunction going on when I'm about to get as close to having sex as possible, and here I am looking to steal a moment of quality time with my poor, sweet mother.

The envelopes slip through my fingers like butter. It warms me to think she touched these very things just days before her passing. She lost so much weight those last few months, and, in the end, she was nothing but skin over bones. I try not to remember her like that, her toothy grimace, her smooth, bald head. My mother was a beauty queen in the most literal sense—Miss Lake Loveless once upon a time, the knockout who stole my father's heart. She had long, dark hair she could wrap around her neck like a scarf, and a body that men would routinely drool over. The cancer stole her looks before it took her life, but it couldn't steal her beauty where it really counted, on the inside. She was diagnosed with pancreatic cancer just a few weeks before my twelfth birthday. I'll never forget the long faces. The fear in her eyes that she would never see me blow out another candle.

I shake the bitter memory of those dark days out of my head if only for a moment.

Instead, I focus in on the loopy handwriting stamped across each one of these envelopes. It's as familiar as seeing her face. I pluck the most recent letter out and open it—run my fingers over her precious penmanship before reading.

Dear Reese,

Happy Birthday!

Congratulations, you're in your twenties! It's going to be a magical decade—one laced with just about every new experience under the sun. This is the time in your life where you really discover who you are and what makes you tick, what you believe in, and the things you think are worth fighting for, dying for. But, like most girls your age, you'll spend an abundance of your time thinking about love. There are so many different types of love, and I think we both know that I'm not talking about the kind of love Daddy and I have for you. What you're probably looking for has a far more sensual meaning behind it. I want you to know, you have my blessing. And I hope you find exactly what you're looking for with the exact person you desire it from most. But if it doesn't come, don't let it steal your joy. There's so much happiness all around, so much unexpected wonder in the little things. That's really what I want you to appreciate—the joy and the ecstasy in the little things. Find the ecstasy in life where you can. It's in those moments you really live. All those other gaps in time are just filler until the next bout of delirium. You could find it just as easily in the silence as you could anywhere—it could be in the face of a perfect flower, in the scent of a fragrant spring morning. It could be in a kiss from a beautiful boy. All of those sweet moments make one hell of an adventure. And if life doesn't offer you an adventure—make one happen.

Enjoy every moment.

Every precious breath is a thing of beauty. Cradle those you love in your heart, bury them there, and never let them go. Life is too short to forget about them even for a moment.

Love you forever,
Mommy

Tears run down my cheeks in long, hot streaks as I carefully replace the letters under my mattress. It was that last line, the one about burying the ones you love in your heart and never forgetting them that set the tone for my entire last year at Yeats. After grieving my mother once again, the next person I thought about was Ace. It was him I knew I never wanted out of my life, and I spent the entire livelong year pining after him like the lovesick schoolgirl I was. By Valentine's Day I had mapped out exactly how this summer would go down. I would have begged on my knees if I had to, but I was determined to have him.

And, tonight, I will.

Mostly.

I skip downstairs to find the house empty. A lone vase sits on the table with two-dozen long stem roses spilling out from it like a bloodied waterfall.

A pink note sits on the table next to them, and I snap it up.

These came while you were gone.
~Ken

I pull the little white card from between the roses, and my thumb snags on a thorn and starts to bleed. I touch it to my lips and let the salty brine linger over my tongue before reading the card.

Reese,
Sorry about last night. Let's talk.
Warren

I bury the card between the knife-sharp stems and walk right out the door.

It's my time with Ace, and I wouldn't miss it for the world.

&)C&

I traverse the backwoods road to Ace's family cabin, in heels no less, just to keep Warren from spotting me. Not that I care what Warren thinks, but if I'm seen out with Ace night after night people are going to talk, and God knows Loveless is as small a town as any. You'd think gossip were the most powerful currency around the way people kept an eye on it like it was in the Dow.

The smell of campfires burning from around the lake lights up my senses with the scent of smoky apple wood, hot dogs, and something sweet layered just beneath that. I love this mystical spell that only the mountain can cast—it brings out a fairytale atmosphere. The fires create a smokescreen with reality and makes this entire evening feel like I've crawled into a dream. Maybe I'll wake up after all this, still in my dorm with the curtains drawn tight. But here I am on the way to see the only boy I've ever loved. It's not a dream. It's my new reality. This is the exact kind of midnight magic Ace accused me of that first night in the lake, and soon I'll be experiencing it with him in the very best way.

I never thought Ace would cave so easily, and it makes me question whether or not *his* brain is the one malfunctioning.

The door to his cabin is wide open, so I lean in. "Knock, knock," I say into a hole in the screen. The house is lit up a bright peach, and I can make out Neva lying on the couch, watching TV. Her pale leg hangs over the side, and she has a long, black dress on that reminds me of Morticia from the Adam's family.

"It's open," she grumbles, so I let myself in. The air gives off a mix of refried oil and cigarettes, which doesn't surprise me since both Neva and her dad are notorious chain smokers.

Neva inspects me from her supine position, never bothering with hello or even a middle finger. Go figure. I guess she's going soft.

Her hair is ratted out over her head a good six inches, and her lids are covered in a dark, maroon eye shadow giving her that bruised effect I'm sure she's after.

Neva didn't morph into Satan's spawn until about six months after she severed ties with me. I'm still not sure why the hell it went down the way it did. We played with Barbies all the way until fifth grade even though we swore we'd never tell another living soul and, honest to God, I questioned for months after she kicked me out of her life if it was some kind of Mattel-sponsored fury. I let Brylee in on our secret once, and I wondered if she said something. It was easier to try and blame Brylee for the split, all those years ago, especially since the only other alternative was myself.

"So"—I try to sound cheery—"you'll never guess what I found the other day while digging in my jewelry box?" My throat constricts because I've said more words to her just now than I have in the last four years combined.

"Gold bullions?" She doesn't bother with a smile, she just douses me with her death rays because, apparently, it's par for the course.

My heart thumps. Neva just spoke to me directly, and it feels like a hard-won victory.

"It was that heart necklace we used to wear." I touch my throat as if I have it on. "You know, the one that's broken in half? Mine said 'Best' and yours said 'friends?'"

"Yeah, I know." She gets up and starts walking past me. "Why don't you put it on and hang yourself with it?" she bleats as she takes off down the hall.

Ace appears in her place and frowns over at her until we hear the slam of her door. He reverts his attention and rakes over me with those soulful eyes—just a hint of sorrow layered underneath.

"Holy shit," he mumbles under his breath as he rides his gaze from my head to my feet. "You look hotter than a Texas sidewalk. Get over here, girl." He gives an approving grin as he wraps his arms around me.

His dark hair is combed back. He's fresh from the shower with his minty breath, his crisp white T-shirt. I press his rock hard body to mine and linger a moment before pulling away.

"Neva might see," I whisper. I wouldn't put it past her to use this to hurt both Ace and me.

He ticks his head back toward his bedroom and leads me over. Ace shuts us inside without bothering to turn on the lights. He leans in and lands a hot kiss on my cheek before hitting pay dirt right over my mouth. I moan into the artful, lingual exchange. Ace knows just how to move his tongue to make me want to linger in this very position all night long.

My insides detonate. I've wanted this for so damn long, and now I'm dying because it's too much to handle.

He pulls back and tracks his hot kisses down the side of my neck.

"I thought we were going to the boathouse?" Not that I care. I can have an orgasm right here on the spot—hell, I'm halfway there already. Screw the fact that Neva is in the next room daydreaming about me swinging from a tree by way of our friendship necklace. I've wanted Ace for so long he's all I see, hear, and breathe.

"We are." Ace runs his hands wild over my curves a moment before flicking on the lights.

A single white daisy has materialized in his hand, and he wears a bashful smile.

"I wanted to give you this first."

My mouth falls open at his thoughtfulness. It's perfect. A gift from Ace means miles more than anything Warren could ever gift me, more than anything I'd ever want from him.

"I love it." And, I want to add, *I love you, too.* "Thank you."

"You're welcome. Picked it myself." His cheeks darken a shade. "You deserve about a dozen more." He adds that last part almost as an apology.

"I don't need a dozen. You already gave me the most perfect one." I hike up on the balls of my feet until our lips collide. I swipe my tongue over his, slow at first, then hard and anxious. We exchange explosive kisses until we're both insanely ready for what comes next.

∞∞

Ace speeds us over to the boathouse, and I laugh as a light rain pelts us on the way up the porch. He unlocks the door and scoops me up in his arms, carrying me over the threshold. Ace lands his lips over mine, and I giggle through a delirious sea of kisses. Here I am with Ace, of all people, the boy I ran field races with, the boy who pretended to eat my mud pies fresh from the yard. The boy I couldn't take my eyes off the past five years alone. This is truly panning out to be the best summer of my life.

Ace lands me back on my feet and fiddles with something on the table. Before I know it, the soft glow of candlelight illuminates the darkness. It's only then I notice the tiny touches that have taken place since last night. A vase full of wild flowers sits on the table, and my heart melts at the sight. Ace handpicked each one of those just for me. He didn't have his father's assistant arrange for them to be delivered to my home, nor did he bury a sterile *I'm sorry* note among the thorns that would eventually draw blood. I shake Warren and his roses out of my head and take in the rest of the tiny boathouse. An old blanket I recognize from the time I spent at Ace's house as a child sits folded at the edge of the bed. I remember snuggling with it whenever I spent the night. His mother once told me she bought it at an outdoor market in Mexico way back when, but that was before she tore out his father's beating heart in front of the family and took off. She tore out Neva's heart, too, and I'm assuming Ace's.

"This is amazing." I brush my hand over his chest. "Candles? Flowers? And—a blanket?"

"I thought you might get cold." He shrugs off his efforts like they were no big deal when we both know they were— candles, flowers, and bedding aren't things a typical guy would remember to bring along on a date. Not that what we're doing classifies as dating.

I run my fingers through his hair in one clean sweep and take in how stunningly gorgeous he is. His chiseled face, those high cut cheeks, the dimples that don't know when to quit, and his demanding eyes that lay over me like hungry, blue flames.

"Why would I get cold, Ace?" I bat my lashes into him hoping he comes up with the right answer.

"Because"—his dimples go off like a warning—"tonight you're going to take off all your clothes."

A dry laugh rumbles quiet in my chest.

Right answer indeed.

Ace

"You ready for this?" I throw in a lopsided grin in the event this was a set up from the beginning. Not that me or my dick want it to be, but a part of me might find it more realistic.

"Ready and willing," she whispers it so low, I hardly believe her.

"I'm not sure I'm ready." There, I said it. I fessed up like a pussy, and she can make of it what she wants.

"What?" Her brows pitch as if they were ready to morph into birds and fly right off her forehead. "You can't back out now." She bites down on her lip like she might cry. "You're my special someone, remember?"

"I'm not backing out." I hook my arm around her waist until her body is pressed tight over mine. If I had it my way, this would be enough. No need for speed because we'd have an entire lifetime to explore one another. I'd trade in a quick and dirty summer for a lifetime of loving Reese every single time. Besides, Reese has been my special someone for as long as I can remember. "With all of my heart, body, and soul I'm on board," I assure her. "But I'm not going to lie, I'm worried this is going to change things—that you'll wake up in the morning and hunt me down with a baseball bat once you come to your senses." I'm only half-kidding. Actually the fantasy involved a hunting knife, and we had mind-bending sex over a bed of pine needles before she hacked my limbs off, starting with the most productive member, the one between my legs.

"Not happening." Reese doesn't waver. Those pale eyes of hers spear from the shadows like flashlights. "There is nothing about this I'll regret in the morning, unless, of course, you bail on me." She cinches up my T-shirt as if she were about to teach me a lesson. And, God knows, I wouldn't be opposed to getting knocked around by her—a wrestling match sounds right up my alley. "Besides, there's no one I'd rather do these things with than you. I mean it. I want this." Her voice quivers, and if I didn't know better, I'd swear she meant each word on a whole different level, the level I'm already on, the one I've been on for as long as I can remember.

"I want this, too." My heart slams against my chest like it's protesting the idea—protesting the fact we're toying with it, not to mention what we're about to do to her heart. I pray to God I don't accidently break it. I'd die before I let that happen.

My fingers work their way down her thighs as I slowly lift the dress right off her body. She holds her hands in the air a moment longer than necessary and lets me inspect her like this, exposing herself to me like a prize.

God.

Reese Westfield has a body that spanks the shit out of any other female I've had the privilege to look at. She highlights the best attributes that the female anatomy has to offer and brings glory to her maker all at the same time.

"We're really doing this?" I ask, giving her the last minute out if she wants it.

"Oh, it's on." She gives a dark laugh. "Are you man enough to lead the expedition, or do I need to recruit someone else?" She presses her lips together, but her smile still rides up the sides. Reese never was one to hide the way she feels around me. She wants this, and, for whatever reason, she wants it with me.

"Take off you bra," I try to say it soft, but it comes out a command. Reese plucks it off, and the girls spring out like a pair of happy melons. Oh fuck. "I'm going to bury my face in those in a few minutes." I give a wry smile and watch as her mouth opens, and she chokes on her next breath. My gut starts to twist because I'm all through with giving her any more outs. I want this just as bad as she wants me to believe she does. "I think you like it when I talk dirty to you, Reese." I skim her hip with my finger, and a gasp strangles out of her. That's what she wants—a dirty, bad boy to ride out the summer with, and I just so happen to fit the bill. Hell, maybe the fact I don't have two coins to rub together gets her going. But right about now, I'm not into analyzing how my lack of finances might factor into things. I'm simply in, sunk, ready and willing to be whatever the hell she wants me to be, so long as my tongue gets to go where its wanted to go all these years. I'm good with it.

Reese moans out a *yes*.

"I thought so." I pump a dry smile. It takes all of my self-control not to move as quick as my body wants. I promised Reese a summer she'd never forget, and I plan on delivering in every fucking way. I'm pretty sure ravaging her on night one isn't how to go about it. The strategy was to figure out what makes her want to detonate, and judging by the way she's quivering for me, waiting for my next move, I think I just found the key. "Take off your panties, nice and slow." I press out an easy grin before letting it dissipate. "I want to watch," I whisper, twisting a lock of her hair between my fingers. I used to fantasize about touching her dark, smooth hair, pressing my face into it and getting lost, and now, here I am.

Reese tries to catch her breath as she hitches her thumbs into her waistband.

If barking out commands all night drives her wild, then that's what I plan on doing. But when it comes right down to it, I want to fall on my knees and worship at her perfect feet, make love to her for seven days straight as a token of my undying affection. But that's not what this summer is about. That's not what it may ever be about.

When we were kids, Reese and I would play a game. She would ask me questions and each time I got the answer wrong she'd sock me in the arm. I knew every one of those damn answers and never gave the right one just so I could feel her tiny fist pummeling into me again and again. Sometimes you take the pain because that's all you think some people will ever give you. Anything is a gift from Reese.

"I *want* you to watch." Reese swivels her hips like a seasoned stripper while her black lace underwear melt in a puddle at her feet. She starts kicking off her heels, and I steady my hand over the back of her thigh.

"Why don't you leave those on?"

She lets out a breath in lieu of an answer.

"Do you like this? Me telling you what to do?" I dig my fingers into the back of her hair, and she closes her eyes and moans like a dove.

"Maybe," it barely crests her lips before she turns her head into my hand and buries a kiss in it. "A little—*more* than a little."

"I think you're just about ready." I tilt her chin gently until she's looking right at me again. "Lay down on the bed." I walk her backward until her knees buckle, and she lies flat in the middle. I whip off my shirt. "Slide your legs back to your hips." She lifts her knees, and I straddle myself just shy of her feet. "Open for me, Reese." I don't take my eyes off hers. It feels like a dare, and a part of me wonders if it is. Reese parts her knees just enough for me to glide my hand down if I wanted. "More, I want to see you."

The back of her head digs into the pillow as she arches her body. Reese is already lost in the pleasure of it all, and I haven't even touched her yet.

I smooth my hands over her thighs, carefully pushing her apart at the knees until I have a bird's eye view, and my heart jackhammers into my throat.

Fuck.

"You're perfect, Reese, you know that?" I touch my fingers lightly over that tender part of her, and she bucks forward, her eyes squeeze tight as if she were already there.

"Hold on." I pull her legs down gently and glide over her smooth body until our lips are less than a breath away. I thought that might spring her in the right direction, but Reese is ready to shatter, and there's so much more I want to do with her—share with her. I land my lips over hers with just a simple swipe, and Reese presses me in by the back of the neck, gliding her tongue over mine eager and greedy. My stomach cinches. My dick perks to life because, holy hell, Reese Westfield is gorging on me with her hungry kisses, and I couldn't have asked for anything better. I float a kiss to her ear. "You're going to come for me tonight."

She gives a hard groan while raking her fingers through my hair.

"And, after that, I'm going to take you home." I press a kiss into her ear, and she shudders beneath me.

"What if I don't want to go home?" She grazes her teeth over my ear, and I pull her in tight and hold her like that. "What if I want to make you come?"

My chest rumbles with a dull laugh. There is nothing I'd like more. "Tonight is all about you. How about next time I show you how to get me there?"

She lets out a heated breath, and her chest quivers under mine.

"How does that sound?" I plant a kiss just shy of her ear without thinking twice. I don't know how she expects me to mechanically love her as if this were some routine, some meaningless one-night stand. If she's here, in bed with me, my natural inclination is to shower her with kisses, to love every inch of her with my mouth and hope she'll return the favor.

She buries a nod into my neck.

"But right now I'm going to map out your body with my tongue." I take a playful bite out of her earlobe, and she lets out a small cry that wrenches my gut. There's no way in hell I'm going to be able to hold out tonight. I'll deserve a trophy if I manage to walk her to the door, let alone drive her anywhere.

I lean up and take her in as the candlelight illuminates over her perfect features, her dark hair sprays out around her like a black wreath.

"God, you're beautiful, Reese." I steal a kiss off her lips and trail my mouth down her neck. "Open for me just like before."

Reese glides her knees up and nestles them on my back.

"I'm going to kiss you in places you've probably dreamed about being kissed." I sink a little lower and scoop her breast in one hand. "I'm going to put my lips over you right here." I rub my thumb over her nipple and watch as she swallows hard in anticipation. My lips part as I land my mouth right where it's wanted to be for so long. I let out a dull groan as I bury as much of her soft flesh in my mouth as I can handle.

"Ace." She moves beneath me with a sigh, and my dick hardens to granite.

My tongue finds a home over her, and I roll her nipple around in my mouth for a good long while. This is heaven.

Reese and me together at last, and, yet, in a way, we're not together at all, not where it counts. I'm just someone filling in the blanks for her, showing her a good time for a few short weeks.

My lips glide down her velvet smooth body as I trail lower, past her hips, to the inside of her creamy thighs.

"Get on your elbows," I whisper into her. "I'd hate for you to miss anything." My lips twitch just this side of a smile as she props herself up.

Reese looks over at me with her lips parted, her breathing erratic.

"I'm going to touch you right there." I graze over the soft curls at the base of her hips, and she flexes into me. "Then I'm going to kiss you—right there." I sink my hand lower until my fingers lose themselves in her heated slick.

A hard groan comes from her, and I retract my touch as I sink even lower on the bed. I spent the last part of the afternoon removing the footboard that I figured would stand in the way of our platonic efforts this evening. Personally, I think Reese Westfield gives new definition to the word platonic. But I'm not complaining.

I glide my hand to her thigh, before trailing kisses over her knee, across her smooth-as-silk shin and down to her slender foot. I pluck off her heels one by one and run my finger over the arch of her foot until she flinches. I catch her by the ankle and pull her back to me, kissing her foot with a smile.

"That tickles." She thumps me on the back with her kneecap.

"Maybe I like to hear you laugh." True story.

"Yeah?" She rasps it out sexy as hell, and I die a little looking up at her with her sleepy eyes, that look of lust ripe on her face. "I thought you might be a little more interested in hearing me scream."

I rumble out a dull laugh. "Maybe I will." Her toenails call to me, painted hot pink just like candy, so I plunge them into my mouth and suck down on each one as she lets out a gasp followed by a string of giggles. I trail my lips back up her thigh in a line of fire and lunge in for the gold, landing my lips over the most delicate part of her without warning, and she lurches up and digs her fingers into my hair.

Holy shit.

Reese Westfield tastes like sugar—like perfection, and, if I hadn't already lost my fucking mind tonight, I've officially jumped into the deep end. This is it. I love Reese, and, as much as she probably never wants to hear those words, I can't go barking out orders like some drill sergeant anymore. I want to pour all of my affection into her, just hoping she'll return the favor.

I ride my tongue over her in waves, pausing every now and again to genuinely make out with her pleasure points, rolling my tongue over her just like I did with her mouth a few minutes before. Her panting increases, she scratches at my shoulders, crying out for a release, and, selfishly, it's the last thing I want to give her. I want this very act to go on for an eternity, but I know it can't. Not one thing we do will exceed this bittersweet season, and in a few short weeks, she'll be leaving for Yeats once again.

I sink lower and plunge my tongue deep inside her, and my balls ache to join the party. I press in and out, until I'm loving her like I've dreamed of a thousand times before, burying the groans in my chest because it's all too fucking fantastic.

"*Ace.*" She lets out a hard breath, and I glide back to her pleasure point, flicking my tongue over her sweet spot until her body spasms into mine. She holds my head locked down in that position before evicting me from my post and cinching her knees together.

"I guess we've met our goal for the night," I whisper, a dull smile riding on my lips. I swim up beside her and hold Reese in my arms, her heated body still quivering into mine. "Did you like that?" I press a kiss over her cheek as she shivers into me.

"Nope." She twists around with her eyes glowing like fireflies. "I loved it."

Reese loved it. A smile cinches on my lips for a brief moment as I tighten my grip around her. I want to hold her like this all night long. It might be game over to her as far as her body goes, but I'm hoping somewhere in the exchange her heart piqued its interest for me just a little. Tonight was magic, and I never want her to forget it. I know for a fact I won't.

I land a careful kiss just over her temple and keep it there in an effort to stop the words *I love you* from slipping from my lips.

But, God, I love Reese Westfield.

Every single day, I do.

ᔕᑎᑕᔕ

True to my word I drive her home, albeit at five-thirty in the morning once the sun has already kissed the lip of the horizon.

"Good night." Reese snuggles into me as I wrap my arms around her.

"Good morning," I counter, pressing a kiss over the top of her head.

Reese looks up at me, her mascara slightly smudged, her hair rumpled and sexy as hell. I remember all those nights she spent at my house when she and Neva still hung out. I remember getting up at the ass crack of dawn just to plant myself in the living room to watch her sleep, memorizing her sinewy limbs, her long, mirror-like shards of hair. I wanted her even then.

"You're perfect," I whisper.

"I'm not perfect." Her chest rumbles with a quiet laugh. "Not even close." She touches the side of my cheek with her hand. "But you are." Reese leans in. A desperation grows in her eyes as she struggles for a moment. "Ace, I..." Her mouth closes, entombing the words she was about to say next.

"Go ahead." I rub my arm up over her shoulder, encouraging her to finish. "You're safe. You can say anything you want." I damn well know what I want to hear, and I can't help but think she was about to say it—say I love you. We're on the cusp of something beautiful, something bigger than a summer fling, something that takes being someone special to a whole new level. If she says those words, I'll drive her right back to the boathouse to finish what we started.

"It was stupid." She shakes her head. "I'd better go. If Kennedy thinks I'm missing, she'll call Warren then Brylee, and I'll have to tell the whole world I spent the night in the arms of the best looking guy on the planet." She bites down on a coy smile. "I wish we could tell everyone." Her eyes widen at the prospect, and I get lost in the blue flecks that swim in a sea of silver.

"But they wouldn't understand, right?" I brush the hair from her face and land a simple kiss over her lips. "Summer flings—*special someone's*—are sort of hard to explain in general."

She nods as her affect dims just this side of tears. "You are special to me, Ace." Her eyes glitter like the surface of the lake when the sun hits it just right. "You'll always be more than a fling." She presses a hard kiss over my lips before bolting out of the car, and I never did get a chance to say anything in return. Her door closes, quiet as a whisper, and I drive back down toward the house, smiling like a goof.

The rim of the lake glistens a bright pink as it drinks down the salmon-colored sun. A duck takes flight over the unblemished sky, and I exhale a breath at the beauty of it all. Everything looks more defined, more satisfying to the senses— more real.

I park in the driveway and note dad's truck is still missing. Looks like two Waterman's scored last night, let's hope it's not three. Not that I consider what I'm doing with Reese a game. She might. It doesn't mean I do.

I head into the house to find Neva on the couch with a blanket wrapped around her, cartoons playing softly on the television.

"Where were you?" Her hair is twisted in a rat's nest on top of her hair. Her makeup is dripping halfway down her cheek giving her that zombie vibe she's been after these last few years. Sometimes I seriously miss the cute little kid she used to be.

"None of your business." I head to the kitchen and start a pot of coffee, tossing in a few extra scoops to intensify the pick me up. "What has you up so early?"

"I always get up early, but you wouldn't notice." She grumbles something under her breath, and I miss that last part. "So, were you with her?"

My arm freezes, midair, as I'm about to reach for a mug. That goofy grin is itching to make its reprisal.

"Yeah, I was with her. We were just hanging out." I turn on the coffeemaker like it's no big deal. "We must of fell asleep."

"Just hanging out, huh? Where? In your car?" She sounds incensed that it could have happened at all, let alone in the Cougar.

"No, not in the car." I head over to the table and flip open my laptop. "Again, it's none of your business."

"Well I sort of feel like it *is* my business." Neva snaps like she's about to start ripping off heads. I glance up just in time to see the fire in her eyes.

"All right, I give. What's the deal? You cut Reese out of your life, and now, you want me to join in on the fun? Too bad. It's not happening." Not now, not ever.

"Yeah? How about some family camaraderie? What happened to all that I've-got-your-back-no-matter-what bullshit you fed me when Mom died?"

My heart stops because for a minute I think maybe I blocked out some huge life event.

"She didn't die, Neva. She *left*." I cut the air with my words as if I were somehow using my mother to deflect the blow she wanted to inflict on Reese and me.

"Same difference," she huffs as she tosses the blanket to the floor. "I guess I could have figured that you'd be the next in line to abandon me."

"How am I abandoning you by hanging out with Reese?" I rub my eye until it feels like it's going to invert into my skull. I'm too fucking tired to do this shit with her.

"Did you sleep together?" Neva's voice rails through the air and saws over my last nerve.

"Not in the biblical sense." Not yet anyway.

"Then why did she come here dressed to impress with her feet pressed into her fuck-me gear?"

She did, didn't she? A dull smile rides low on my lips at the memory.

"Look, I know you don't like her. I get it. For whatever reason she's your mortal enemy. But, for the record, I've never once heard her say anything bad about you. And that's true as shit, so get off my fucking back."

"Right." Neva drills into me with those raccoon eyes. "She's only screwing my brother. I think that goes a little further than talking behind my back to her stupid ivy-league friends."

"You're friends with all the same people."

"And I know for a fact they think they're better than us." She picks up a magazine and glances over it before tossing it to the floor. "Look, I know you were with her last night, but I also know she's pretty serious with her *boyfriend*, Warren. He told me so himself."

I don't bother glancing up, just finish perusing the Yeats' rowing team's homepage to see if they've added my name to the roster yet. "Don't believe everything you hear. They're not that serious."

"Then why did he show Brylee and me the engagement ring he bought for her? He said he was going to pop the question on the Fourth of July."

My insides boil with heat. I shut the laptop and stare at the chipped cabinets for a brief moment.

"Really?" I straighten in my seat, trying to remember if she ever mentioned breaking things off with him the other night at the Blue Crab. "I doubt it'll happen. Even if he does, she won't say yes."

"Why's that? Because she's so in love with you?" She storms over to the table with the look of mockery ripe in her eyes. Neva leans in and bares her fangs in a sarcastic smile. "You'll never be anything but some cheap throwaway toy to someone like her. Just watch—she'll be engaged to Warren McMoney by summers end, and she'll have you chopping the firewood to heat their happy home. That's all you'll ever be to her is some tool she fucked for the hell of it."

"Shut up," I say it low. My palms flattened over the table to keep from turning it over.

"Fine. I'll keep my mouth shut," she shouts as she stomps her way down the hall. "But I'm only trying to stop you from getting your heart broken. You may not have my back anymore, but I sure as hell have yours."

The slam of her door goes off like a gunshot.

"Fuck," I grunt, before heading outside to clear my head.

A smooth, clean line bisects the water, and I recognize the kook stroking through the lake. It's bright and early, and Warren is already doing laps like he's training for the Olympics.

"What the hell." I jump into my canoe and paddle out until we're parallel.

"You and me," he shouts, pointing over to the buoy at the distal end, and I give a thumbs up.

We start neck-in-neck as we race over toward the forest end of the lake. Warren and I have done this a million times. Hell, I credit myself for getting his sorry ass into rowing to begin with. Way back when, it was me who spent hours training him before he took flight on his own, and now, here we are, going at it like the prize was Reese herself, only Warren wouldn't know that because he thinks he already has her—owns her.

I pull out a good twenty feet, and he never catches me. We spin around, and he points to the other side, and we do it all over again.

Warren and I glide up onto the white sandy beach of Pleasure Point and roll out of the tiny boats. My muscles are on fire, and I can't catch my breath.

"Dude," he pants. "You must have wanted that bad. I don't think I've ever had my ass kicked so hard." He slaps his stomach as he lets out a howl.

"I usually get what I want." Not quite accurate but in this case, with Reese, I hope to God it's me who's the last man standing. "So what's up? What's going on in your life, bro?" I'm not sure what I'll do if he fesses up to wanting to pop the question. There's no way Reese and I could carry on this summer charade unless she clears the air with him—that is if she wants to.

"Just the same bullshit day after day—doing an internship for my dad, playing lackey."

"Cool." My stomach loosens with relief. He didn't even mention her. Maybe she's not that important to him.

"I'm having a big party next week, you up for some bro's and hoes? We got to get you laid, dude."

"The party sounds good. I might have plans though." A vision of Reese moaning beneath me bumps through my mind, and I don't fight it. "Don't worry about me. I'm pretty damn lucky these days. And you?" I know for a fact he's not getting any.

"Got me a wild one. Sucks me off like it's nobody's business." He gravels out a laugh, and I flinch. "She's got some douche on the side, and I don't even fucking care, man. It's sort of an open relationship right now, anyway." He gets up on his elbows and stares off at the water. My stomach pinches tight, and that cup of coffee I just downed burns through me like battery acid. Why do I get the feeling I'm the fucking douche. "Reese and I will do the whole monogamy thing once we tie the knot, but for now, it's a summer of sowing some serious oats if you know what I mean. We both know we're buckling down come fall."

Shit. Is that what I am? An oat?

"She's really okay with that?" I find it doubtful.

"Hell, yes"—he cinches his head back a notch—"she's the one that suggested it. Don't let that sweet, innocent routine of hers fool you, Reese is nothing but a bad girl waiting to let loose. It's her best kept secret. But don't tell her I said so. I'll deny it every single time." He gets up and jumps back in his canoe. "Do yourself a favor and find yourself someone like Reese. Life doesn't get any better than that." He sails off, and I watch as he pumps his way toward his father's overgrown house.

I thought I did find someone like Reese.

Now I wonder if I know Reese at all.

5

Catching Shadows

Reese

"So?" Kennedy stares at me from over the rim of her coffee cup. Her nose is bunched up, her lips set to a snarl, giving her all the drama of a demon, and her ears peak back like an elf's. I'm guessing over breakfast isn't the best time to let her know I think she looks like a demon elf. "How's the big *race* for your virginity?"

Kennedy has long since dubbed herself the keeper of my V-card. As soon as she lost hers, she put mine on a timer.

"It's getting pretty heated." That's like saying the surface of the sun is a little hot. I want to keep all the orally delicious details to myself, but a fire rips through me, and I'm pretty sure she can see it blistering over my skin—goose bumps in the shape of a thousand little penises.

She pumps a dry smile like a lioness ready to pounce her virginal prey.

"Spill the semen, like Ace did," she insists.

"I'm not discussing bodily fluids over breakfast with you."

Kennedy is fresh from the shower with her white plush robe pulled snug around her body, her hair wrapped in a towel two feet above her head like a pile of whipped cream. She smells sweet like sugared pears. It reminds me of a dessert my mother used to make. Mom would boil the pears once they began to bruise and sprinkle brown sugar over them. I still do it now and again just to keep her culinary traditions alive. Only next time I'll pretend I'm boiling Kennedy and her foul mouth, and I find that mildly amusing.

We sit at the table, overlooking the lake, and my eyes keep catching on the yellow and orange tents that materialized overnight across the way. There are so many camps up here in the summer, but mostly they're all on the other side, which is nice since they tend to get rowdy. Somewhere in the recesses of my mind I think of Ace and me sneaking off to a tent of our own—nothing but God, and sky, miles of evergreens, and not a dollar bill or Warren in sight.

"So what's up with you and McCarthy?" Kennedy chooses to carry on her interrogation of my private life, and I don't know why. I don't make it a practice to ask about the state of *her* vagina, not that Warren has anything to do with mine but still. "He's been asking me a million questions."

"Nothing's up with Warren. I told him the other night I think we should see other people." True story and he didn't even bat an eye. Something tells me he's been on board with that idea a lot longer than I care to know about.

"You broke up with him?" Her mouth elongates into a perfect oval. It's so rare to see Kennedy shocked by anything, and that alone sends a mild panic railing through me.

"*No,*" I say it slow to defuse the gossip bomb just dying to go off in her. "You see, I would have had to be going out with him in order to break it off. One cannot break off something that technically never began." I give a satisfied smirk because that was some serious ninja word-fu I just did there.

"Okay, Confucius, you can relax." She lowers her dark gaze into me and gives a knowing smile. "For the record, I don't think he heard that whole part about you seeing other people. That boy is insane when it comes to his little, *Reesie pie.*"

"For the record"—I mimic her tone—"Warren has never called me that ridiculous nickname once, and if you ever use it in public, I'll tell everyone you smoke tampons recreationally."

"How do you know what he calls you while he's fucking my brains out?" She kicks me from under the table, and I shake my head at her stupid attempt at humor. For one, I sort of wish he was launching grey matter through her ears because that would solve a hell of a lot of problems for me right now.

"Would you be quiet?" I roll my eyes while Kennedy laughs her turban off. "And he's insane if he thinks we were ever together to begin with. Paternal expectations do not a relationship make."

"And what about Ace?" She settles down just enough to dig her fingers into her eyes. "Does he think you're together? Are you *his* little, Reesie Pie?"

I wish.

"He wants to keep things status quo," it sails from my lips robotic. "He likes having me as a friend." It guts me just to say it, to think it. After all, I'd swear on my life that his tongue catapulted us well past the friendly phase of our relationship. Maybe Ace is just afraid to admit it, the way I am. Who am I kidding? Ace has always been fearless. I'm simply feeding his boner addiction for the summer.

"And what happens once August rolls around?" Kennedy swivels her finger around the lip of her mug in a never-ending circle, sort of the way my mind cycled in a never-ending loop over Ace all last year.

"I guess we go back to the way things were." God, how I hate the way things were. I like yeast infections more than I like the way things were with Ace and me. "But what I really hope is that nothing goes back to the way it was ever again." I come to just as the words slip from me.

Crap. I just gave Kennedy an inch, and she's going to—

"Oh my, God." Kennedy's eyes widen, her forehead wrinkles, perplexed. "I call bullshit. You are so falling in love with him." She shakes her head. "Oh crap." She belts out a laugh. "You've always been in love with him haven't you?"

A bang emits from behind followed by footsteps, and we turn to find Beverly and Dad storming the room with their suitcases.

"Who has Reese *always* been in love with?" Bev darts over to Kennedy and gives her a long, moaning embrace.

"Daddy!" I jump up and wrap my arms around him tight. It feels like a small eternity since we've seen each other last. It's like seeing a ghost, and a part of me believes Mom might be the next person to barrel through that door. But I'm not that lucky today. I'll never be that lucky again.

"Hey, princess." He plants a kiss over my cheek. His hair shines like glass. It's silver as a nickel, clean and white, no signs of yellowing. Dad's face glows with a smooth even tan, and that tiny dimple by his eye cuts in as he smiles down at me. "Now what's all this talk about love?" He gives a quick wink. "Speaking of Warren, how's my boy doing? I hear he's been running the show while I've been away."

"He has," I say, shooting a quick look to Kennedy. "Rumor has it he's working very hard." At committing an assault against your daughter I want to add but don't. I haven't forgotten the fact Warren tried to mow my field with his weed whacker. There's no way in hell I'm giving him a pass on that one. In fact, I think I should kick his boys around the lake a time or two to get the message across. Not that I want to spend a moment of my time bothering with Warren or his wandering wiener.

"Good. About time he starts pulling his weight around the office." Dad presses in another kiss. "Yeats has one of the best law schools in the country. I think he'll make a fine addition to the firm one day. Until then he should blow off all the steam he can." Assholes always do. "Enjoy academia while you're able, girls. The corporate world is a cold, cruel place to be."

I want to tell him that the whole world has been a cold, cruel place to be since my mother died, but now with Ace filling my days, my *nights,* it feels a lot less scary.

Just the thought of Warren setting up shop at the law firm feels like another link in the chain that will permanently bind us together. I curl into my father's chest, so he won't see the disappointment blooming over my face. I'll never be rid of Warren in my life. Not that I really care. A part of me just wants him to find someone and be happy, the way I found someone—sort of.

"I missed you," I whisper as I tighten my arms around my father's waist. He feels solid as a tree trunk, immovable. He smells of cedar and leather, and I take him in, trying to memorize the way he feels and smells so that when fall rolls around, I can hold him in my heart.

Beverly drops her purse on the table with a thud, jolting me out of my moment like an ax falling over my neck. "You'll never guess what I bought in Milan." She pets Kennedy's hair as if she were an exotic animal. Beverly and Kennedy look more like sisters thanks to all the Botox, the nip and tuck, the Pilates before dawn, but Beverly keeps her jet-black hair cut above the ears with long sweeping bangs up front.

"A new Louis Vuitton purse?" Kennedy hops when she says it like a child on Christmas. "The oversized one I want as a beach bag?" It's a sad day when a handbag that costs more than some used cars is relegated to fun in the sun.

"*No.*" Bev swats away the thought like she were vying for an eco-tote from the dollar store. "We can pick one of those up over lunch one afternoon if you like." She taps her acrylic nails over the veneer of the table and creates a death rattle. "I've finally found a decent replacement for this God-awful table."

I glance up at my father. This is the final material piece of my mother that's left in this house. She loved this hunk of mahogany as if she grew it from the ground and hewn it herself.

"It's a done deal." Dad holds up a hand. "It's already being shipped."

"But this is Mom's table," I say it low for my dad's ear only, but the room stills because the passive-aggressive bitch in me made damn sure everyone around us heard.

"Oh, hon." Beverly pours out her faux sense of sorrow, thick as vomit. "I'll have it stored for you, and when you and Warren buy your first home, we'll have it ready and waiting." She winks over at me, and I wonder if that's her socialite way of saying F.U. and your dead mother's table, too. "See? You're already on your way to starting a family of your own." She tilts into a peaceable smile. Deep down inside I'm convinced she knows I'm not into Warren. Maybe that's what she and Kennedy discuss over lunch before they buy overpriced beach bags. "It'll all work out. I promise."

I don't think it'll all work out. What I do think is that my Step Bitch isn't quite done booting my mother out of my father's life. When Beverly moved in, she had the wrought-iron railing plucked right off the stairwell and replaced it with sheet glass and a metallic track that lined the top, and now it has no more feeling than a rain gutter. As soon as she took over the house, she systematically removed every last piece of my mother that I cherished and replaced them with cold, unfeeling works of questionable "art." I can't bear the thought of losing this table to some faraway storage unit. They might as well bury it in the cemetery right next to my mother. I don't want to wait until I finish with graduate school one day and finally move out to see it again. God knows I'll never share a home with Warren.

"Speaking of homes"—Dad nods out the window at the neighbor's property—"the Nicholson's house is up for sale." The exact one nestled between our house and the McCarthy's.

I roll my eyes at the thought of shacking up with Warren, now or ever, and sandwiched between our parents no less. Just the thought makes me want to stab my eye out with a fork.

Nope—not happening.

I'm so head over heels in love with Ace, I can't see straight.

This is the start of something spectacular. I can feel it.

Ace Waterman is the one for me, and there is no other—never was, never will be.

A few, lazy, Ace-free days slip by. Gavin hauled Ace into the backwoods in order to chop down an entire Connecticut forest. And now that the emergency hacking spree is over, we can resume our regularly-scheduled debauchery and bring honor to the good name of summer flings everywhere. Well, almost.

I swivel around in my chair, more than slightly irritated as I stare at my desk.

Normally I keep track of important things like when my papers are due, when I'll be having a quiz, and when my period might interrupt one of the most exciting weeks of my life. But despite my meticulous attempts at mapping my life out on a calendar, I totally forgot that red witch was due to shoot right out of my fallopian tubes. This pretty much ruins things for me tonight, but it doesn't mean Ace has to suffer.

Brylee sits on my bed whittling a banana into a bona fide penis while I watch the careful attention she puts into her pornographic art.

"You should go on tour or something," I muse. "People would pay to see this. They'd call you the Penis Peeler. You'd be a hit in galleries all over the country. Society is sick as fuck, but don't you worry your pretty little head, you fit right in," I say as she unearths the fruit's true phallic form, complete with ridges and what looks like a vein running down the middle, a tip that looks more like a crown. "Maybe you could sit outside of the general store with an empty coffee can? I'll seed you some tip money."

"You're a riot." She squeezes the poor thing until it launches right out of its casing and into my chest. I let out a short-lived scream followed by a rather swift eviction of the sticky mess. "That's a dick's favorite thing to do." She presses out a manufactured smile. "Come right at you."

"That's disgusting," I say, still plucking the mess out of my tank top.

"Tell it to Ace." She gives a light kick to my knee. "So, you break things off with Warren?" She unties her bathing suit top at the neck and accidentally flashes me before redoing her strap.

"What's with everyone today? First, Kennedy—now you? We were never together. He's fine with me seeing other people. We've discussed it—I kicked his balls, I believe the topic is no longer on the agenda." Somehow I don't believe that. I doubt I could have a Warren-free summer let alone a Warren-free lifetime.

"In theory? Or do you know this as a fact?" Brylee leans in as if there were a real need for an answer.

"Fact. Besides, I'm not advertising Ace anytime soon. He made it clear we're BFFs forever, remember?" I wipe my chest down with a tissue. "Warren is yesterday's news. He needs to find himself someone new to blue ball him."

"You ever going to tell Ace how you really feel?" Brylee's eyes glitter up with tears. Her lips redden as if she were sorry for me in a severe way. Looks like I'm not the only one PMSing around here.

"No." I push out a sigh as I fall back on my pillow. "We're in such a good place right now, I don't want to ruin things."

"I know right?" She mocks, landing beside me. "I mean, that little pesky thing called the *truth* has fucked up more relationships than I can number."

"Be quiet."

"Promise me something." She nudges her thigh into mine. "You'll tell him the truth at the end of all this madness."

"At the end of all this madness," I parrot softly. I think about it for a second. "I mean, at that point summer will be over." I shrug, trying to reason it out. "It's not like I'll see him until next year. I'll be home for Christmas, and that's when he sees his mom." Ace and I can play hit and miss for the rest of our lives if we want to.

"Nobody remembers anything in a year." She's goading me, but I go with it.

"I guess you're right." I chew the inside of my cheek until I'm about to draw blood. "Yeah, I think I will tell him how I really feel at the end of summer." A spike of adrenaline surges in me at the thought.

"Pinky swear?" She holds out her hand.

"Pinky swear." I hook my little finger over hers, and we shake on it. Suddenly it feels as if a boulder has been lifted from my chest, and I can breathe again. I hadn't felt this light in so long. I had forgotten how good it felt. I'm walking on air, and it's all because I'm finally going to tell Ace Waterman exactly how I feel.

My phone goes off. It's a text from Warren, and I groan.

You up for dinner? I get off early tonight. Blue Crab?

"What should I tell him?" That giant ball of granite rolls right back over my chest as I stare at his words.

"Just curious"—she pokes me in the knee—"are you allergic to the truth?"

"No. Maybe." I type, **Not feeling so hot tonight. Some other time**, and hit send. "There. That's not totally a lie. I started my period today. I always feel like crap the first day I start."

"You do realize that by tacking on, 'some other time,' you're stringing him along."

"Please." I pull back to get a better look at her and that blonde, wide-eyed innocence she's faking just for me. "I'm being nice."

"Yeah, well, eventually you'll have to be a lot less nice. Face it, you're going to have to dump his ass."

"Mmm." My dad floats through my mind. "If our lives weren't so intertwined, I would have put Warren in his place a long time ago. Besides, there are plenty of girls who are after Warren. I'm sure he's already into someone else. And, if he's not, he'll get the hint I'm not interested when I successfully manage to avoid him at all costs this summer." I thump my finger over my lips. "Hey, didn't you once say you thought Warren was hot?"

"Yeah, but we were like fifteen, and it was the night I got drunk off wine coolers for the first time."

"Maybe you should take up drinking wine coolers again."

My phone blinks to life. **Damn girl all this time apart just makes me want you more. Tomorrow you're mine.**

"Told you." Brylee shakes her head in disapproval. "You should try the truth. You never know, miracles might happen."

"I find that hard to believe."

I wish I could *try the truth.* But not any truths I might have to share with Warren.

It's Ace and our truths that take over my mind and heart. Telling Ace that I love him would be the most amazing thing in the world, especially if he confessed to feeling the same.

It would be magic—a miracle.

Ace

Gavin backed a tractor behind the cabin and dumped a shitload of red fir into the clearing. I've been splitting logs since two, and I'm sweating like a hooker in church. My back hurts like hell as if Gavin parked that tractor right over it before he left.

I land piece after piece on the mauler and split the soft wood, easy as slicing butter.

"Ace Waterman."

I turn around to find Brylee waving, making her way over with two large iced teas from the general store. A short-lived smile pumps from my lips because I know one of them is just for me.

"Thanks." I take it from her and down it in a few quick gulps, sort of the way I imagine what being with Reese the first time will be like. The other night keeps running through my mind like a dream I was lucky enough to experience firsthand. "Grab an ax," I tell her. "We'll knock this out in an hour," I pant through a smile. I'm teasing. I wouldn't make Brylee lift a finger around here.

"I've got an ax to grind all right." She purses those ballooned-out lips at me. She's pissed to hell, and I know I'm in trouble. Brylee and I commuted to Collingsworth Community College all last year to save on gas. I know all of her pissed off expressions, and this happens to be the one she reserves just for me.

"Spill it." I land on the bench and pat the seat next to me.

"A little birdie told me that you're having yourself a real good time this summer." Her sky blue eyes blink in disbelief.

Reese and Bry are pretty tight, so I expected this on some level. Hell, I'm hoping the only bird around here is Brylee because, God knows, I'm hoping she'll sing and let me in on how Reese might really feel.

"And?" I may have mentioned to Brylee on one or more occasions that I was into Reese. Heavily.

"Have you told her how you feel?" The wind picks up and tosses her hair into her face a moment. She hitches it behind her ears, and it trims her face like a haystack.

"Nope." I swallow hard at the prospect. "Thought about it, but I'm not sure I'm ready to go there. Things are moving pretty good right now. She say anything to you?"

"Yes, and I'm embarrassed to repeat it."

I give a little laugh. It takes a lot to embarrass Brylee.

"Look"—she slumps down—"just promise me that at the end of this crazy summer, you'll tell her how you really feel." She closes her eyes a moment too long.

"I don't know. Reese was pretty adamant we stay friends. I'd hate to ruin anything."

"It won't ruin anything. You never know, she might have been dying to hear it all along."

"Do you know something?" My adrenaline spikes at the thought of Reese dying to hear anything that remotely resembles that.

"I know Warren texted her while I was over there. He still very much considers himself a contender." She glances down at my dust-covered chest, my dirt-stained Levis. "Don't let him out charm you. Make this a summer she'll never forget, and who knows? She might go insane and beg you to make her yours forever." Brylee bears into me like there's an underlying threat in there somewhere.

Making Reese mine forever—I like the sound of that.

"And if she doesn't feel the same?" I ask, still inspecting her for clues as to how Reese might really feel.

"Then you'll both move on—the end. Reese would never cut you out of her life. You and I both know that." She rubs my back as if she's already consoling me. "I just want to see you happy for once, and, sometimes, telling someone how you really feel is a step in the right direction. You never know, she might be right there with you at the corner of delirious and happy."

Delirious and happy. That's exactly how Reese makes me feel.

Brylee gets up and starts heading back down the dusty road before turning around. "Oh, and heads up. Her Aunt Flo just came into town for a visit."

"Who?"

"Her period."

I crimp my lips. Did I want to know that?

"I prefer some chocolate, a warm blanket, and a movie on days like that." She shrugs. "Just saying."

"Chocolate, warm blanket, movie... got it."

"Massages. *Foot* massages!" She drifts down the road. "S'mores!"

Aunt Flo, huh? That's all right. I'm just thrilled to spend time with Reese, and, if I get to comfort her in the process, even better.

Guess I'm off to do some shopping.

ЮСß

In the evening while the residue of the sun still lights up the sky like a lamp, Reese knocks on the door.

"Come in," I call from the kitchen. I'm just about done loading up an oversized picnic basket I dug out of the shed.

I step into the living room and find Neva glaring over at the most beautiful girl I've ever laid eyes on—Reese Westfield. Her hair is slicked back in a ponytail. She has on a pair of grey sweats and her Yeats T-shirt. Her face is freshly scrubbed, and she looks about thirteen, and mighty fucking cute.

"Hey beautiful." I wrap my arms around her waist and land a gentle kiss over her lips. Neva lets out a groan like she just witnessed a puppy massacre.

Screw Neva. What the hell does she care? She certainly doesn't care about my opinion where it really matters. I told her months ago that the douche she's dating is a loser, but she didn't bother to listen.

"Fuck you both," she belches it out like some demon on steroids.

"Um"—Reese cuts a quick glance to my sister—"hi yourself." She starts in on a tempered smile as if she's relieved our secret is out, at least at my house anyway.

"Ignore her," I whisper. "I've got a surprise for you tonight."

"Really?" Reese bounces on her toes. "I can't wait." She tilts her head to the side, gazing at me as if I told her I was going to take her to the moon. "You didn't have to do that. You're all I need."

"Oh fucking gag me." Neva jumps up like she's pumped for a fight. "Why don't you find some other idiot to cheat on your boyfriend with? Why is it you're picking on *my* brother? I doubt this is a coincidence. I think you're lower than pig scum for what you're trying to do." She storms off down the hall and slams the door to her room.

"Nice seeing you, too," Reese says it low for my ears only.

"I'm glad *you* turned out all right." I lay my hand over her shoulders as we head out to the car.

"What's that?" She eyes the picnic basket in my hand and gives a knowing smile.

"Part of the surprise. You up for an adventure tonight?"

"Sure. I'm up for whatever. Tonight is all about you. Remember?" She runs her hands down over my hips and sinks a little lower.

"And what about you?" I'm hoping she'll tell me. I'd hate to rat Brylee out as the period police.

"I'm out. My body decided to pull the curse card, and I'm vexed with the details of being a woman tonight." She lays her head over my chest a moment. "Sorry."

"Don't be." I pull her in by the waist. "Then, I'm out, too." There's no way I'm going to let Reese pleasure me while she's feeling like shit. "Tonight's about being Reese and Ace. How's that?"

"Reese and Ace." She breaks out in a grin as she tightens her grip around me. "I love that." She hikes up and lands a lingering kiss over my lips that blows any platonic implications out the window. She tries to pull back, but I follow her with my mouth, and we engage in something deeper, my tongue chasing hers, playing catch and release. It's heaven like this with our mouths fused together—her affections pouring into me, desperate and aching.

"Why are you so nice to me?" Her eyes flutter into mine like twin pools of water.

"Because no one deserves it more." I walk her over to the car and open the door for her. "You up for some camping?"

"Are you kidding?" She practically squeals her way into the seat. "I've been dying to go camping since I was a kid.

You'd think we'd do it all the time, but Beverly is allergic to the idea."

"Perfect." I hop in, and we take off. Tonight is all about Reese and me. Just holding Reese, staring at the sky, breathing God's own breath.

If this isn't heaven, I don't know what is.

ℬℭ

I pull in along Fox Road and follow the trail all the way up until we have a good view of Pleasure Point Marina. The sun is getting ready to set as it lays its reflection over the water in pink and silver tails. The boats shine like miniature jewels, like a whole string of Christmas lights. I kill the engine, and we hop out.

"The facilities are that way." I point down at the public restrooms about a hundred yards away.

"This is amazing," Reese says as she stretches her long tawny limbs, and I pause for second to watch the way her arms touch the sky, her legs elongate over the earth like a shadow. I open the trunk and pull out the popup tent my dad bought for Christmas a few years back.

"You look amazing tonight," I say, handing her the round disc. "Toss that in the clearing over there, would you?"

Reese throws the tent in the air, and it explodes into its proper form, mid-air, landing on its bottom just the way God intended.

"No way! That was too cool!" She bubbles with a laugh. "You make every moment magic, you know that?"

"It's easy when you're around." I graze her lips with mine, and she pulls me in by the back of the neck. A small moan gets locked in her throat as she swipes her tongue over mine in achingly slow circles. Her moans increase in volume as we part ways.

"You're the best kisser ever, Ace Waterman."

"That's because I'm kissing you."

We get settled in the tiny tent, overlooking the lake, and I start a small fire out front before turning on my laptop.

"Are we surfing the net?" she teases.

"I thought maybe at the end of the night we could watch a movie. Just you and me under the stars."

"Sounds perfect." Her eyes catch the light from the fire, and I try to memorize her with the flames dancing in her eyes. "And until then?"

"I'm glad you asked." I pull forward the picnic basket and unleash the chocolate fest on her.

"Oh my, God! How much do I love you?" She glances up as if she caught herself off guard, and a thread of sorrow swims between us.

"I had a feeling chocolate was the way to your heart." I pull her onto the blanket and land another one over our shoulders to keep the chill off. Not that we need it, but Brylee suggested it, so I figure if it's what the neurotic blonde doctor ordered, I'm not going to fight it. Besides, I want Reese comfortable. I'm not sure what "Aunt Flo" entails other than the basics, but I want her to feel good, safe, and, most of all, loved.

"Everything about this is perfect," she whispers. "You know the last time I did something like this was with my mom." Her face pinches with grief a moment. I remember the hell she went through losing her mom like that. It killed me then to witness it, and, it was on the heels of that, my own mother took off.

"Sorry." I pull her in close until she's settled in my lap. "I really liked your mom. She was better than mine, by a long shot."

"How's she doing, anyway?"

"She's okay. She's got her new and improved family—Daniel's five, Jenny is turning three." Neva calls them the replacements.

"What about that guy she married? He still around?" Reese threads our fingers together and brings my hand up to her lips for a quick kiss.

"Vic*tor*." I break his name in two equal parts when I say it. "Yup. He's still hobbling about. He broke his foot, and it never healed right, so he's on disability. My mom's been asking about my dad more and more. A part of me wonders if she wants her old life back, but she's got little kids and an injured husband, not much I could do to help her. She's working at the bank to make ends meet."

"Wow." Reese settles into my chest. "Who would have thought? It sort of caught me off guard when she left like that, but, then, not too long after I was given the boot by Neva, so I never did find out the real story." She spins into me and wraps her arms around my waist. "I'm glad you came out unscathed."

I'm not so sure about that, but I hold back. No point in dragging us any further into the dysfunctional Waterman dungeon tonight. I'd rather put the focus right back where it belongs, on her.

"So tell me how you're doing, you know, after losing your mom. How you've been dealing with it."

Reese locks her eyes over mine, and the air around us grows stale with silence. Shit. I never should've ventured there. I knew it was iffy. I hope to God I can bring her back out of the pit.

"Thank you." She lowers her gaze a moment.

"For?" Obviously for ruining her night.

"You're the only person who's ever asked me that in all these years."

Shit. "Really?"

"Yeah, really." She lays her cheek against my chest and starts spinning her finger over my shoulder in a circle. "It seemed like my dad started dating Beverly right after, and soon my mother was reduced to a picture on the wall. And after he and Bev married, Mom was the picture in the drawer. Anyway"—she gives a hard sniff—"she did this really cool thing those last few weeks she was alive. She wrote me a letter to gift me on each of my birthdays. That way, I'll always have a little piece of her with me."

Now it's my turn to give a hard sniff.

Reese looks up, and her mouth opens. "Oh my, gosh," she whispers, wiping away my tears.

Great.

"You really do care about me," she marvels.

"Of course, I care about you." I wipe my face down with the back of my arm and start massaging her shoulders so she won't have to look at me weep like a pussy. "I think what your mom did was incredible. And if you ever need anyone to hold your hand or sit with you while you read those letters, I'd be glad to do it."

"You would?" She glances up at me. "Thank you. I might take you up on that. And, by the way, your fingers are magic." She taps her shoulder for me to continue.

"So I've been told." Crap. Not cool to mention other girls when you're with the only girl you care about.

"I'm sure you have. Maybe I should talk to some of them and get some references before we venture further into the bedroom." She tickles my ribs when she says it.

"References, huh?" I'm only slightly amused.

"What do you think they'd say?" She spins to take me in fully.

"They'd say give him back."

"Am I keeping you from someone?" Her brow rises as she offers a sexy-as-hell smile.

"Nope. I'm all yours, Reese." Forever if she'll have me.

"Good." She sinks her arms further around my waist. "And, I think you artfully changed the subject. What would all those girls that Ace Waterman slept with have to say?"

My chest rumbles with a laugh. "They'd say he has magic fingers"—I lean in and whisper directly into her ear—"and a magic tongue."

"That I'd have to agree with." Reese blushes ten shades of red.

"They'd also say sleeping with me is just as addictive as chocolate." I give a wry smile because I'm starting to feel like an ass while marketing my dick. "Anyway, back to the letters. I want to read them with you if you'll have me. I mean that."

Reese sags into me. Her head curves downward over my chest. "I'm sure soon enough you'll be with someone special, and she won't want you hanging around me while I read my dead mother's birthday cards."

"Doesn't matter, I'll be there. There's not a person on the planet who could stop me."

"Not even your special someone?" She bows her head, and I gently run my fingers over the back of her neck.

"You're my special someone, Reese." I freeze. My fingers forget how to move for the next few seconds, and all I hear is the crackle from the fire.

"Sure, for the summer." She taps her shoulders, and I continue with the massage. "But come fall, you won't be on the market long. You're one of a kind."

I lean in close to her ear. "So are you."

Reese spins into me and scratches at my chest. "I guess that makes us *two* of a kind."

"That's the best pair."

Reese gives a slight nod as the mood grows all too serious.

I bow into her with a kiss, and our lips meet as her hungry mouth devours mine. Reese and I share kisses that span the better half of the night. We crawl into the tent and pick out a movie, but we don't watch it. Instead, we fuse our lips together until sunrise.

Reese is my addiction.

Always has been.

Always will be.

6

Spitters are Quitters

Reese

The next afternoon, the hard line of the sun streams in from the driver's side window as Kennedy and Brylee steal me away for a girls' day. I tell them all about the dreamy date I had with Ace last night and get lost in the whir of scenery as Kennedy races us down the mountain for our mandated spa day. Ace let me know he had some things to take care of today but asked if we could reenact our camping adventure later tonight, so, of course, I said yes.

I pluck my phone out of my purse to text him something obnoxiously cute to remember me by like *my tent or yours?* or *I can't wait to have S'more fun with you!* but my battery is dead. Perfect. I toss it back in the black hole of my bag and note my wallet is missing. Crap. I must have forgotten to transfer it from my backpack. I'm terrible about that. It's precisely why I never switch purses. I've had to walk away from many a latte at the coffee counter because I happen to travel without any cold, hard cash, or in my case, cold hard plastic in my pockets.

A car honks as we narrowly avoid a head-on collision, inspiring Brylee to take over the wheel from the backseat, righting us into the proper lane.

"Pay attention fucktard," she snaps at Kennedy. "A facial won't be necessary after you launch our heads through the windshield. Chill out or pull over, and let me drive."

"Keith and I broke up last night." Kennedy growls into the road as if it were Keith himself. Her expression dims, she looks hollow as a porcelain doll without a soul—not that she's wicked or evil. "I should eviscerate him in his sleep."

There goes that theory.

"What happened?" I'm not too stunned by the update on her rocky relationship. They seem to part ways regularly just to keep things interesting, but I hold back the commentary in the event this is panning out to be the real deal.

"Joanna Knickerbocker happened."

Brylee groans. "Joanna Knickerbocker always happens."

Joanna helped facilitate the break up of Brylee and her then boyfriend, Ryan Johnson. I believe a hammock and a couple of blunts were involved.

"Charlie texted me a picture of him doing body shots off her stomach." Kennedy looks like she might be sick. "So I sent it to Keith, and he texted back, suggesting I *deal with it*."

I suck in a breath. "What'd you say?" I know for a fact how Kennedy "deals" with things. Kennedy knows how to skirt a felony with the best of them. Keith is lucky if he still has his man parts attached. And, if he does, he should cherish them because it won't be long now.

"I told him it was fine." A wicked grin plays on her lips. "After all, he explained that he and Joanna go way back, that they're just *friends*."

"Body shots with friends?" Brylee is unimpressed. "You should've told him that Joanna is friendly with a *lot* of people—that she practically invented the fine art of skiing."

"What the hell are you talking about?" I squint into Bry, partially because I know I'm about to get schooled.

"You know." She averts her eyes at my stupidity. Brylee has long since been kind enough to spell things out for me. "It's when a girl helps out two guys at the same time with their—"

"Stop." I slam my hands up over my ears and repeat the words, *skiing is a wholesome sport*, over and over, until my heart stops palpitating from her wayward verbal assault. That's the thing with Bry, not only does she call it like she sees it, but she sees far too much for me to ever care to know.

"It is fine." Kennedy smirks. "Because right after I told him that, I had Charlie slit his tires."

"That's the sister I know and love." I'd offer her a high five, but judging by her NASCAR driving skills, all fingers are required on deck.

Kennedy takes a sharp turn as we head toward the chi-chi day spa Beverly likes to frequent.

"I hate cheaters," she laments as she screeches into the valet parking queue, nearly taking out the attendant.

Brylee pops her head between the two of us and openly glares at me with her eyes jetting out like hardboiled eggs. "I hate cheaters, too."

"Would you stop?" I balk at her. "I'm not a cheater. And don't do that thing with your eyes. It's freaky."

Brylee raises a penciled brow at me. "Nobody said you were."

I'm *not* a cheater. But if I'm not, why do I feel sick to my stomach when I think of Ace and Warren taking up the same breathing space?

Maybe I should break things off with Warren—just to be clear. I guess that's me admitting we're sort of together.

I hate it when Kennedy and Brylee turn out to be right.

ॐ✿

The Lux Spa in Collingsworth is a modern day architectural marvel. The facility, itself, is enshrined in jasper and gold thus garnering Beverly's seal of approval for its fusion of precious stones and alloys. The entire place holds the heavenly scent of lavender and the memory of fresh ocean breezes. There's even a seventeen-foot statue of Michelangelo's David in the foyer that we traditionally pause to worship because his anatomy is so stunningly vulgar.

Brylee looks up wide-eyed and amazed. "His dick is as long as my forearm." She says it as a fact.

"My new boyfriend." Kennedy declares while she steps underneath him and snaps a selfie.

"So"—Brylee hooks her elbow with mine as we make our way to the check in—"what happened after dark? Are you holding back the dirty deets?"

"Nothing," I'm quick to say as we store our purses and shoes into our lockers and exchange our clothes for plush, white robes. "He was a perfect gentleman." The memory of his tongue smoothing over mine for hours sends me into a private heat wave. "We kissed." I stop short of adding it was no big deal because every part of me knows full well it was a very *big* deal—as big as David's man hammer, but I choose not to drag Kennedy's new boyfriend into the picture.

Ace and those things we did last night come rushing back to me. It felt comfortable, familiar—we were Reese and Ace just like old times with some tonsil hockey thrown into the mix. My face heats up ten degrees. I may have accidently told him that I loved him, and he confessed that I was his special someone. Only, it sounds better than it was because we were both talking out of context.

"You *kissed*?" Kennedy flashes her boobs to get a rise out of me, and I avert my eyes at her sophomoric efforts. The truth is I've seen her boobs more than I've seen mine. Kennedy likes to resort to flashing when she's fresh out of ways to offend me. "Did he whip it out and let you hold it?"

"I'm ignoring that. And, by the way, your nipples are like twelve times the size they're supposed to be." There. Maybe if I give her a nipple complex, she'll lay off on the bazooka assault for a while. I shake out my hair as we head into the salon. "Like I said, Ace is a gentleman." We take seats next to one another as an attendant wheels over a footbath to each of us. "Oh, this feels good," I groan as my feet slip into the warm, soapy water.

"Is that what you said to him?" Kennedy snickers into Brylee.

"Laugh all you want girls, but I got the real deal in Ace."

"More like the real *limited time* deal." Kennedy holds my gaze a moment too long.

"Are you cruising for a bruising?" I'm only half teasing. I'm not above going street on her ass right here in the princess lounge.

"Calm down. I'm just saying you can change that. Once summer wraps up, tell him you'd like an extension on your contract. If you play your cards right and *blow* him away, then he'll practically beg to keep you around."

I mull it over a second, giving her a pass on the BJ innuendo. Anyway, checking Kennedy on the corruption that comes from her mouth is pretty much useless. There are no bounds to Kennedy's crudeness.

"File an extension huh?" I look over at my raunchy stepsister. "Way to make my love life sound like an unpleasant IRS transaction."

"Nevertheless"—Kennedy rolls her head over her neck—"make sure you're good in bed. That way he'll come back for more."

Brylee moans in agreement. "I bet Joanna Knickerbocker is brilliant in bed." She shakes her head in disgust. "I bet she swallows."

Kennedy jolts to an upright position as if Brylee just spewed some serious insanity around the room. "You *spit*?"

"You *swallow*?" Brylee matches her tone for tone.

"Would you both knock it off?" I hiss. "You're causing a spermtacular scene. If you don't keep it down, they'll ejaculate us right out of here."

Kennedy rolls her eyes. "Well, it's either *or* sister. If I were you, I'd make up my mind right now where your lingual loyalties lie." She glances up at the ceiling a moment. "And no matter what—make sure you kiss him after. That's the test of a real man."

Brylee groans at the visual, and I let out a breath. Because sometimes, there's just nothing left to say.

Kennedy's phone goes off, and her affect brightens. "Well, looky here." She wags it in my face a moment. "A text from Warren McCarthy. *Bring Reese by the office around five. I have a killer surprise. Don't tell her.*" Kennedy annunciates each word before punching something into her cell and hitting send.

"What did you say?" The words speed out of me in a panic. She's all over the place today no thanks to Keith and his insatiable urge for body shots.

"I told him I'd have you there with bells on." She gleams a black smile, and my heart sinks. "That I wouldn't say a word."

"Perfect." I'm plotting my revenge already. I sense a tragic separation in the works for her favorite pair of Prada shoes. It wouldn't be the first right-footed heel I've used as a paperweight.

Brylee bubbles out a laugh as the attendants start in on our pedicures. "Looks like someone has a date with her 'boyfriend' tonight."

"I guess tonight's the night, then." I swallow hard then glare at Kennedy for ruining a simple bodily function for me.

Spit or swallow. I shake my head. I don't know what I'll do when I get to that point with Ace. But I do know what I'm doing with Warren tonight, and it doesn't even remotely involve procreation or any of its liquid facets.

"Prepare to comfort him, girls," I purr. "Tomorrow morning, Warren McCarthy is going to have a serious case of the break-up blues."

Then, maybe, Ace and I can take things to a deeper level. Maybe Ace will give me that relationship extension sooner than I think.

I sink into my seat and try to relax as the attendant scrubs my feet like she's sloughing Warren, himself, off my body.

I push all thoughts of Warren McCarthy and our "date" right out of my mind. Instead, I think of Ace and lose myself with the only pressing decision I want to have at the moment, and that just so happens to involve my gag reflex.

ະ໐ଓ

After hours of primping and pampering and having our hair and makeup done to the hilt, we reconvene in Kennedy's Range Rover and prepare for the long drive home.

Kennedy leans into the rearview mirror and makes a face. "On a scale of Mother Teresa to transvestite, what do you think?"

"Oh, hon"—Brylee gives a guttural laugh—"just mentioning yourself in the same breath as Mother Teresa is an unforgivable sin."

"You would know," she counters. "Anyway it doesn't matter. Unlike Reese here, I won't have two men vying for my affection tonight."

Ace runs through my mind, our secret hideaway in the woods—Gavin's boathouse—chocolate. This summer is rife with delicious secrets. I can hardly wait to see him tonight. Maybe I should do something amazing for him? Take him somewhere and show *him* a good time.

Kennedy drives for a few minutes before pulling into a parking spot and not until I look out the window do I realize what she's up to.

"Shit," I mutter, staring at the tall office building of Westfield and McCarthy. It sits nestled in a hub of skyscrapers in downtown Collingsworth. The gilded sign with my family's surname right next to Warren's sits prominent on the outside, and just the sight inspires a roll of nausea to push through me. I forgot all about my breakup date with Warren. I spot Dad's black sedan gleaming in the early evening light, and, for whatever it's worth, it adds a safety measure.

"Let's get this over with," Brylee huffs as she gets out of the car. You'd think she were the one responsible for twisting Warren's balls off in the next few hours the way she exemplified exactly how I felt.

I glare over at Kennedy a moment. "I'll deal with you later."

"You'll *thank* me later."

As if.

We get out and head into the air-conditioned building where Daddy waits to greet us down in the reception area.

Odd.

"Hey, hey, the gang's all here." He pulls all three of us into an embrace, and I take in his spiced cologne. Dad has always been kind to Bry. Brylee feels every bit as much family as Kennedy if not more. "Rumor has it one of you lucky ladies has something special waiting for her on the rooftop. Shall we?" He teases just as the elevator opens, and we hop inside.

"The roof?" I shoot a quick look to Kennedy and Brylee. What the hell could be happening on a rooftop? Could Warren be threatening a swan dive off a twenty-four story office building? Not likely. Plus, I doubt my father would be grinning like a goof at the thought, also we're lacking an entire emergency response squad, so there's that. Whatever the hell it is, this isn't going to end well. Rooftops and breakups never go hand in hand.

"Promise me something." Daddy pulls me in by the shoulders. "You'll have the time of your life tonight?"

"Oh, I will," I assert. Just as soon as I get back home and finish off the evening with Ace. Although technically I plan on gifting Ace the time of his life. In about an hour, I hope to have no memory of this rooftop experience. Besides, I suddenly have a severe craving for heady kisses and chocolate, and they both involve Ace.

The doors whoosh open, and an obnoxious pelting sound thumps through my skull.

Dad escorts us out, and to my fucking horror, I spot Warren standing fifty feet in front of a helicopter that looks as if it's ready to whisk us away at a moment's notice.

"Oh, no." I grip onto the nearest hand, which happens to belong to Kennedy.

"Oh, *yes!*" My father proudly chides.

Warren comes over in his neat three-piece suit, his hair slicked back with a heavy polish. His strong, tangy cologne permeates the area before he does. He pulls me into a hard embrace and lands a wet, sloppy kiss on the side of my cheek.

"You ready to be whisked away on a magical mystery date?" He barks out a laugh as if it wasn't a question at all.

Dad slaps him on the back and offers me a quick hug.

"Beverly and I have taken care of everything. I one hundred percent approve of this outing." He clamps his hand over mine. I wonder if he would have approved of Ace and the outing we had last night—any outing with Ace for that matter. "Go and have the time of your life. Make some great memories." He gives a quick wink to Warren before leading Kennedy and Brylee back toward the elevator.

No, no, no!

Brylee turns and gives a solemn wave. Kennedy glances back and rolls her eyes.

Just crap. This is worse than I could have imagined. It was going to be difficult enough having to tell him that we should see other people, as in never see one another again, while I thought Kennedy was going to be waiting for me out in the hall. I sort of envisioned Kennedy and Brylee taking me out for margaritas after because that's what girls do once they sever ties to a longtime tagalong that the world thinks she's dating—get shitfaced with tequila. Okay, so maybe we were dating a little bit.

"Let's get moving." Warren pulls me all the way to the helicopter, and before I know it, I'm buckling up and throwing on a pair of headphones so I can communicate with both the pilot and my soon-to-be ex-boyfriend.

Perfect. In the event I was afraid I wouldn't have an audience when I told Warren I didn't love him, the universe has now solved that problem, too.

We rise through the sky and wobble our way over Collingsworth. I pretend to marvel at how miniaturized everything looks when all I really want to do is shove Warren and his goofy grin out the window. Although, I suppose if it were Ace next to me, I'd be venerating his efforts for gifting me with a luxury date of aerial proportions, so I cut Warren some slack in that department.

And a break up in the sky? Really? Maybe I'll be the one parachuting to earth without the proper equipment to get me there safely. Warren could easily plead insanity, and God knows he's got the backing of a topnotch legal team—hell, my own father might even vouch for him. Obviously, I'll have to wait until we land.

We're probably just going to take a quick tour of the city. Dad took our family and the McCarthy's on one of these a few years back, and I remember thinking it went by pretty quick. One minute we were in the air, and the next thing I knew, we were landing, just like that. Only then we had a totally annoying couple in the back that kept making out, and Beverly offered to pay both Kennedy and me a hundred bucks each if we would stop turning around. Of course, Ken didn't obey the almighty dollar, but I managed to parlay a nice pair of Ray Ban sunglasses out of the deal. I glance back in the event I missed the fact there's a pair of lip-locking passengers taking the trip with us and jump when I spot my leopard print carry on nestled next to a duffle bag.

Holy. Shit.

"We're just taking a quick tour of the city right?" I bleat into the mini mike that hovers around my lips like a bee.

"That and then some. Good deal, right?" Warren's arm slithers around my waist and despite his effort to feel me up, I sigh with relief. I mean we've already seen half of Collingsworth in the time we've been in the air. If we race up the mountain, I could still squeeze in a nice picnic under the stars with Ace over Pleasure Point. Last night was the stuff that dreams are made of. I had no idea you could have a romantic time without sex being the main objective. It's like being with Ace has already taught me so many things about love, and, yet, we've still got miles of great memories to make up ahead. I sigh dreamily, and Warren rewards me with an unwanted kiss.

Gah!

I pull back as a nervous smile twitches on my lips. I forgot how freely Warren doles out the kisses. In truth, I haven't kissed him since we've come back this summer, and now that some time has passed, it feels a little foreign, more than a little intrusive. And why do I suddenly feel like I'm being held against my will?

The helicopter picks up speed, and we rise even higher until the city fades into a sea of haze. I bet we're getting ready to land on top of some posh restaurant, and then I'll fake being sick so we can put the kibosh on this quasi-kidnapping.

A shoreline crops up on our right, which indicates that both Collingsworth and Loveless are well behind us—hell, the entire state of Connecticut is turning into a tiny speck.

"What city exactly is it that we're touring?" Why do I get the sick feeling I could have easily replaced city for country?

Warren slips his well-manicured hand over my knee before sinking it between my legs.

"We're going to New York for the weekend, baby! Just you and me." He offers a toothy grin, his tan skin is just this side of orange, and suddenly I want to vomit on his pricy Dolce and Gabbana patent leather shoes.

I carefully return his hand to his lap, but it springs back to my knee.

New York.

Something tells me I'll have to pull off an Alcatraz-worthy escape to make it back to Loveless tonight.

Crap.

I am definitely not in a New York state of mind.

❧❦

"This hotel is the shit!" Warren holds the door open for me as we step into the elevator. My head is still ringing from the sound of the rotors. My brain feels as if a hornet's nest has dislodged in it. And despite the fact that I've got mild cramps and a migraine on the horizon, my mind is buzzing with a thousand clever ways to kill Warren and make it look like an accident. I swear if his fingers travel to my inner thighs, one more time, I'll reenact the ball-breaking moves I employed on him just last week.

We step off onto the penthouse floor with plush navy carpeting as he wheels my suitcase down the posh hall toward a room with double doors.

"So what are you thinking? We'll change and go to dinner?" My voice sounds like I'm hearing myself from the inside of a fishbowl.

Warren slips the plastic keycard into the door and gives a wicked grin in lieu of an answer.

"We *are* going back to Loveless tonight, right?" I insist because obviously I refuse to the let the hotel room and luggage offer me a clue.

"After you." He holds out his hand, and I breeze past him into the darkened room. Warren picks up a remote and points it at the wall, and the room magically fills with the sound of a lovesick sax while a thousand electric candles illuminate the area, exposing an oversized loft-piled bed. In the center of the gargantuan space a table is set up for two with a pair of silver domes over it.

Oh, God.

I take in the opulent display as if it were a crime scene.

Ace had real candles at the boathouse, and the music came from our own hearts, our passion tore up the room, and the only thing we were hungry for was each other.

Warren manhandles another remote, and the fireplace roars to life like an untamed dragon.

"Nice touch." I let out a helpless sigh and take in the surroundings once again. "Well, we'd better get to dinner I'm starved." Maybe if I speed things along, I can wade my way through this nightmare and still make it to Loveless by midnight.

"First—a dance." He snaps up my hand, and I make sure to maintain a comfortable distance. This is Warren after all.

I've known him since we were babies, for as long as I've known Ace—funny how I sort of have polarized feelings for the two of them. I try to think of a time that Ace and I shared a dance, and not one occasion comes to mind. It breaks my heart. But it also gives me something to look forward to.

"What's going through your mind?" Warren leans in and sniffs into my neck like a predator. He's immaculate looking tonight with his power suit, his hair slicked back in thick, caramel waves, his fresh tan, even if it is a fake bake. I know for a fact there are a ton of girls who would sell all the eggs in their ovaries for a chance to shack up in New York for the night with Warren. It just so happens that I'm not one of them.

I pull back and take him in as he awaits my answer. I'm sure as hell not going to say Ace Waterman, but I want to.

"Just missing home, that's all." It's the truth. I'll have to tell Brylee I'm not allergic to it after all.

His hands sink past my waist and round out my bottom. He's sending some pretty serious signals that I'm prepared to ignore.

"I don't travel well." I raise his hands an inch before they find a home in the hills and canyons he's not welcome to.

"You're still pissed about the other night." His chest bumps as he huffs it off. "Did you get the flowers?" He looks perplexed that I could still be angry after he followed up his failed penis plunge with the biggest bouquet that money could buy. Things went from horny to thorny in a single bound, sort of like they're about to now.

"Look"—he knocks his head back exasperated—"that's what New York is all about. I'm making it up to you."

"Great." I try my best to drag him over to the table. "Consider yourself forgiven. Now, let's eat."

I scurry to my seat and whip off the dome only to find my favorite crustacean staring back at me with the tail already neatly pieced off just waiting for me to give it a butter bath. I think Warren would have done miles better to have sent two dozen red lobsters instead of roses. If I were even mildly riding the fence, I might be swayed by deep-sea culinary delights, but I'll take chocolate and wildflowers any day if it means I get Ace in the end.

"You sure know what I like." I dig in. If I have to eat a sacrificial meal to spur this hostile takeover along I'm pretty damn glad it comes equipped with a shiny red spine and beady little eyes.

"Of course, I know what you like." Warren reaches over and places his hand over mine just as I'm about to dive into the first golden delicious bite. "And I know what you need." His eyes fix on mine, and now my appetite is waning. Why do I get the feeling I might want to save one of these claws for use once he starts chasing me around the furniture? "I'm all about giving you the best. We're going to have an entire lifetime of this shit, Reese." His jaw squares out. Warren looks like one of those underwear models they bronze out and blowup over Times Square. Sometimes I wonder if I'm the only girl on the planet who's not attracted to him. "You realize we're not like other people. We're so fucking lucky." He shakes his head as he starts in on his meal.

I pop the luscious bite into my mouth and contemplate his theory. "I guess you're right." I don't mind talking through a mouthful of food. In fact, the more I disgust Warren and kill any fantasy he might have of me being his plus one on any of his future hostile dinner takeovers, the better. "But I kind of like the simple life. Camping, a nice crackling fire, picnic baskets—massages." Specifically the kind Ace gives with his tongue, but I leave that part out.

"Camping?" He ticks his head back a notch as if I suggested we scan the corner for cockroaches and eat them for dessert. "This is as close to camping as I'll ever let you get." He gives a greasy smile. "And, in just a little bit, I'll be giving you a massage you will never forget right in front of that kickass fire." He flicks his tongue in the air, and I straighten in my seat.

Dear God, deliver me from Warren.

He picks up the wine and fills both our glasses to the rim. "Knock some back, would you? Tonight is special. We're in New York City, baby. And, in just a little while, we'll be working those mattress springs. I think it's about time we take it to another level."

I stare at the broken lobster and muse at the fact he feels like my only friend in New York right about now, and I suddenly don't have the heart to eat him. For a moment I contemplate running to the bathroom and calling Ace to help figure a way out of this mess until I remember my phone has conveniently died. Besides, even if Ace offered to drive here to get me, he wouldn't arrive until morning. I would never ask him to drive all night. It's not like I'm some damsel in distress. I can certainly hold my own. I mean I'll just get another room—

A gasp gets locked in my throat when I remember the fact my wallet is still snug in my backpack next to my bed. Perfect. I'm officially trapped in New York with Warren and his wandering hands while visions of mattress moves dance in his head.

I bet that's what Dad meant by he and Beverly "took care of everything," as in ran up my battery and hid all my credit cards. Nice. Not that my father would do that, but, dear God almighty, I sure like spreading the blame for my idiocracy.

"What's up?" Warren is already on his fifth glass of imported vino which I'm betting is a good thing. Maybe he'll pass out for the night, and he won't have to face the world's most expensive rejection. And I do plan on doling it out sooner than later.

"Nothing, really. I was just thinking I should probably hit the sack. My head has been on fire ever since we got off that thing, and I've got these insane cramps." I double over and let out a horrific groan.

"Well then let's get you to bed, little lady." Warren does his best impersonation of a cowboy, and this mildly alarms me. He whips off his jacket and scoops me up in his arms. Before I can process what's happening, he's on top of me with his tongue halfway down my throat, and the mattress rodeo has officially begun.

"Get off!" I try to push him away, but he's suddenly morphed into a wall of granite. "I can't have sex with you. I'm on my period."

"What?" He jumps off as if I were on fire. "Shit. That's fucking disgusting."

"It *so* is." I decide to go with it. "In fact, I turn into a red fountain at night, so you might want to sleep on the couch."

"*Shit.*" He hops off the bed so fast, you'd think I just gave him head lice. Warren examines his dress shirt, for stains no doubt. "We're here until Sunday. You'll be over that shit by then, right?"

Sunday?

"Nope," I sag into the feathered bedding as if I were disappointed myself. "I'll have it for another six days straight." Okay, so I may have stretched the truth, but it's really none of his damn business how long my body decides to punish me in advance for the luxury of having children.

Warren groans as if he's having his balls mauled off by a rhino.

"Heavy—*heavy*, bleeding." I nod.

"All right, all right." He covers his ears. "I fucking get it." He snatches up a pillow and heads to the couch.

There's that.

The next day sucks. I mostly shop while Warren mostly tags along like he's actually enjoying it which makes me feel horrible on several levels because, for one, he's buying, but if I'm going to break things off with him, we might as well keep our friendship intact. He won't even hold my hand due to the red plague that's racking my body, so, all in all, it's panning out to be a rather platonic experience—far more genuinely so than the one I'm having with Ace.

Early Sunday morning a helicopter picks us up on the roof, and we do the entire first day in reverse, only its Warren who drives us back to Loveless from our father's legal offices.

I don't have the balls to look at him all the way up the mountain. I keep waiting for a lull in traffic, or a lull in my panicked brain to break up with him officially, but it feels like that moment never arrives, and, before I know it, Kennedy is waving at me from the balcony of the house.

"Thanks for the trip, Warren," I say, and he gives a brief nod, the look of frustration rife on his face. "It was a really nice thought."

"Yeah, whatever. We'll get it right." He snarls into the window.

I get out and watch as he drives down the street before turning and glancing over at Ace's cabin. His car is tucked in his driveway, and just the sight of that old Cougar warms me.

It's so nice to be back in Loveless—even nicer to know I'll be seeing Ace in just a little while.

Ace

The sun shines bright over the lake, pressing its heat over Loveless, hot and smothering as if someone stuck a magnifying glass in the sky just to intensify the torture. It's been three long days since I've last seen Reese.

Brylee came over Friday night and let me know the tricks Warren had up his designer sleeve. She told me that Reese forgot her wallet, that her phone was dead. As soon as she filled me in I thought about heading to New York and trying to find her myself. That image Reese painted of Warren trying to force himself on her haunted me all weekend. But she handled him then, and I knew she could do it again if it came right down to it. There was obviously a phone in her room. She could have called the police if things got out of hand. I guess what I'm most worried about is that Warren somehow managed to rekindle the flame. Maybe Reese discovered that luxury hotels and helicopter weekends are something she prefers to a popup tent and a rusted-out Cougar.

Neva shuffles over to the kitchen and scoffs into the fridge, while I sit staring out at the lake.

"Warren's back," she purrs. She's been rubbing their weekend getaway in my face every chance she gets. "But you already knew that, didn't you?" She plucks out a soda and offers me one, but I refuse. She's got on her death mask, with the white pancake makeup, the black soot rubbed in large, dark circles around her eyes. She's head to toe in full Halloween mode with her thigh-high combat boots and a lace top with nothing but a metal studded bra underneath. I think she slept that way.

"Why don't you put some clothes on?" I growl before darting a quick glance over at Reese's house.

Neva comes in close until her head is practically on my shoulder, and we're both looking out at Loveless together.

"Has she given you the finger yet?" She teases. "I bet little Miss Money Bags didn't have many clothes on this weekend either. I bet she and Warren might even have some big news to share with everyone, real soon."

"Doubt it."

"Heard he's having a huge party on the Fourth—he even invited *me*," her voice rises when she says it. "I'm thinking that's the perfect time to announce an engagement. Don't you? Just think of all the fireworks that went off between those two this weekend. I think a sparkler is in order—I'm betting it'll take at least five carats of bling for Reese to even consider it. She's got expensive taste. People like us could never please her."

"Enough." I shake my head. "If you think it's making me crazy, you're wrong. If Reese really wanted to marry the guy, I'd be at their wedding, cheering them on. This isn't about me. It's about what she wants." I press my lips together because I'm pretty damn sure I just lied to this cartoon version of my baby sis.

"What the hell is wrong with you?" Her voice booms through the cabin, rattling the windows and mugs. Dad stumbles out of his bedroom looking like a zombie with his hair spiked up in every direction.

"What the hell is going on?" His eyes are downturned from dragging his ass out of bed far too early, no thanks to Neva's morning riot.

"Nothing's going on." I spot Reese out on her balcony and turn from the window. My heart is already picking up pace. I can't help it. My adrenaline spikes each time I think of her, let alone see her.

Neva shoves me in the arm until I look up at her. "Reese Westfield is cheating on her boyfriend with Ace. Just try to deny it."

"I don't know what the hell you're talking about." I shoot a look to the fireplace as the memory of Reese's tongue over mine, bumps through my mind. "We're just hanging out once in a while. Nothing unusual about that."

Dad's chest expands. He pats his jeans down until he yanks out his wallet and replaces it in his pocket. He snatches his vest off the hook and slips it on.

"You got school in a few weeks," he says, plucking a cigarette off the sink and sticking it between his lips. "Lots of girls over at Yeats. I wouldn't mess with anything that Loveless has to offer."

"Tell him to stay away from her." Neva waits for Dad to follow her command, but he doesn't. Dad needles me with a sorrowful look that suggests he might be siding with Neva after all. She speeds over to him, her hair bouncing in that rat's nest she has it teased up in. "You never believe anything I say. Nobody ever does. They're *together*. She's using him, and he's getting sucked in. She's going to chew him up and spit him out. She's going to break his heart."

Dad looks up with a depleted smile. "Do yourself a favor, son." His eyes plead with me a little too hard. "Find yourself a nice girl that has eyes only for you. It's not worth it to fool around with someone who's not willing to give you their full attention." He steadies his gaze across the way at the Westfield's house and sighs. "Neva's right. She'll only break your heart."

My phone goes off. It's a text from Reese. **Can we get together? I would love to explain everything. I've missed you to pieces.**

"I bet that's her." Neva shakes her head as if she's readying for a fight.

Dad tips his hat over at us before flopping it on. "I gotta get to work. Try not to kill each other while I'm gone."

No sooner does the screen shut than I text Reese back.

Let's do it. Missed you, too.

Neva snatches the phone and examines it.

"What a joke," she hisses before handing it back. "You're nothing but a dirty little secret to her. Does she know you're leaving in a few weeks?"

"Nope." When the coach called and said practice started the second week of August, I figured I'd run down to campus and check into a dorm. I get my key on the first. I was going to ask her to come with me last Friday, but she said Kennedy was taking her out. I guess I'll hang onto my surprise just a little bit longer. If Reese finds out I'm headed to Yeats in the fall, it could cloud the rest of the summer. Maybe part of the appeal is she won't have to face me ever again if she wants. I'd hate to ruin that option for her, or more selfishly to the point, ruin things for me.

A polite knock erupts over the door, followed by the sweetest *hello* I've ever heard in my life.

Reese.

She's back, and my whole world feels as if it's falling into place again.

ಬಿಂಛ

Neva pushes the screen into Reese as she zips past her. "You better watch your back," she shouts before racing off toward the general store.

"Ignore her," I say, pulling Reese inside for a moment. Leave it to Neva to ruin a perfectly beautiful morning.

"So, do you forgive me?" She bites down over her cherry-stained lip, and her eyes moisten with tears.

"There's nothing to forgive." I press out a grin that's been vacant from my face since she left. Reese hops up on my hips and wraps her legs around me as if she wanted to be there all along.

"God, I missed you." She lands her soft lips over mine and indulges in a kiss that tastes like cotton candy and strawberries. I let out a moan that swims toward the lake like a siren, so I shut the door and enjoy the hell out of the moment, running my tongue over hers like a promise of things to come.

"Missed you, too." I pepper the side of her face with kisses that trail all the way up to her ear. "You have a good time?"

"Anything but." She makes a face, and it's only then I notice she has on her bathing suit under her shirt.

"You want to go for a ride?"

Reese gives a dangerous smile. I have a feeling she would let me take her to the edge of the universe if I wanted.

I drive us out past Pleasure Point to the dunes on the distal end of the lake where the roads turn to crap and you might have to consider four replacement tires after the visit. But it's a private beach, and that's the point of this afternoon, some serious and much-needed privacy at least on my part. Selfishly, I want Reese all to myself without Warren's prying eyes, or anyone else's prying eyes for that matter.

The white sand looks pale as salt, and the water glistens a glacial blue. I keep forgetting how gorgeous the Eagle's Nest dunes are. Of course, Reese is the one who's making its beauty spring to life. Without her here, it would be just another lonely trek to the desert end of the lake.

I park under a rolling oak and pluck out a blanket and a paper bag I filled with sodas and chips on the way out the door—a far cry from the five star meals she was no doubt treated to this weekend.

Reese wraps her arm around my waist as we find a spot under a spreading tree and lay out the blanket. The sunlight dapples around us just enough to ensure me I'd better keep the both of us hydrated just so we don't pass out.

"You know what my favorite part of today is?" She stretches over the blanket before pulling off her T-shirt and shorts. Her hair falls around her tanned shoulders, and her eyes glow like silver flames.

Holy shit. I stare wide-eyed at her barely-there red bikini. Reese Westfield has a body that doesn't quit and curves for miles in all the right places. She clears her throat, and my gaze pops right back up to her eyes. Caught red-bikini handed.

"What's your favorite part of the day?" I take off my shirt before landing on the blanket next to her.

Reese glides in beside me, her cool thigh grazing over mine.

"Coming home and seeing you." She lands her slender arms over my waist, and I lean my head into hers. Reese starts in on the whole story, and I give a sorrowful laugh when she tells me she felt like the lobster was her only friend.

"You'll always have me." I pull her in tight. "At least you caught a show and got some shopping in. It wasn't a total loss." And, yet, if she were there with me, there's no way I could have taken her to see a Broadway show or outfitted her with a new wardrobe. We'd probably have to hit the dollar menu and hightail it to the library for entertainment. Not really, I'd empty out my bank account to show her a good time. We'd tour the city, climb to the top of the Empire State building—climb each other in a fit of passion.

"It was a total *kidnapping*. And I swear if that ever happens again, I'm not boarding the helicopter, or the train, or the cruise ship he's commandeered. I'm through being nice."

"Warren is just being Warren," I say, as she slides over into my lap. Her skin warms against mine, and I drop a kiss over her forehead without putting too much thought into it. "We've both known him forever. Plus, your dads are linked at the hip, so keeping your distance isn't a reality. I get it."

Her mouth falls open as she glances up at me. Reese's eyes are the exact shade of the sky today, and I want to always remember how she looks, nestled here in my arms.

"Ace"—she lowers her lids a moment—"thank you for understanding. A part of me wanted to knife my way out of that room and, yet, the other part of me wanted to be nice—I mean he made a serious effort. He apologized for what he did. But obviously he thinks we're more than friends." She shakes her head. "I pretty much gave him the cold shoulder anytime he came near me, so I think maybe he got the hint. He was pretty frustrated when he dropped me off."

"I bet." I didn't mean for that to slip out. That conversation I shared with him comes back to me. He mentioned being with someone wild and, at the time, I wondered if he meant Reese. "So, you and he..." I let the words hang in the air to see if she wants to go there. Really, it's none of my business what they've done together.

"Nope." She runs her finger over my chest. "I mean we've kissed. His hands have tried to score a touchdown all on their own, but I'm just not that into him." Her lids hood over with grief as if maybe deep down she wishes she were. "It's some twisted dream of my dad's for me to end up with him. It's ridiculous." She shakes her head.

"Sounds like a lot of pressure."

"Oh, it is. Most of the time the only reason I don't tell Warren to stay the hell away is because of my dad. I know he really likes the synergy our families have—the businesses, the countless vacations we've taken, and, now, it's like some fantasy to have Warren and I both at Yeats."

She buries her face in my chest a moment. Her lips brush against my skin, and I take in a breath at how damn good it feels.

Reese leans up and brushes her lips over mine. "I wish you were going to Yeats."

"What would change?" I cinch my lips in a crooked smile.

"I don't know." Her eyes widen a moment. "We could continue to do things like this." She leans up and sears a kiss off my lips. Her eyes remain closed long after she pulls away.

"That would be amazing." For a moment I contemplate telling her I was accepted, that I made the rowing team right alongside Warren, but I don't want to complicate what we have, so I keep it to myself. "So what's it like at Yeats?" I run my fingers over the length of her arm before landing my hand flat over her belly.

"Lonely." She lays her hand over mine and leans in to kiss my bicep. "Lots of wild girls and boys but I try to steer clear from those—tons of parties. I thought about maybe joining a sorority, but after discovering that Kennedy wasn't a one of a kind, I decided not to."

"You should find someone to hang out with, maybe get a boyfriend." Shit. I meant me, but now, she's going to think I'm pushing her off on some faceless junior.

Reese bubbles out a laugh, and the soft skin on her chest ripples in tune with her rhythm. "I don't need a boyfriend to make me happy, Ace." She slides down until her head is in my lap. Reese smiles up at me while using my dick as a pillow. "You make me pretty happy, though." She tugs at her bottom lip with her teeth. "I'm excited to be with you." She glances at her thighs. "I'm all done down there—short and sweet, just three days. But I thought maybe we could make this afternoon about you." She reaches up and drips her fingers slowly off my chest. My heart drums, fast and furious, I'm sure she can feel it.

"You make me pretty happy, too." I run my fingers through her hair. Her chest expands. Her tits ripple as if they were trying to break free from the eye patches she's shielding them with. And, right on cue, my dick ticks to life beneath her.

"What's this?" She teases nestling the back of her head into my crotch until she yields the full effect. "You really are glad to see me, aren't you?" She giggles as if it were the funniest thing in the world. "Looks like we have a very hard problem we're going to have to solve." The smile slides right off her face. Reese grows serious, her eyes widen like a silver sky.

"No problem solving necessary." I readjust myself, and Reese leans up beside me on her elbow. "Just give me a minute, and I'll shape shift back to your regularly scheduled stud." I hope. Not sure it's possible but it was worth the lip service.

I pluck at my shorts as her tits campaign hard for my attention. Looks like this bad boy isn't going anywhere.

"I want to see it," she says it sweetly. She's looking up at me from under her lashes, biting down over her lip with those paper-white teeth.

"It's not a pet." I hold back a laugh because it sort of is.

"It can be," it sails from her lips smooth and sultry. "I'll *pet* it if you let me."

In the shade her skin looks perfectly bronzed, her bathing suit bottom catches my eye, and I want to run my hand over her velvet thighs, land my fingers in all the right places.

"Reese." I lean back on my elbows, considering her offer. It's not like anyone ever visits the Eagle's Nest. We're secluded with a bed of pines all around, nothing but rolling oaks filling in the blank spaces. I doubt we'd be discovered anytime soon.

"Please, I want to." She pulls the string to my board shorts and unties the front. Her fingers comb out the laces, and before I know it she's excavated my hard-on, and lands it between us. It does look like a pet, one big, oversized, hairy beast. "Wow. Impressive," she whispers, a soft giggle ripples through her chest, and I start to lose it.

"*Reese.*" I arch back, unsure of how the hell I'm going to alleviate the pressure, short of tossing off in the bushes, and, right about now, I'm not entirely opposed to the idea.

She runs her fingers along the length of it, and I give a hard groan.

"You're amazing." She looks up and holds my gaze, her mouth parted like a seasoned seductress. Reese easily puts to shame any number of the girls I've been with. Never in my existence have I felt so fucking turned on. "I'm going to kiss you right here." She runs her finger over the tip and my throat locks off.

Shit.

She blinks up at me innocently. A dirty smile waits to break loose on her lips. "Do you want me to kiss you there?"

"Yes," it rasps from me.

"You like this, don't you, Ace?" She holds her voice steady and calm while running her fingers over my cock soft as a feather.

A dry laugh rumbles from me. She's doing exactly what I did to her the other night, and she's a hell of a lot better at it.

"Ace." She leans over and brushes the tip with her lips, and it takes all my strength to not to give a shout of approval. She looks up, licking her lips. "I don't know how to do this. I want you to teach me." Reese bows her head and glides her mouth over the entire length of me.

Oh fuck. I let out a moan as if I were in pain.

I dig my fingers in her hair, guiding her in a steady rhythm. I offer just enough encouragement, but she goes down on her own, and I'm pleasantly surprised she's able to take just about all of me in without bringing her breakfast up over my balls. I've never had a girl go this far down before. I'm more than impressed as she runs her tongue over me, sucks me down like she's about to digest me. Her cool fingers slip lower still, and before I know it, the boys are in on the act.

I can't take it.

"*Reese,*" it hisses out of me as I thrust my head back. It feels so fucking good. I want it to last forever. A heated rush blows over me, and I can feel the storm cinching up inside me until my entire body feels as if it's about to shoot out of my dick. "Reese." I pull her shoulder back, but she gently restrains me by the wrist. If she's looking for the full experience, I'm not about to fight her.

"I'm coming." I struggle to push her off, but Reese maintains her position and— fuck. She swallows down every last bit. I shudder over her hard, digging my hands into her hair, holding back the groan that's trying to knife its way from my vocal cords. I tremble to completion as her lips throb around me until she finally pulls away.

Shit.

Our eyes lock, and I don't know what to say.

"You can throw up if you have to." Maybe not that.

Reese touches her fingers to her lips. Her eyes widen as if she's considering it.

I pull her to me, and we fall over the blanket, her face buried in the crook of my neck.

"Hell, Reese," I pant. I've never had a girl do that before.

"Did I do okay?" She glances up. Her eyes are watery, and I'm praying to God it's not tears of regret forming in her eyes.

"You did better than okay." I press a kiss into her hair. "Don't ever do that again."

"What if I want to?"

"You won't," I tease, stroking my fingers down her back. "If you ever want to venture there again, I'll pull you out of the line of fire, and, if not, feel free to spit."

"Spitters are quitters." She scratches at my stomach, and our chests rumble with a quiet laugh.

"You know what I can't quit?" I tuck a kiss in just behind her ear.

"What's that?" A lock of dark hair glides over her face, smooth and glossy like a ribbon. I pull it back and take in her beauty.

"I can't quit you."

7

Last Dance

Reese

The lake rises and falls as a steady stream of boats glide over the water. The smoky scent of the grill infiltrates my senses.

Last night, Ace and I stayed at the Eagle's Nest long after the sun set. We held each other and talked for hours. I told lame jokes, and he was nice enough to laugh. It was comfortable. That's the best part about being with Ace—everything always feels so natural. There's never an awkward moment, no forced conversation, even the long gaps of silence feel easy as breathing.

Kennedy convinced me to head over to her beach party this afternoon. I know for a fact she invited Ace to come down because she told me so herself. She called him the special guest of honor just for me.

I spot Brylee down by the waterline. She's already set up a place for us by the edge where we can dip our toes to keep cool, so I head over and plop down beside her. The sun shines its harsh glare right over the lake, turning the water into one giant spotlight. The entire shoreline is crawling with Greeks from Yeats who made the trek up the mountain. I spot Warren walking over with both Gavin and Ace, and my stomach turns.

"Looks like things are about to heat up." Brylee tickles my foot, and my entire body jerks.

"Here's the old lady." Warren lands on the towel next to me, a beer already in his hand. "Take it." He tries to pass it to me. "You need to mellow out a little."

"No thanks." I guess he hasn't thawed out since I put the freeze on his balls last weekend. I suppose his next plan of action involves large doses of alcohol and the hot afternoon sun. Come to think of it I haven't eaten anything yet, so I suppose it wouldn't take much to get me wasted.

Kennedy bounces over in her teenie-weenie barely-there bikini, and I cut a quick glance to Ace to see if he's noticed. But Ace's eyes are firmly planted on me, with a warm smile on his face to boot. Ace has a way of making me feel like the only girl in the world simply by looking at me.

"So you guys have to be social." Kennedy is quick to chastise us. "None of this 'we're locals' shit. Our friends hauled ass to Loveless to spend time with us. I want to show them that we know how to entertain."

"Turn up the music." Brylee cranes her neck up at my sister. "Give them enough beer, and they'll entertain themselves."

"I've got a killer speaker you can use," Gavin offers.

"Bring it," Kennedy barks, still in drill sergeant mode.

Gavin hops up and disappears toward the parking lot. Gavin is a nice guy and hot as hell—but not in the "for me" kind of way—for Kennedy. Maybe this is the year we both leave the country club boys for some downhome decent mountain loving.

"Hey, we should play chicken." Brylee nudges into me.

"We should *not* play chicken." The last thing I want to do is wrap my legs around Warren's neck in front of Ace. Wait, who says I have to choose Warren? "On second thought, I call Ace." I glance up at him, and his eyes widen a moment, his lips tug upwards, but he's slow with the smile. Ace is perfection with his deep-set dimples, those glowing eyes that give the blue of the lake a run for its money, and that dark, thick hair, I could lose all day running my fingers through it, burying my face in it like a pillow.

"And"—Brylee kicks into me with her knee—"I call Warren. Come on, McCarthy." She yanks him up by the fingers. "Get ready to dominate out there."

"You wish," I say, dusting the sand off my thighs as I jump to my feet.

"We *will* dominate." Warren pulls me in by the waist and smirks over at Bry. "Only you'll be on the losing team. It's my old lady and me." He slips his fingers over my left boob and gives a squeeze like he expects it to honk.

I suck in a quick breath and glance back to find Ace looking like he's about to murder someone.

"Would you stop calling me your old lady?" I push Warren back a good foot.

"Would you stop being such a little bitch?" He reaches over and rumples my hair so hard my head knocks forward.

Ace steps in and pushes Warren flat on his ass. "Don't you fucking touch her."

Warren jumps up and lands chest to chest with Ace, both of them primed for some serious guerilla warfare as a small crowd gathers.

"*Dude.*" Warren butts his chest into Ace. "You don't tell me what I can and can't do. Reese knows I was shitting around."

"Do you, Reese?" Ace doesn't take his eyes off Warren, just presses in with a hard glare.

"Yeah, it's fine." I touch my hand to my throat. "*I'm* fine. No fighting, please." I take a step toward the two of them.

"I'm going for a swim." Ace sweeps over me with heavy eyes before wading in and diving into the lake.

Gavin comes back and helps Kennedy hook her phone up to his speaker until the sand vibrates to Coldplay's *Yellow*. Some kids from Yeats start swaying to the beat, and the mood elevates around us.

Warren speeds off toward the coolers, ticked as hell, and I watch as he pounds beer like water.

"Old lady, huh?" Brylee shoulders up to me. "I take it you didn't break things off with him yet."

"It's kind of odd knowing I have to break up with someone I was never really officially with to begin with." I spot Ace's dark hair glistening in the lake.

A girl from Alpha Kappa crosses his path while doing the backstroke, and my insides feel like they're being boiled in oil. She bumps into his chest, and I can hear her high-pitched laugh carry all the way over to my ears like a curse. It guts me to think he might find her pretty, that he might want her in general.

"You know, I think I'll go for a swim." The cool water runs up my thighs as I speed in and dive under. I move like a seal all the way over until I graze against Ace's leg and pop up next to him.

"Hey, beautiful." Ace gives his signature killer grin, and my insides melt like candle wax.

I blink the water from my eyes and glance to shore. Gavin and Warren are back on the sand next to Brylee along with a bunch of people I don't recognize.

"I'll race you to Boulder Island." I cock my head, doing my best to flirt openly. It feels good to be with Ace in public even if I am a hundred feet from shore.

"It's on, but you'll never win." His dimples dig in and out. "I'll even give you a ten second lead," he teases.

"Oh, I won't need it." I glide my fingers up the inside of his thigh. "Ready, set, *go*." I dive toward the overgrown rocks and missile right past him. Our fingers touch the blue granite at the exact same time, and I laugh as I submerge myself one last time.

Ace helps hoist me onto the heated rock and starts leading me to the back.

"No, this is fine," I say, pulling him to the flat surface that faces out toward Kennedy's huge summer bash. "I don't have anything to hide." We find a spot that's partially in the shade, provided by a lonely pine shooting from the center of the mass group of boulders and take a seat.

Ace scoots in until our shoulders touch. "I don't like the way he talks to you," he says it low as if there were a chance Warren might hear.

"I don't either." I make a half circle over the rock with my toes. "He's just being Warren." I shake my head as I pick up a twig that's drifted from the pine.

"I don't hear him talking to anyone else like that." Ace cuts me a looks that lets me know he'd knife Warren's balls off if I let him.

"Nor should he." I swallow hard. The truth is, I don't know how to get rid of Warren without turning this into some kind of familial and business meltdown. "I think we should change the subject." I rock into him. "We should talk about *us*."

"My favorite subject."

"Mmm." I moan into him. "You always know what to say. Is that what they're teaching you down in Collingsworth? How to Treat A Lady 101?"

"Nope. With you it just comes natural. So what do you want to talk about?"

"I want to see if you're still into doing this with me—you know—our special summer thing."

"The non-fling?" He teases. "Hell, yes. You still on board?"

"Yes. *God*—yes. In fact, I'm ready and willing to press on." I drip my gaze down his body and sink it into his lap a moment. "You know—really be with you." I've waited my whole life to be with Ace.

"Okay." He dips into a nod.

"Okay?" I look up at him from under my lashes. "As in right now?" I tease. "You think Warren would want to watch?"

Ace rumbles out a laugh. "I bet he would." He closes his eyes a moment. His dark brows create clean lines that frame his face. "Boathouse. You and me, Fourth of July."

"Really?" My entire body seizes at the thought of finally being with Ace in that special way. "That's just in a few days." My toes curl at the thought.

"I know," he says it low, sad. "Are you okay with that?" He glances down at my bikini bottom as if it were the forbidden zone.

"I'm more than okay. I'd let you have me now if you wanted." It comes out far too quiet and serious, pulling us down to a place I'm sure we don't want to be. "It could be my official break up with Warren. You know, a performance piece." I pinch a quick smile.

Ace and I share a quiet laugh.

"That might be the ultimate F.U." He rocks into me. "But I think the Fourth is perfect. That gives us a few days to finish being Reese and Ace, and then we can start something new."

"Something new." I nod into the idea. "I like the thought of starting something new, but we'll always be Reese and Ace."

"No," he says it sad, measured. "This is going to change everything between us. Nothing will ever be the same, Reese."

I hold his serious gaze as if it were made of blown glass.

"It's going to be incredible," I whisper.

"It will."

ஐ൙

The afternoon wanes into evening, and all the hard bodies, and those of the silicone-enhanced variety, are still busy partying on the edge of the lake. Kennedy has the entire event catered by the best Mexican restaurant in town, and it smells like heaven as they grill the street tacos right here on the sand.

Brylee dances next to me and pulls me in until I'm moving to the music right alongside her. Ace and Gavin had to leave earlier to head to work, but they said they'd be back by evening, and now I'm stalking the shoreline like a predator for the hottest boy in Loveless. I haven't said a word to Brylee about my special date on the Fourth because Warren planted himself between us for the better half of the afternoon. But, he's gone now, and I can't wait another second.

"Guess who's going to see some real fireworks this Friday?" I swivel my hips against hers like I'm flirting.

She pauses for a second as she narrows her gaze into me. "If I didn't know better, Westfield, I'd think you were hitting on me." Brylee shakes out her blonde mane before wiggling her chest in my face. "So is that when we're going to take the plunge and migrate to the other team?" She chest bumps me, throwing me off balance.

"Not you and me." I avert my eyes as I sway to the music. "Me and someone *special*."

"No way!" Brylee squeals so loud that an entire group of got-the-clappa's turn to look at us.

"Yes, way." I motion for her to keep it down.

"So is that how you do it? You pencil it in?" She smears it with sarcasm. "Sex on Friday." She holds up a finger to say something else, and Neva pops up behind her looking like a zombie.

Shit!

I straighten.

Honest to God, Neva scares the crap out of me, but what scares me even more is Brylee's inebriated need to repeat what I just said.

"Who's having sex on Friday?" Neva doesn't bother to keep her voice down just as Warren comes up behind her. "Oh, let me guess." She leans in, and I can smell the Jack Daniels on her breath. "You and—"

Double shit!

Without putting much thought into it, I clock her.

The crowd gasps. Neva knocks me to the ground and begins railing away at my face with her fist. I try to bat her off, but Neva sits hard on my stomach and takes the air from my lungs with one severe bounce. She gives my hair a good yank just as I feel her body lifting off mine. Warren plucks her away, but she lands a foot in my eye before I can move.

"Shit!" Ace pulls me up and draws me into him, and my entire body sighs with relief. I wrap my arms around him, burying my throbbing face into his chest.

Neva lets out a scream, and we look over.

Warren hustles her toward us. "You fucking dislocated her jaw." He cuts me a hard look as if I deliberately did this to piss him off. Little does he know I was just trying to save him from hearing that I was turning my virginity in to Ace come Friday—that all of the money in the world isn't enough to make me want to lie down for him.

"Let's see it." Ace pulls her hair back, exposing a nice split in her lower lip, a jagged line of blood runs clear down to her chin.

Oh, God. In no way did I ever want to hurt her. Okay, so maybe a small part of me did, but never like that.

"I'd better get you to the clinic." Ace tries to pull her in, but she growls at him as if she were rabid.

If I didn't know Neva before her walk on the wild side, I might actually be afraid of her—I sort of am anyway.

"Dude." Warren pulls her back and examines her closely. "She might need stitches. Anything more than a band aid, and they're going to send you down the hill." He cringes into her. "I'll take her. It'll be faster in my truck."

"My car is plenty fast." Ace expands his chest at the thought of being cut off at the vehicular balls by Warren of all people.

"No it's not." Warren pushes Neva toward the sidewalk.

"I'll come with you," Ace offers.

"It's a two-seater. We'll be right back." He leads her off toward his house, and I can't help but breathe a sigh of relief. I feel bad for Neva, but with both her and Warren gone, I feel lighter than air.

The music shifts its rhythm back to Coldplay's *Yellow,* and I lower my lashes into Ace. "I spent the entire last year listening to this song on repeat." While dreaming of him, but I leave that last part out. I remember agonizing at the thought of having to spend each day without the possibility of seeing that dark hair, those eyes like polished sapphires.

"This song reminds me of you." He presses out a sly grin, and his dimples dig in deep.

Joanna Knickerbocker bops up in a pair of pasties she's trying to pass off as a bathing suit, her round bottom hangs out of her bright pink shorts.

"Ace Waterman," she purrs into him. Her blonde hair is pulled back into a sleek ponytail, and she actually looks pretty with her face kissed by the sun, her lips glowing a soft peach. "Dance with me!"

My stomach pinches just witnessing the exchange.

"He can't dance with you," I say, gurgling a silent laugh while looking right into his eyes. "Because he's going to dance with *me*." I pull him along until we're buried nine deep in a sea of bodies. Ace slips his hands around my waist. "I was just thinking the other day how we've never danced," I whisper into him.

"Sure we have." He brushes his lips over my ear, and a dull ache travels all the way down to the most intimate part of me. "Remember the night you loaded my pillow with toothpaste, and I chased you around the cabin?"

I belt out a laugh. "That wasn't dancing, that was called running for my life."

"No, it was dancing. We were just moving really fast." He presses me in by the small of the back, and I catch my breath as his stomach sears over mine. "Do you remember what I said to you that night?"

"What did you say?" I tilt my head back and catch Warren up on the ridge in his truck. The smile glides from my face as he stares me down. He takes off so fast, a trail of dust rises in his wake.

Ace leans in and touches his cheek to mine. "I said I forgave you because one day I'd have you right where I want you."

My chest heaves for a moment because, for one, Ace remembered, and two, it sounded beautiful coming from his lips.

"And where's that?" I pull back to take him in, his navy eyes, those deep wells in his cheeks that wink at me in turn. Ace Waterman is perfection.

"Right here." He leans in and rubs his lips over my ear. "In my arms."

Ace

The bodies only seem to grow in number as the sun sets.

Kennedy pulled Reese back to the house to ice her face, and I haven't seen her for a good half hour. I shake my head at the thought of Neva and her damn left hook. I plan on giving her a fucking earful in the morning. I don't want anybody touching Reese, not Warren and for damn sure not Neva.

Funny how things work. I used to come to these parties just to see Reese, and now, we're meeting up, stealing kisses on the side.

I groan as I head to the food line. Gavin had me chopping a shitload of walnut this afternoon, and my muscles kill just to move.

Brylee makes her way over just as I'm loading up on tacos. I plan on wolfing them down in record time. According to Neva's text, she'll be another couple hours in the E.R., so as soon as Reese comes back I plan on stealing her away to the boathouse for another dance—a private one we can both enjoy.

"Hey, hot stuff." Brylee snatches a taco from my plate and takes a giant bite.

"Have you seen Reese?" I glance out at the crowd.

"I just talked to her. She's changing into something that's guaranteed to drive you insane. You do realize that girl is crazy about you."

"She's just having a good time." I shoulder up to Bry as I continue to pan the crowd. "She specifically signed up for fun, and that's what I plan on giving her."

"A little bird told me that you plan on giving her a lot more than fun on Friday." She bumps her hip into mine, and the rest of my food goes flying.

"Nice." I toss my plate into the trashcan next to me. "And, yes. Did she sound excited?"

"Hell to the yes. Oh, hon, you don't even know. This is bigger than prom." She bats her lashes a ridiculously long time. Brylee straightens out, and her demeanor shifts. "Why don't you do everyone involved a favor, Waterman..."

I know what she's going to say, so I look away.

"I don't want to rock the boat," I whisper. "If she's happy like this, then so am I." The last thing I'm going to do is slam her with my feelings, especially since we were pretty clear about maintaining a friendship right from the beginning.

"So you're content just being fuck buddies?" She glares into me with her arms folded tight. Brylee knows I hate that term, and to associate it with Reese seems almost blasphemous.

"Don't say that." I look around to see if anyone else heard. "What we have is different—it's special. She just wants to cross that bridge with someone she feels comfortable with, and this is the summer she wants to do it." I swallow hard. "She recruited me." I'm not sure that's an upgrade from fuck buddy, but I like the argument. Maybe, at the end of the day, that's all we would have been this summer. "It's special to the both of us. We're best friends." It's like I can't keep my mouth from moving while trying to justify the situation.

Brylee tilts into me with a look that suggests I've just fed her one line of bullshit too many.

"Reese and I are best friends." Her hardened stare bears into me. "Should I be fucking her?"

"Yeah, well, she didn't ask you. Did she?" I scan the crowd for Gavin now. I'll do just about anything to ditch Brylee and her ball-busting campaign.

"Exactly my point." She nods while staring me down as if this should mean something.

I'm just about to ask her to sharpen the lines, tell her I'm a guy and can't read between them when a light tap emits over my shoulder.

I turn to find Reese, and my heart stops. She's wearing a skintight dress, the exact color of her skin, short as hell with her cleavage blooming in front. Her hair is loose around her face in perfect waves, and her eyes glow like streetlamps in this dull light.

"Remember that marble collection you used to have?" Her tongue licks over the rim of her lips like quicksilver. "I wondered if you still had it. Maybe you could show it to me?"

Brylee groans into us. "Would you two get a room already?" She calls out for Kennedy before dancing off in her direction.

"Sorry. I told her," she confesses. "Do you hate me?" She tilts her head, and her dark hair fans out on one side like a giant feathered wing.

Reese pulls a smile from me without even trying. "I could never hate you." And there is no bigger truth.

Reese threads her arm around my waist, and we walk boldly through the crowd like a couple. I wait until we hedge the upper ridge before pulling her in tight.

The lake and the lights from the party glitter down below, and it feels as if we're on top of the world from this vantage point.

"Marble collection?" I press my lips over her forehead as a dull laugh rails through me.

"I'm serious. When we were kids, Neva and I used to sneak into your room while you were out and touch all your things." She flirts with her eyes, and my body starts to tremble. I want her so damn bad it hurts.

"All my things, huh? You weren't allowed in my room." I give her ribs a quick tickle as we make our way onto the blacked trail that leads to the cabin. I wince when I spot Dad's car parked next to mine. A part of me wishes he were down the hill, getting his rocks off with all the local MILFs—anything but this.

"Yeah, well, that's what made it so fun—knowing that we weren't allowed." Reese looks up at me from under her lashes, her eyes siren out like stars. "Sometimes it's the forbidden things that I want the most." She hikes up on the balls of her feet and kisses me hot over the lips, but her words swirl through my mind like a flying hatchet. Is that the draw? The fact she knows her father—most everyone in Loveless wouldn't approve? "Anyway"—she rubs her hand over my chest—"I loved the giant blue one you had. It was the exact shade of your eyes." She looks down a moment. "I used to hold it and stare at it for hours."

She noticed the shade of my eyes way back when?

"So what you're really saying is that you want to gouge out my eyes and hold them hostage for hours." I lean my head over hers as we make our way to the porch.

"That would make me sick and disgusting, and you're equally sick for thinking it up." She steals a kiss as we make our way to the porch. "Thanks for making my skin crawl."

"I've got about another dozen scenarios designed to do just that." I plant a kiss just shy of her lips. "In a good way, of course."

"Well, then"—she pulls me in as if she's trying to meld our bodies together—"you're welcome to make my skin crawl anytime you like."

I pause just shy of the door and give a sad smile into her. Reese is perfect. She has everything, and her future sparkles like gold, even I can see that. I don't get what she wants with me, but I'm glad I'm the one holding her right now and not Warren.

"Come here." I pull her in gently by the cheeks and land my lips over hers. My body shakes, my insides detonate, and I lose it. I plunge my tongue into her mouth in a hungry bout of passion. Maybe I am the forbidden fruit, but at this point, Reese is too, and if all we get is this one quick burst in our lives, I plan on enjoying the hell out of it.

"Take me to the boathouse," she whispers directly into my ear, and my dick ticks like a bomb.

"That's the plan." I skim her cheek with my lips. "But first I need to get something. I'll be quick." I turn around and spot Dad heading to his room from the murky screen. "Maybe wait here. I should probably tell him about Neva."

"Shit." She covers her mouth.

"It wasn't your fault." I brush my thumb over her cheek.

"But it was." Her forehead breaks out in a series of worry lines, and her mood takes a nosedive.

"Neva is always asking for it. I'm sure you wouldn't hit her unprovoked. Hang out one second, I'll be right back." I land a careful kiss over her lips. "I want to make sure tonight at the boathouse is memorable."

She pulls me back in by the chin. "What's the game plan?"

"I'll give you a hint, it involves strategic body placement."

Her tongue touches over her lip. "I like the sound of that."

"I figured you would." I pull another kiss off her, and my stomach bottoms out just thinking of the ways I plan on loving Reese on the Fourth. "And trust me, you and I will both be winners tonight."

Her face breaks out in a hotter-than-hell smile with a promise in her eyes. I don't want to let her down. If a good time is what she wants, that's what I'm going to give her.

I dart into the house to hunt down Dad and give a brief knock at his door. The sound of mumbling penetrates through the wall, so I walk in. The light from the TV illuminates the room a dull grey while he nurses a beer in bed.

"Neva fell. She hurt her jaw."

"Aw, shit." He wipes his face down with his hand. "She out there?" He hops out of bed and jumps into his jeans.

"No. A friend took her to the E.R. to get cleaned up. She should be home any minute."

"Sounds good." He fishes his phone off the nightstand. "I'll see how she's doing."

I head to my room and snatch the jar of marbles that have been sitting on the top shelf of my desk for the better part of a decade and blow off a thick layer of dust. The last time I messed with these was the week Mom took off. I spent the rest of that year moping in front of the TV, and, after that, they just sat and rotted. An entire slew of memories rush at me as I head back out to Reese. I give a wry smile. I knew she and Neva used to sneak into my bedroom the second I turned my back.

A quiet rumble of voices emit from the front, and I see Reese standing there looking defensive. I whip open the screen to find Neva and Warren glaring at her.

"Oh, hi." Reese startles when she sees me. "I was just coming to see if Neva was all right, and they pulled up as soon as I got here."

Nice save. Still not sure why she feels the need to lie. It's just Warren. Neva already knows.

"What happened?" I step into my sister, but all I can make out is the giant bag of ice, covering her mouth.

Warren pats her on the shoulder. "She'll live. Nothing but a bruise."

"Thank God." Reese lets out a breath of relief, and her chest expands in that skintight dress of hers.

"Like you care." Neva bumps into her hard with her shoulder before barreling into the house. Looks like Neva is ready to take their rivalry to a physical level, not that Reese didn't, but I'm sure it was warranted.

Warren shakes his head after Neva.

I take him in with his lavender Polo—the collar popped out, his plaid shorts, his penny loafers with the penny shiny side up, and I want to deck him for no reason.

"Let's get out of here." He wraps an arm around Reese and starts leading her off the porch.

And, there they go. I place the stupid jar of marbles on the railing as the moonlight prisms through them like a bunch of dying fireflies.

Reese turns around. There's a look of longing in her eyes, and I'd like to think it's because she'd rather be with me.

"Um"—she chews on her lip, not budging a single step further—"I'm not really up for Kennedy's madhouse right now. It's a little noisy for me." She never takes her eyes off mine.

"You want to hang out and watch TV?" I offer. "I could put on a movie. We could eat popcorn—maybe play monopoly." Warren cuts me a death ray of a stare. "You could hang out, too, if you want." I extend the offer, and my gut flinches. Fuck. Way to bring the awkward to the table.

"Actually I'm having some people over at my place." Warren nods me in the direction of his house. "Gavin's there doing his best to get laid. Who knows, you might get lucky, too."

Reese gives a little wink. "I'm sure there are tons of girls that would practically beg for you to take them. Come with us."

Take them? Come with *us*?

A blistering heat rushes through me, and this time it's because I'm more than a little pissed—only it's not at Reese—it's at me for ever thinking we could be anything more than a summer fling.

"Yeah, sounds good." I pull out my keys as Reese hops willingly into Warren's truck. I wait until they're clear down the street before I even start the engine.

Looks like Neva was right all along.

Suddenly it sucks to be "just friends" with Reese Westfield.

I wish the whole world knew how I felt about her.

Hell, I wish Reese knew, and something tells me it wouldn't really make a difference.

$\infty\heartsuit$

The last time I was at the McCarthy's house was over two years ago during another similar socially awkward event I got roped into. And, if I remember correctly, the reason I was there that night was also because of Reese. The only reason I've ever gone to any of their parties was to see her. There's something seductive about Reese in her element. She outshines the crystal, her smile sparkles, her entire person gleams. Only seeing her in Warren's house tonight is going to be about as pleasant as peeling off my skin. She'll be far from my arms, and it makes my dick and me both want to weep.

Gavin nods into me as I walk into the great room. His hair is slicked to perfection, and he's got his trolling for hoes douchebag shirt on. But I'm not interested in Gavin and whether or not his dick is going to find a nice tight place to call home for the night. I'm too busy taking in the mega estate that the McCarthy's not-so-humbly call home.

"Crap," I whisper. "I forgot how huge this place is." From the outside it's mammoth in size with the appeal of an oversized chalet, but inside, it feels like two solid football stadiums could sit nicely in here.

"Yeah, well, Reese doesn't strike me as a size matters kind of girl."

"Watch it." I turn to find her sitting on the floor with Brylee and a few other girls while Warren and his friends hit the hard stuff at the bar. I'm still not sure what I'm doing here other than helping Reese cover for being on my porch to begin with.

A group of girls bombard us and set in on the small talk. A blonde with a ponytail and pink bikini glides her shoulder up against mine. She's sending all the right signals, but too bad for her because I'm not in the market for a good time. The only good time I want to have is with Reese, and it looks as if that's being denied, too.

"So where you from?" She flutters her fake, moth-like lashes and grazes my chest with her boobs. I can feel her nipples right through the fabric, and it feels like I just cheated on Reese, right here in the open.

I take a step back, but she charges at me again. "From here—from the lake. Actually, I don't live on the lake, I live near it—well, pretty near it. And you?" Shit. I look past her at Reese, and she's still twisted in the other direction while Brylee glares at me from over her shoulder.

The blonde goes on and on, and I nod politely without understanding a single word that speeds from her lips. I try to revert my focus to Gavin who seems to be holding the attention of every other girl in our circle with a story of a bear.

"All right." Warren gives a loud celebratory hoot. "Let's get something on the fucking boob tube." He cuts out the lights, and the oversized television blinks to life. Everyone finds a spot to sit and relax, and lucky for me, the blonde bounces away with her friends.

"Over here!" Brylee waves at Gavin and me, and we head toward the back where she and Reese are sitting against the wall. Warren is taking up an entire couch on his own while pouring a steady stream of beer down his throat. He'll be knocked out in less than ten minutes at the rate he's going. It doesn't look like he's all that concerned about where Reese is sitting or if she even has a chair.

"Right here." Reese pats a spot next to her on the floor, and I readily comply. We lean against the wall as the lights go out.

The movie starts, some stupid sci-fi flick about a town that gets eaten by flying sharks. I've already seen it about a dozen times and enjoyed it each and every one.

Gavin reaches behind him and tosses a blanket to us then chucks one over to a group of girls who have been complaining the AC is on too high.

"Suck it up." Warren barks from the front.

"Nice." Reese rolls her eyes while covering herself to her neck. "Here." She throws it over my knees, and I scoot into her, effectively making a tent between us. "Sorry about this," she whispers. "I bet you had great things planned." Her teeth graze over her lips as if she were hungry for those very things.

I give a quick nod. "Damn straight, I had great things planned." I give a dirty grin. And in just a few days I plan on unleashing them all.

Reese takes up my hand under the blanket, and I rub soft circles in her palm until her eyes roll to the back of her head as if that's all the affection she needed to set her off. I let go and run my hand up along the inside of her thigh. It's so fucking dark in here, especially in the back, I doubt anyone would notice if we went at it full throttle—not that I plan to. Half-throttle maybe. I run my fingers under her dress, and she scratches at my thigh in approval. Her knees open for me just enough, and my hand glides south into her wet slick.

Shit.

I cut a quick glance to her.

No fucking underwear. A slow-spreading smile crops up on my face. Looks like she had a surprise of her own tonight. My chest thumps with a dull laugh as I continue to look straight ahead. I bury my finger, in her, and brush my thumb up over her folds until she's digging her nails into my leg. I take my time, just staring straight ahead as if I were immersed in the low-budget flick Warren decided to regale us with. I work over Reese, slow and easy, for several more minutes until Reese bucks beneath the blanket and strangles my arm in the process. I can feel her body vibrating beneath me, her heated breath as she pants to completion. I tug her dress down and warm her knee with my hand until that oversized shark on the screen eats the entire damn town.

Reese rolls her head into me, her lips twitching with a smile she's too shy to give. "Thank you," she mouths, and I can see the color rising to her cheeks even in this dim light.

I cut a glance to the front, and nobody moves, every single person is either nodding off or transfixed on the oversized screen.

I lean over and steal a kiss right off her lips, easy as pocketing a precious McCarthy heirloom. But Reese was never meant to be Warren's. She was meant to be mine. I can feel it.

By the time the movie finishes, half of the room is asleep, including Warren who's still clutching a beer in his hands like it's all he needs and lucky for him because I'm pretty sure that's all he's going to get.

Reese and I head outside with Gavin and Brylee.

"So what did you think?" Brylee looks over at the two of us with a sly look in her eye like maybe she knows.

"Great movie." I sock Gavin in the arm for the hell of it.

"I wouldn't know," he holds Brylee at the waist. "I wasn't watching." They take off up the street whispering into themselves, and it sounds like Reese and I weren't the only ones having some fun on the side.

"I'll walk you home," I offer.

"Sure." She wraps an arm around me as we walk the dirt trail just below the houses. You can still hear the party down on the lake even though it's almost one-thirty. I'm surprised my dad hasn't come by to fire a warning shot in the air. He's not into anything above a sneeze taking place after ten o'clock—especially not on the lake.

"Did you have good time?" I dip a kiss over her temple and take in the sweet taste of her skin.

"Thanks to you it was the best."

She pulls me in, and I dig my fingers in through the back of her hair. This feels right. Like we really are a couple. But I know we're not—that summer will end and exemplify just that.

"You want to go to the boathouse?" she offers.

"It's late. You've got to be tired."

"I'm not tired." Her eyes plead. "I feel like we missed out on our alone time together."

I do, too, but I'll be the last to say it.

"I know"—her eyes catch the moonlight and glitter like their own constellation—"follow me." She takes my hand and leads me up the stairs to her house. The porch light blinks on, exposing us as we make our way up the walk. I've seen them go off at all hours of the night. I know it's a motion sensor, but still, my heart jumped into my throat, and I half expect her dad to run out with a shotgun. Reese is getting bolder, holding my hand, taking me home—I wonder if that's a good sign or, more to the point, if she's getting careless in her cover up.

We make our way to the back and up a series of stairs that lead to the second story.

"My dad and Bev sleep downstairs." She gives a sly smile as she unlocks the door and lets us in. It's dark with the exception of a thin rail of light emitting just above the floorboards. I've only been in this house a handful of times and that was to help her dad install a new hot water heater when the last one blew out in the middle of a snowstorm. I've never been upstairs, for sure not in her bedroom.

"Kennedy's love shack." She points to a shut door, and the faint sound of panting emits from inside. "Freaky, right?" She gives a quiet laugh. "It's probably Keith. They broke up like five minutes ago." She leads us all the way down the hall to a set of double doors at the end, and we slip inside.

Reese turns on the lights then flicks them off just as quick, but the curtains are wide open allowing the moonlight to stream in. I can still make out how huge the place is.

"It was my parent's bedroom," she says, locking the door behind us. "Bev made my dad add a new master suite downstairs, so I got the killer room." She shrugs. "It makes me feel closer to my mom. I'm sure that sounds stupid."

"No." I pull her in and hold her like that a good long while, our hips conjoined, her warm belly over mine. "You're a sweetheart, you know that?" I pull my lips along her cheek until I fall into her heated mouth. Reese plucks at my shorts until they hit the floor, and I'm standing there with my cock in the air like a hat rack.

A wicked grin buds on her lips. "I didn't bring you here to show you what a sweetheart I was." She pulls my shirt off, nice and slow, and takes a step back examining me like this, my skin washed blue from the night. "That was really nice what you did for me back there," there's a hint of sarcasm in her voice. "And, I want to pay back the favor." Reese pushes me against the bed and drops to her knees.

"You don't have to do this." I stroke her soft hair as she looks up at me.

"Open for me," she teases, tapping at my thighs until I'm straddling her on either side. She runs her tongue over the tip before lunging down over me.

"Oh, shit," I whisper.

Reese goes off on me like she's been skillfully trained in the fine art of giving head. She dips in low, and I'm just waiting to hear her gag. Her cool fingers graze over my balls, and I suck in a breath through my teeth. Reese has got me going, she's waking up all my senses, and it's too damn good to not want to share this with her. I reach down and carefully pick her up onto the bed. I lie down opposite her and plant a kiss on the inside of her knee, and she groans. Reese puts her perfect mouth back over my cock while I meander kisses up her bare thigh, lifting her dress over her hips with a simple glide of my hand. I bury a series of kisses in that sweet spot of hers I was loving earlier tonight while she continues the most fucking fantastic blow job in the history of the universe. I flick my tongue over her until she's scratching at my back again. Reese tastes like sugar, like fucking candy, and I can't get enough. I wait until she's hyperventilating before I explode, and this time she pulls away. Her body spasms into mine, and we tremble together as she clutches my neck in a chokehold with her knees. I kiss her thigh, and she quivers before pulling me up next to her on the pillow.

"That was unbelievable." She leans in and nibbles on my lower lip.

"You're unbelievable." I wrap my arms around her.

Reese reaches down and pulls a giant comforter over us, light as air.

"Stay tonight. I want you to." She looks up at me with those big silver eyes as the moon kisses her features, turning her skin the same beautiful hue as her eyes.

I want to tell her that I love her but hold back.

"Well, if you're going to twist my arm." I rumple her hair, and my chest thumps with a quiet laugh.

"Thank you." She dots my lips with a kiss and twists into me until we're spooning. "Ace?"

"Yeah." I flick her earlobe with my tongue before kissing the back of her hair.

"What if everyone knew?"

I stop breathing for a second.

"Then we'd have to own it," I whisper. "Then it'd be real."

"It's already real to me." She shivers as she says it, and I warm her arm with my hand.

"It's already real to me, too." I plant another kiss to her cheek.

I hold Reese like that until her breathing steadies into long, shallow breaths. A seam of moonlight falls over her desk and illuminates a picture of her and Warren at the beach. His arms are firmly around her waist sort of the way mine are now. Reese can deny it all she wants, but after what happened tonight it's pretty clear she and Warren are still a couple.

I try to fall asleep, but that picture keeps calling to me as the moonlight screams over it with a harsh glare. It says *you could never be them. She never hid Warren.*

I pull Reese in tight and breathe into her soft, silky hair. Our time together is running through my fingers, swift as sand. Summer is going to come to an end sooner than either of us realize. I only have a couple weeks before I have to get to Yeats. I wonder what she'll do when she sees me there. Will everything really go back to how it was? Can it?

I don't think so.

We're either sealing our love or killing our friendship.

Either way, nothing will ever be the same.

8

Fireworks

Reese

On Wednesday, Ace was stuck down the hill helping Gavin gather firewood or whatever he has him doing. They had to spend the night in Sherman, which is at least four hours from here, and won't be back until late this evening. All I know is, it was hell without him, and that was just one day, but tonight he's all mine.

All last year I shed tears over my pillow because I missed his smiles, those insanely deep dimples you could dive into, the way he would wave from across the lake and, now, in a few short weeks, it all goes back to the way it was. I can only imagine those impossibly long, lonely nights without him will sting that much more—now that there are kisses to miss, his warm, strong hands roaming over my body, his amazing tongue. But tomorrow is the Fourth of July, and I'm going to spend it in the most special way possible with the boy I love.

I sigh into my pillow before reaching down and pulling out my mother's letters. I shuffle them in my hands like a deck of cards, smoothing my fingers over each one as if it were her skin. God, I miss her. This is an indescribable ache that transcends physical pain. It hurts in a jarring way, like a Charley horse or a foot cramp that catches you off guard, and your world stops in that moment, and nothing exists but the pain. It's that way all the time. Some days I wish I could pull my pillow over my head and never get out of bed, and, if it weren't for these letters, I wouldn't have made it through a single day.

I pluck out the very first one she gave me, the one she had me read the day after her funeral.

The fragile parchment unfolds in my hands, the outer edges already stained from a waterfall of tears I shed those first few months. I still cry when I read her letters, the only difference is they're happy tears. Each time I open one, it's like she's holding me in her arms again, and, for a brief moment, the world starts up again, and everything is how it's supposed to be—almost.

My dear sweet baby girl,

Reese, you know how much I love you—how outrageously much I think the entire universe of you. I beg of you to hold on and be strong. Know that one day far, far away from this day, I'll hold you in my arms again and dry your tears forever. But, until then, you've got a lot of living to do, missy. In no way do I want you moping around the house, or losing yourself in front of the television. I want you visiting friends, playing with your hula-hoop, and turning cartwheels in the yard. I want to hear your sweet laughter all the way up to Heaven. And most of all, I never want to see that precious smile leave your face. You are not a victim and neither am I. This is simply my time to go. I'm lucky in a sense because I was given a pretty accurate measure of when I'd be leaving the planet. It gave me time to create gifts for you through letters. You'll be getting one from your father each year on your birthday until you're a ripe old age. I'm sure you'll get sick of me repeating how much you mean to me, to be a good girl, but I want to remain in your life somehow and this is the only way I could figure out how. I hope you won't mind my yearly intrusion. I hope you'll come to look forward to them and that they will never be a source of pain to you. I have a special letter for your wedding day (should you choose that road), and I have a special letter for the day you think you've fallen in love. I'm sure it'll be more than embarrassing to ask your father for that one, so I've labeled it "special recipes." Feel free to ask for it anytime.

One more thing I want you to know, don't worry about missing me. Missing me will only bring pain. Try to focus on the special moments we shared like our walks to the park, sitting at the edge of the lake and watching the sun dip down over the back of the mountain, camping at the Forbidden Falls. Those moments and thousands like them are a part of who we were, who we are—not the grief, not the pain. Don't let the sadness pull you in—emerge from it with a smile when you relive each of those special times we shared.

I love you, forever.
You'll always be my special girl.
xoxo
Mommy

I hug the letter tight and pretend it's her. I can smell her perfume on the paper. She was so light in my arms those final days. This doesn't feel that much different. She knew I'd fall in love one day, and she wanted to participate in some small way. My soul sings just thinking about her giving me advice.

Special recipes.

It's time to find my father.

ଽଓୡଷ

The house is quiet as a tomb. Kennedy sits in the den watching television, so I poke my head in from the kitchen.

"Have you seen Bev and Dad?"

She ticks her head toward the window. "At the McCarthy's, helping to get things ready for tomorrow."

"Why would they be helping?"

Kennedy looks depressed as hell, not at all like her chipper self.

"They're hosting for clients." She tucks a pillow beneath her neck and turns to face me with her eyes laced with crimson. "No one does a firework show better than Loveless, so why not."

I bite down over my lip debating whether or not I should call her out on the fact she's been crying. Ken isn't one to share her soft side. Confronting her on a meltdown often comes with a price.

"You're right," I say. Last year Dad and Warren senior held a picnic at the park, and it was bland as oatmeal. "Fireworks are always a good call. Speaking of fireworks..." I let her in on the fact I'm on the final frontier of becoming a woman and hold back a laugh because I know she's going to zing me with some sarcastic remark.

"Really?" Kennedy pats a spot next to her, and I flop down on the couch. "I think that's beautiful." She wraps her arms around my waist and lays her head on my shoulder. "And, now, for the rest of your lives you'll both think of each other on the Fourth of July. It's like the whole country will be having barbeques and lighting off fireworks in honor of your special night—forever."

"Very funny." Although not half as clever as I would have pegged her for because it just so happens to be romantic as hell.

"No, I'm not trying to be funny. I mean it." She pulls back and gives a hard sniff.

"What's going on?"

Her mascara is smeared along one side, and she's got track marks in her foundation where her tears once flowed.

"It's Keith. I know we're over, but it's like we just won't let it die. Sort of like you and Warren."

"What are you talking about?" A part of me wants to push her off the couch in an effort to set her straight. Warren and I are nothing like her and Keith. "How many times do I have to tell you that I'm not into Warren like that?"

"Oh, really? Then why did you let him take you to prom in high school? Oh wait, *every* dance in high school? Why did you go with him to Vale for a part of your winter break and Cancun just after school let out?"

"Those were all group events."

"No, they weren't. I was there with Keith, and you were there with Warren. Sure there were a few stragglers, but you and Warren always sat together, always had dinner. He kissed you until you were both blue in the face. The only thing you never did was sleep with him, and, rumor has it, he's got a line of skanks a mile long to satisfy him. But, for whatever reason, he always floats back to you. You're his anchor, whether you like it or not." Kennedy narrows in on me with her accusing stare. "For God's sake, Reese—you keep a picture of the two of you in a heart-shaped frame on your desk."

"Shit," I hiss at the revelation. "I don't know. In my mind it never went down like that. We had the same friends, so we hung out." I turn and bury my face in her neck. This is it, the final unveiling of a truth I had been hiding even from myself. Warren and I had happened, we were still happening, and, as much as it hurts to admit, I'd keep the ball rolling forever if I knew it pleased my father. My mother crushed us with her death. I hated her for leaving, especially since she lit up our lives like an oil lamp. And then, in an instant, she was gone, and keeping my father happy had become my life's work. "I don't know how to do it. It'll kill Daddy. Besides, I told Warren we should see other people, and it's like he didn't even hear it."

"Please, Reese, don't string people along for the sake of your dad, he's got my mom. Maybe if you accept that, you'd see he doesn't need you trying to balance yourself on a rolling log when what you should really do is drop in the water, swim to something more stable." She pulls me back until we're eye to eye. "You need to have a serious heart to heart with Warren. Let him know he'll find someone special one day like you did." She gives a wry smile. "Only don't say that last part. Just leave it in a happy place."

"Got it." I rub her back. Kennedy's sweet honeysuckle perfume comforts me. "Did Keith leave it in a happy place?"

"No. He didn't. He found someone else." Tears fall fast and loose. "I guess that's the funny thing about relationships, people always think they're with the right person until they find out they're not." She gives a hard sniff. "Anyway, enough about me." She takes a breath. "As for your dad, have a nice sit down with him, too, and explain to him that Warren just isn't the one. I mean, it's not like you didn't try. Sometimes when love taps you on the shoulder, you don't always find who you expect on the other side. That's one of the nice surprises life has to offer. Warren will still be a part of the family."

A clatter comes from the kitchen.

"That's Dad," I whisper. My heart races like a prisoner who just climbed over the barbed wire. "I've got something to ask him, but I think I'll hold off on the Warren speech until I can process it a little more."

I go to get up, and she catches me by the wrist.

"It's okay to have your excuses, Reese." Her eyes spear right through me. "Just know you may not always have them. The sooner the better. Life has a way of unleashing the truth in the most inconvenient way. I should know. The more I learn about Keith and Joanna, the more I'm figuring out it wasn't a one-time deal."

"I'm so sorry." I pull her into a hug and hold her like that for a long time. Kennedy is right, the sooner I tell my dad about Warren the better. Then maybe I can tell him how I feel about Ace. If my father approved, it would mean everything.

"Get out of here." She pushes me up. "We'll talk tomorrow before the real fireworks go off."

The real fireworks. Just the thought of being with Ace buoys me with excitement, and I bump into Dad as I fly into the kitchen.

"Um..." Crap. "I was thinking about baking something for tomorrow. Do you think I can have Mom's *special recipes*?"

Dad raises his brows. "Sure. I thought you'd never ask. You know, it's the only letter I don't keep in the safety deposit box at the bank." He heads back to his bedroom, and I follow. "Of course, I had the teller make a copy of each letter and put them in separate locations in the event the bank disappeared overnight in an act of God. I promised your mother I'd keep them private just between you and her. I've never read them, but I'm hoping one day you'll have mercy on me and show me one or two." His features sag a moment, and I can see the grief prickling on the edges. "I do miss her." He pulls me in by the shoulder and presses a kiss over my head.

We walk over to his bedroom, but I linger by the door. I find it creepy to be in the room he shares with Beverly knowing the things they might do in here, although I doubt it's anything like what happened with Ace and me the other night. That was downright dirty magic.

He returns from his closet with another envelope that matches the ones I have upstairs. My mother's loopy handwriting greets me across the front.

"Special recipes," he chimes.

"Great." I fan myself with it a moment before kissing my father on the cheek. It'll most likely be the last kiss from his little girl. I bring the envelope to my lips and take in its warm scent as if it were my mother.

I'm on my way to becoming a woman. And, now, I'll have my mother's words of wisdom to guide me.

❦❧

My thumb and forefinger create small circles over the envelope for a long time. The paper warms beneath me until it's hot to the touch.

I can't do it.

Instead, I tuck it away with the rest of her letters and swear to myself that I'll read it in the morning. If it is my last night as a girl, I may as well save my mother's life-changing advice for my life-changing day. Tomorrow a whole new world opens up for me, and I might as well start the day off with a word of advice from my mother.

Around nine-thirty, after Ace has a chance to shower and wash all his woodcutting efforts from Sherman County off his body, he meets me down by the gnarled oak at the base of my house.

It's dark out, the moon is hardly a sideways sliver, but those are the best nights in Loveless because you can see the stars spray out like pinholes, trying desperately to expose the glory of heaven. Beverly once said it reminded her of a shattered crystal vase, and that pretty much solidified the fact that Beverly could see the negative in just about anything.

I run over to Ace and wrap my entire body around him, and he spins me while landing a dizzying kiss over my lips.

"I missed you like crazy," he whispers hot in my ear. He smells good and clean like spices and mint, a slight woodsy scent mingles in the background.

"You did?" I give a playful tug at his ear. "I missed you way more than you could ever miss me."

"Doubtful." He swoops in and picks me up.

"So"—I draw a soft circle over his chest as he carries me over the dirt trail—"are you as excited about tomorrow night as I am?" I gaze up at him. He's so stunning. He presses against the night sky with his dark hair catching the light of the moon, picking up blue highlights. His dimples go off, and he's trying to withhold a smile but it breaks free anyway.

"More than you'll ever know."

"What's the plan for tonight?"

"I thought maybe we'd hang out—be the awesome Ace and Reese for one last time." He bears into me with a slight hint of sadness as if he missed the old us already.

"Hey"—I swat him gently over the shoulder, and my heart ticks a notch at how muscular he is, how rock solid he is in all the right places—"won't we be awesome after tomorrow?"

"After tomorrow, we'll be extraordinarily awesome." He dots a quick kiss on my forehead. "In fact our awesomeness will be impossible to contain. The entire mountain might quake just having us both on it at the same time."

"Sounds epic."

"It will be."

The curve of his bicep twitches as he maneuvers me over toward his cabin. I run my finger up the thick cords of his neck, over his jawline, and up through the ridge of his nose.

"I wish I were an artist," I whisper. "I'd sketch you—mold a bust of your beautiful face just so I could take you with me wherever I go."

"You have a way with words. I'd say you're more of a poet."

"I don't know. I'm terrible at rhyming."

Ace lands me on my feet just shy of his car and swings the door open for me.

"Not all poems need to rhyme. Just write from your heart." He lands a careful kiss over my lips. "Like a letter with a little more feeling."

"A letter with a little more feeling." I blink back instant tears. "That's exactly what my mother wrote me. Poems."

Ace tilts into me with a sad smile. He takes my cheeks up in his hands and draws me toward him. "Sometimes, Reese"—he brushes his lips over mine just enough to make me ache for him—"you can write a poem with a kiss."

And that's just what we do.

The boathouse is quiet, still, as if we've just stepped into our own private universe. There's so much peace here without any of the drama that Warren affords or the stress of trying to maintain an image my father might approve of. Here, I'm able to shed them both like dead skin. My entire being feels invigorated escaping reality this way with the boy who stole my heart.

Ace starts a fire in the potbelly stove even though it's still pretty warm out.

"We can just start taking off our clothes if it gets too hot," I tease while bouncing on the bed.

"The candles alone won't be enough light for what we're about to do." He smolders into me with those glowing eyes. "The overhead light would blind us. I thought the fire might be a happy compromise." He opens the windows off the back, and a nice breeze flows in making the gauze curtains flutter like a pair of ghosts. I can't help but note the romantic implications of it all. Whether Ace is aware of it or not he's a born romantic.

He comes over and sits beside me on the bed.

"For what we're about to do?" I tease, running my hand up his shirt. "I like the sound of that." But more specifically I like the way he blisters over the palm of my hand, the smooth ridges of his abs that lie hard as concrete under his skin.

"I'm glad you like the sound of that." He plucks my hand out and kisses it sweetly over the top. A smile tugs at his lips. "Get on the floor."

"Yes, master." God knows I'm up for Ace barking out orders tonight and me complying. I'd do anything Ace wanted as long as we could be together, as long as I ended tonight and every other night in his arms.

I kneel down on the center of the rug and he takes a seat on the floor, opposite of me, pulling something out from under the bed.

"What's that?" I slide next to him, observing the familiar jar in his hand. "I remember those." It's filled to the brim with colorful marbles, mostly clear ones with swirls of blue and red in the center. It may as well be filled to the brim with my childhood. I wish I could open the lid and fall back into those haze filled days when my mother was still alive, baking special treats for my father and me in the kitchen.

"I thought we'd take it slow today. Go old school." He wraps his arm around my waist and his cologne intoxicates me. He spills out the tiny glass spheres between us, and picks up the oversized navy beauty, clear as midnight. It's the exact color of his gorgeous eyes. "This is the shooter." He spreads the marbles out with his hand. "Any marble you shoot outside this ring is yours." He traces the outer edges of the braided rug, about a three-foot circumference. "The one with the most marbles wins."

"That's it?" I've never played marbles before, and certainly it always seemed to have something more to it, but I'm all for easy. "That sounds easy enough. I like the simple things in life." I take the shooter from him and roll it in my hands.

"You like the simple things?" He tilts in observing me as if he learned something entirely new.

"Yeah, I do. I guess you could say I'm the anti-Kennedy. She needs designer labels just to breathe, and I couldn't care less as long as I have sunshine on my back—peace in my heart." I reach up and run my fingers through his hair. It's still damp from the shower and slick. "She needs security. I need love." I swallow hard, reverting my gaze to the carpet. "So who goes first?"

His eyes are still pressing into me, heating the entire right side of my body like an inferno I've accidently gotten too close to. But I can't seem to face him. I let the L word fly from my lips, and now it's fluttering around the room like a bat getting ready to tangle itself in our hearts, things are bound to get messy, and we'll have to cut it out—cut each other out of one another's lives as collateral damage.

Ace picks up my hand and intertwines our fingers, soft, without pretense. "I think you deserve love, Reese. That's exactly what I told you that first night in the lake. I want you to have it."

Ace didn't mention that he'd like to be the one to give it to me, so I guess love is outside the realm of possibility for us.

My eyes skirt the braided rug that sparkles with the remnants of our childhood. I lean in and shoot the oversized navy eye across the floor and take three marbles out of the ring.

"Now, there's something I love." I give a quick wink collecting my glass winnings.

Ace frowns into me a moment before breaking out into his killer grin. "You're about to go down, Westfield."

He takes the shooter and proceeds to knock a single marble out of the ring, and just barely at that. I reach over and pick it up. It's a chalky yellow, pocked with a thousand little holes that make it lighter than air.

"Hey, this is made out of cork or something. I don't think this counts."

"It was in the pile." His cheek rises seductively as he takes it from me. "All's fair in love and marbles." He holds my gaze this time and neither of us moves.

"I think maybe we should have outlined the rules a little better." My throat dries up as I say it. Ace Waterman is making my panties disintegrate with nothing more than that serious gaze of his—that steady stream of innuendos that I wish meant something more.

"Sometimes it's best to let things play out." He places his hand over mine as he lays the shooter in my palm but he doesn't move. Instead he warms me with his eyes, his skin over mine. "Things have a way of ending up just the way they're supposed to." His fingers pull from mine, achingly slow and my insides cry out to have him, right here over this bed of miniaturized rolling stones.

"Do you believe that?" It comes from me childlike, tragically innocent.

"I do." His gaze never wavers. "I really, really do."

I take in a deep breath as the woodsy scent from the fireplace permeates the air with the pleasant bite of hickory. I wonder what those words mean to Ace, but I'm too much of a coward to ask. Maybe after the summer...

"We'll be friends forever, right?" I ask while trying to shoot an entire mob of marbles out of the circle, and not one of them twitches under my command.

"That's right." His lips press into a line as he shoots into the exact same spot and lands six of them off the carpet without much effort. "I'll always be in Loveless. You know where to find me if you're ever in the mood for an affair." His chest pumps just once.

I shoot at a clear yellow marble and land it on the line.

"It still counts," I say, scooping it up as a win.

"You like to make your own rules, don't you?" He shoots another half dozen off the rug, and I shake my head at the fact Ace is kicking my ass.

"Sometimes making your own rules is the only way to go." Ace might be landing the marbles where he wants them but I've managed to land him where I want him, and tomorrow night, that's exactly where he'll be. Too bad it's not a permanent arrangement. Too bad I'm not better at figuring out how to keep what I win.

We continue our game until I'm effectively decimated, and, as the loser, I have to scoop up all the marbles on my own, but Ace helps anyway.

"Come here." He lands me over his lap and we stare at the fire, listening to it sing its broken song through a series of wild crackles.

"I like it like this." I snuggle into his chest, pulling his arm over me. "In the dark—the fire the only light around. I wish we could end every night like this. You should come to Yeats, and I'll sneak you into my dorm."

"Do you have a fireplace?" His hand smooths up my arm, and a tingle erupts between my legs as if his fingers were there all along.

"No, but for you, I'd move off campus and get one." I dip my hand up under his T-shirt hinting at the fact I'd like the night to end with our bodies wrapped around one another like a vine, but I'm too embarrassed to ask.

"You'd move for me?" He seems genuinely impressed.

"You're worth a move. Of course, you'd have to bring your firewood along. There's nothing like a wood burning fire."

"Knew it." His chest rumbles beneath me as he singes my neck with a kiss. "You're just using me for my logs."

"I guess my secret's out. And it's *log* as in singular." I tickle his ribs. "I hope it doesn't bruise your ego, too much."

"Are you kidding?" He tightens his grip around my waist. "I'd let you use me every day of the year and twice on Sundays."

"Just twice on Sundays?" I twist around until I can get a better glimpse of his blessed by God features. I've loved his gorgeous face, body and soul as soon as my hormones kicked in. "You've had me blushing since I was thirteen, you know that?"

His head ticks back a notch as if it were the last thing he expected me to say.

"No, I guess I didn't."

"Have you ever had any, you know, *special* thoughts about me?" I trace my finger over his jawline.

"Special? Is that the code for dirty? I suppose I could fess up to one or two." He steals a kiss off my lips. "Like that time I locked you and Neva in a trashcan and rolled you downhill. That was pretty dirty."

I give a gentle laugh. "That was disgusting."

"Yeah, but you begged me to do it."

"That's because we were stupid. You should have warned us that our hair would smell like sour milk for a week." My fingers race to the lip of his jeans, and I undo the button. "And, that's not what I meant by dirty."

Ace bears into me with those cobalt eyes. "I know that's not what you meant. You want to know if I think about you at night—if my body shakes at the thought of your perfect face when I'm alone in bed." He slips his hand up my shirt, and I take in a breath as soon as his heated flesh touches mine. "If I've ever relieved any tension by imagining you and I doing this." He lands a kiss at the base of my neck, and I shudder into him. "Or this." His hand sinks low on my waist, then lower still until his warm fingers find a home inside my thigh.

"Yes that," I breathe into his ear. "And now, I want to play a different game." I take a gentle bite out of his earlobe, and let it out slowly by way of my teeth.

"So do I." He gives it in a heated kiss, and my thighs tremble.

Swear to God, I'm one breath away from detonating right here in his arms.

"But"—he pulls his hand from under my shirt and my stomach quivers as he grazes it—"I think if we hold out until tomorrow, it'll be that much more amazing."

I let out an unexpected groan of disappointment, and he breathes a laugh into my hair.

"Now you know how guys feel most of the time." He runs his fingers over my ribs.

"Okay, but after that, I want to be with you every single night."

"Just at night?" He brushes my neck with his lips. "Summer's pretty damn short. I think maybe we should utilize a few waking hours, too."

"I like the way you think." My entire body sizzles at the thought of loving Ace in the afternoon. "I'll tell Kennedy I'm going on a camping trip with friends, and maybe we can spend the night. I'll let her break the news to my dad when he notices I'm not around."

"Camping with friends." He lets out a breath as he rests his chin on my head. "I think we should do it. We should head over to Forbidden Falls and stay for a week."

My body seizes. A week alone with Ace would be paradise. I look up at him as the light of the fire glows over his features in crimson waves.

"You're brilliant you know that?"

He shakes his head. "If I was brilliant I would have said *two* weeks."

If I were brilliant I would have said forever.

"Forbidden Falls," I whisper, nestled in his strong arms.

"Forbidden Falls," he breathes it like an erotic poem right into my ear.

Ace and I are going to make a memory, create an entire series of moments that hopefully neither one of us will ever forget.

I know I won't.

ಐಲಿ

The sun rides high over Loveless on this, the fated Fourth of July in which I gift Ace my virginity. I've been up with the sun, nervous and excited, and scanning my brain for reasons to abort the effort, but, happily, I can't think of a single one.

Outside the entire mountain vibrates with the sound of children laughing. The scent of barbeque is thick in the air by three-thirty.

I stared at that envelope labeled "special recipes" for the better half of the day. My thoughts were laced with the memory of lying in Ace's arms all night and the promise of spending the entire next week with him alone in that tent of his. I can't bring myself to open my mother's letter and risk hearing something that might change my perspective on my special time with Ace. All I could think about was what if she says something outrageous like wait until your wedding night? I've always had a place in my heart that wants to please my mother, both my parents, and that goes double for Dad ever since Mom passed away. But, mostly, I'm afraid Mom's letter will say wait until you say I love you and mean it. I pet the letter and debate for another small eternity whether or not to open it, but by five o'clock I abandon the effort and get ready for Dad's big company bash at the McCarthy's. The entire lake is invited, so I already know I'll be seeing Ace there.

I pay careful attention to my hair and makeup until I accidentally make myself look like a cupie doll with bowtie lips, eyes that are overdone like a drag queen. I scrub it all off in haste and throw my hair into a ponytail. I settle on the string bikini that has the U.S. flag imprinted on it and pull on a pair of my favorite cut offs before examining myself in the mirror—simple yet hot. I'm hoping to have Ace's blood pumping in all the right places long before we ever get to the falls tonight. My duffle bag is packed and ready to go in the corner. The only thing left to do is endure a few hours of family fun.

I bounce my way downstairs and follow the trail of voices to the living room where, to my surprise, I find Dad talking to Warren. But that only mildly shocks me in comparison to the gaping hole I see in the dining room. The table is notably missing, and my heart sinks like a stone. I go over and walk into the bare spot like it really didn't matter, but it feels like a betrayal, like we dug my mother up and found the coffin empty.

"You guys ready to party?" I try to muster all the enthusiasm I can but it comes out barely audible. I hate that the final piece of my mother has been yanked from me today of all days. I wanted to remember this day for all of the erotic pleasure tonight would offer, and now I've burned the image of this bare room into my mind, my mother's treasure extracted, obvious as a missing tooth.

"What the hell are you wearing?" Warren snaps me out of my funk before it can properly set in. His eyes round out over my questionable attire as if I had come down naked. "Go throw on a dress and some pearls or something. Make yourself presentable. Important people are showing up for this."

Warren McCarthy is an uptight asshole. I smile briefly into him because it pleases me to have that fact sail through my mind in front of both him and my dad. Speaking of which, I tilt into my father and wait for him to put Warren in his place because God knows if I do it we're looking at an awkward evening that will start with expletives and probably end with a kick in the balls.

"He's right." Dad's features sag as if he were disappointed that I wasn't smart enough to figure this out for myself. "Sorry, sweetheart. I've got a lot riding on tonight. Warren understands because he's been in the thick of things down at the office. It's just one of those days where you can't afford a single thing to go wrong."

I glance down at my flag inspired bathing suit top, my Daisy Dukes that glow against my summer tan. "I get it." I glare over at Warren in his upturned polo, his signature khakis and penny loafers. "I'll change for you, Dad."

I trot back upstairs and that stupid picture of Warren and I encapsulated in a silver heart catches my attention. I pick it up and rub my hand over him through the glass. Without thinking, I toss it right into the trash.

Dad is right. Tonight can make or break a lot of things.

I, for one, am about to make something beautiful with Ace and break things off with Warren forever.

Loveless shines like a beautiful woman. She wears her best party dress with glittery shoes, her hair and makeup done to the nines for the night.

Kennedy wraps an arm around me as the crowd bustles in every direction on the McCarthy's lakefront estate. It's hot as hell, and I haven't seen one sign of Ace.

"I have to tell you something." She's got that evil twinkle in her eye because whatever the hell she's about to say is going to rock my world and not in a good way. I can tell.

"Wait." I pluck Brylee away from Gavin a second and pull her into our circle. "Sorry," I shout to him before he melts into the crowd. "I have something to say, too." I crimp a smile. "And I want you both to hear it." I fill them in on my faux honeymoon with Ace, and my face fills with heat just verbalizing it.

"A week?" Brylee looks impressed as hell—as she should be.

"A *week*, alone with Ace Waterman?" Kennedy deadpans. "Your dad is never going to let this fly."

"That's why I'm not going to tell him." I dot a finger into her chest. "You are."

"You want me to tell him you're sleeping with the woodcutter while his pipe dream of you getting laid by a McCarthy goes down the company drain? No thanks."

"Eww—and no. Tell him I went camping with a couple of friends from school. Ten bucks says he doesn't even notice I'm gone for the first three days."

"And what about Warren?" Kennedy nods behind me as he fast approaches.

"I'll take care of Warren," I whisper just as he circles his arms around my waist.

His skin glows a deep bronze from logging all that time down at the water. Warren has always been tall and lanky so his body feels leaner, less muscular than Ace's. And oddly I don't feel any sexual ache for his arms to linger around me. It's like having a family member hold me, an older brother.

"What's this I hear about you taking care of me sweet cheeks?" He thumps his hand over my thigh and his breath bowls over me with the strong scent of whiskey. "I got something you can take care of." He lands a sloppy kiss on the side of my face.

"Whoa." I try to ease out of his grasp but it proves impossible.

I scan the crowd, and, sure enough, I catch Ace looking over at the two of us from the white picket fence at the base of the property. He glances away and continues his conversation with Gavin as if nothing ever happened.

Ace is the one I wish was holding me right now, not Warren—never Warren.

"Hands off, please." I try to pry his arms from around me but he only strengthens his grip. Anger rips through me like a fire. "Warren, I'm serious, let *go*."

His arms tighten like a vice. "Ooh, you like it rough, huh baby?" He whispers, sticking his tongue in my ear and flicking it around.

Dad and Beverly pop up in our little circle.

"All right you two." Dad winks approvingly at Warren's barbaric display of affection. "I've got a group of people I'd love for you to meet. In fact, why don't you sit with us at dinner and they can really get to know you."

Kennedy shakes her head just barely, as if she's seen the bear trap I'm about to fall into and doesn't approve.

Beverly links her arm in mine and walks me briskly over to the formal section of the property with its congestion of white tablecloths, waiters in full dress, champagne served in crystal flutes. The McCarthy's hired a decorator to come out and festoon the place with all things Americana, not to mention the expensive floral arrangements dripping in the center of each table—white lilies mixed with blood red roses. It all reeks ode to country club, and I want nothing more than to ditch back into the crowd and find Ace.

Beverly leans in with the mint julep she just downed exuding from her lungs. "I can't underscore how important this is to your father."

Maybe I should get ripped. God knows I'd do just about anything to melt away the next few hours. I'm ready for the real fireworks to begin, and I'm not talking about the ones that are about to shoot over the lake at dusk.

Beverly throws on her overzealous smile as we approach a table full of Dad's prospective clients, the McCarthy's, and Warren himself. I land in the seat next to Warren and pretend to listen as an entire whirlwind of conversation drones on around me for the next solid hour. Try as I might, I can't seem to pay attention. Instead, I find myself sneaking glances at Ace who stands far away at the other end with Gavin, Kennedy, and Brylee. Joanna Knickerbocker slithers her way over and tries to climb Ace like a pole, and, honest to God, I can't blame her. He deflects her efforts time and time again but she's proving staunch and most likely wasted. I think it's high time I intervened.

"Um"—I push my plate back and offer a polite smile to Dad, interrupting his conversation—"I think I'll go out and mingle a bit." I pan the table with a smile that says you will never see me again. "It was really nice getting to know all of you."

I hardly have time to scoot my seat back before my father holds up a hand in protest.

"Warren?" Dad nods into him with a knowing look. "Why don't you bring Reese over to the podium for a moment? Your father and I have something we'd like to say to you."

Warren leans in. "I bet they want to reward me for all the bullshit I've done this summer." He slinks his hot hand around my waist and pulls me over to the makeshift dance floor where there's a glorified pulpit and microphone at the ready.

Dad taps the mike like he's spanking its bottom and sets off some serious feedback, effectively settling all eyes and ears upon us.

Perfect. In the event I was worried Ace didn't get the best view of Warren clutching onto me like a koala bear, we're now front and center with DJ Daddy ready to drop a beat. At least it's getting dark, and we're sort of melting into the evening shadows.

A series of twinkle lights go on overhead and to my horror a bona fide DJ starts in on a slow song that's thankfully turned too far down to dance to. A giant ten-foot screen pops up against the house, and the next thing I know I'm staring at an oversized version of myself, Warren and his father. Crap. Nothing but the best for Westfield and McCarthy.

I twist uncomfortably in my heels. Swear to God, as soon as they reward Warren with a new Corvette or whatever the going rate is for being their lackey, I'm kicking off my heels and dragging Ace to the Forbidden Falls.

I give a private smile at the thought.

"Warren—Reese." Mr. McCarthy looks lovingly at the two of us as if I've somehow added to Warren's success at the office. "It was years ago at the same university the two of you attend now that a good friend of mine and I decided we'd start up a law firm one day." The crowd quiets as he readies to share the rest of his budding bromance with my father. "If we only knew then that one day our friendship would blossom into a legacy, we'd have been a little more sober-minded on the outset." A few random chortles break out in the crowd.

Really? Legacy?

Someone should have suggested Warren senior here check his ego at the door. I'm pretty sure it's never a good idea to make yourself sound like an egotistical maniac when the entire lake is flooded with prospective corporate clients, but whatever. He could recite his grocery list, and I couldn't care less as long as I make it to the falls within an hour. I'm hoping to make a legacy myself.

"Legacy, family…" he continues with tears in his eyes. "Reese, when your father and I first noticed there was a genuine spark between you and Warren, in all honesty, we weren't sure how to feel."

Spark? My insides go rigid. Who has a fucking spark?

Holy shit. I glare into him.

Balls are going to roll if he keeps this up.

I scan the crowd for Ace.

Dad snatches the mike from Mr. McCarthy's obnoxiously wasted hands, and I breathe a sigh of relief.

"I knew damn well how I felt." Dad gives a stern look to Warren and the crowd erupts with laughter. "But, in all seriousness, you've been nothing but a perfect gentleman with my daughter." Not. "And as your love has grown for one another these past few months it's become apparent to everyone around that not only is our business in the process of expanding but so is our family."

Family? Is Warren having a baby?

I shoot a look up at Warren but he's too caught up, nodding at my father like he knows exactly what the hell he's talking about.

"That's why." He pauses. Beverly joins my father and hands him a shiny gold key with a red, white, and blue ribbon dangling from it. "When the Nicholson's home came on the market both the McCarthy's and I knew what needed to be done." He gives a warm laugh. "Warren, Reese, we know you're still off at college and, after that, graduate school waits for you, but because we love you both dearly, and we hope to glean many grandchildren from you one day, we wanted to give you an early wedding gift of sorts." He hands the key to Warren. "Hope you won't mind the neighbors. We've put both your names on the deed." The crowd erupts with cheers as Warren pulls me in and lands a kiss over my lips.

Beverly leans in. "Your mother's table is already in it."

Crap.

I try to maneuver out of Warren's vice grip and run the hell off the makeshift stage—maybe knock some sense into my father, by way of my shoe before I jump in the lake in an effort to forget this nightmare.

"That's very nice of you." Warren takes up the mike, and for a fleeting moment I'm hoping he'll set the record straight— let them know that even if we were to get married one day— which we won't—we would never be insane enough to live smack in between the two of them. Who does that? And who the hell gifts their kids houses—especially in front of the entire community and prospective clients? I think dad would have done better with his corporate contenders if I kept my bikini on and he kept his mouth and wallet shut.

Beverly stands alongside Warren's social hungry mother and they gaze at us approvingly. You can practically see them drumming up a thousand neighborly reasons to drop by unannounced.

"Reese." Warren turns to me, and I can feel my face turning colors. It couldn't get any redder if you pressed it in a hot skillet.

Okay. Breathe. We got this. Warren and I are simply going to decline the gesture. We'll raffle off the house for charity and make both our fathers look like stellar philanthropists in the process. *God*, it's pure genius. I only wish someone would have let me in on the game plan right from the beginning.

I glance at the crowd to look for Kennedy, but Ace snags my eye instead. Just crap. I shoot him a pleading look but I get the feeling he wants nothing to do with me or my leap into real estate right now.

"The first time I said I love you"—Warren starts, and in the wrong fucking direction, might I add—"I think maybe we were six and you had just shoved a stick of gum in my mouth."

The crowd melts in a choir of sighs.

"It was a Popsicle," I stupidly correct. If I knew that sweltering August day would come back to haunt me, I would have shoved it in a far more interesting location.

"Whatever." Warren shrugs it off. He never could stand being corrected. "The point is, I had no idea that the girl I was saying it to would be the exact one I'd be saying it to for the rest of my life."

My stomach lurches and suddenly the prime rib and potato salad I wolfed down a mere fifteen minutes ago are begging to make their reprisal.

"What I'm trying to say..." Warren drops to one knee and the crowd gives a collective gasp.

Oh sweet mother of God.

My entire body freezes. Warren has crossed the last fucking line. My mind tells my feet to carry me the hell away from here, but I catch the expression on my father's face, and not one muscle in my body obeys.

"Reese Abigail Westfield..."

Abigail?

I shoot a look to my father. Unless he knows something I don't, my middle name is still Madelyn. But dad doesn't dispute my misplaced moniker, he simply plasters that shit-eating grin on his face right alongside Beverly and the McCarthy's.

A choking sounds emits from Warren's throat, and for a second I think he's going to puke all over my patent leather FMs, and if his speech is headed in the direction I believe it is, I'd welcome vats full of vomit.

"I guess what I'm trying to say"—he picks up my hand—"Reese, will you spend the rest of your life with me?" He pops open a small velvet box that appears from the inside of his shirt, and I'm equally unimpressed with his magician-like skills as I am with his ambush proposal. Not that proposals are ever *not* ambush, it's just the prospective bride-to-be usually has a freaking clue things have escalated to a matrimonial level.

The crowd coo's, creating its own lovesick brand of delirium as I'm momentarily blinded by the sparkler he's wielding like a threat.

He dips the microphone away from the two of us a moment.

"Are you pissed?"

"*Yes.*" I hear my voice amplify over the lake like a gong, and the crowd erupts in violent cheers.

"You!" I try to snatch the microphone from him, but he passes it back to my father. "You're an asshole," I hiss into his ear.

Dad says something about champagne that sets the crowd off into another round of titters, but I miss it entirely because the only thing I hear is the sound of Warren's balls exploding in my angry fist—or at least I'd like to.

The party shifts back to its pre-marital assault stage as the music gears up with an obnoxious song that gets the entire crowd moving.

"How could you?" I push Warren in the chest and sadly not one person witnesses the quasi violent exchange.

"What the *fuck* is wrong with you?" He grabs ahold of my wrist and whisks me off past the lawn to the dark area near the house.

"Do you really think our non-existent relationship is at that level?" I take the ring off my hand and shove it in his chest.

Warren stares at me for a very long time, his eyes filtering their disappointment into each of mine.

Oh my God. I stagger back a few steps. Obviously he does.

"But we've never even, you know." I glance down at his crotch a moment.

"You're the waiting kind of girl. I get it." He comes in and lands a wet kiss over my lips. "And now that we're engaged. I think the waiting should be over, don't you?" His beer breath blows over me, and I'm getting a buzz by proxy simply off the fumes.

"Warren. I don't think it's going to happen. I just don't think—"

"Look"— he knots up the front of my dress and yanks me in as if he's about to beat the living shit out of me—"you and I belong together. Get your fucking head straight, will you? We've got a sixteen million dollar account riding on this evening. Just put on a happy face and stop acting like everything is always about *you*. Sacrifice a little for once. This is our damn company you're about to take down with your silly little tantrum. This isn't the time or the place."

He shoves me away, and I struggle to regain my footing.

"You're right, Warren, this isn't the time or the place. But I have news for you, when you least expect it, you'll be getting a new asshole," it heaves out of me in a heated rush. "And *I'm* going to be the one to give it to you."

I take off my heels and dive back into the crowd looking for Ace.

I pray to God I can explain everything. I pray to God I didn't piss him off or worse, break his heart.

Come next week, I'm breaking my father's heart, too.

Ace

The rocky mountain road is virtually abandoned as I follow the dirt trail all the way to the falls. I park the Cougar just shy of the towering pines and find a secluded clearing to set up the tent. There's a campground back a good distance with shared restroom facilities, showers, and a snack shack. That's what makes the falls the perfect place to spend an undetermined amount of time—the promise of indoor plumbing.

After Warren's proposal, I couldn't stand to hang around. My balls weren't officially kicked in until Reese bleated out an enthusiastic *yes* for all to hear. I'll be reliving that moment in my nightmares for the next sixty years.

The logs call to me, so I start a fire and collapse right there on the dirt. I can't help but wonder what could have happened if I had done what Brylee told me to do and let Reese in on how I feel. Three little words, I love you. That's all. I could have walked away knowing I did all I could. I would have slept at night knowing she had the facts. And, if she still wanted to be with Warren, I would have been okay with that too—not really, but I could have faked it for about two minutes.

I pitch a rock across the field as the fireworks start over the lake. The screams and laughter from the crowd rise through the air and the cheerful lakefront only seems to exemplify my misery.

"Hey!" A girl's voice calls from behind, and I turn to see the most beautiful sight in the world. "Well if it isn't Reese Madelyn Westfield."

She throws down a small duffle bag and falls into my lap, peppering my face with slow, lingering kisses. She tastes sweet like watermelon, and I'll be the last person to stop her from loving me like this.

She pulls back and inspects me with a twinge of sadness in her eyes. "You know my middle name."

"Does that impress you?" I wrap my arms around her as we look up at the fireworks lighting up the sky in shades of purple and blue.

"Everything about you impresses me." She lays her head over my chest, her eyes drawn up to the sky in wonder. "You know I'm not marrying Warren, right?"

"You can marry whoever you want." I don't mean for it to sound as coldhearted as it does. "I'll cheer you on." I press a kiss over her temple. "I'll always be there for you Reese, always."

Reese looks up at me with those luminescent silver eyes, her dark hair framing her like a shadow.

"You left me," she whispers.

My stomach tightens. She's right. I hightailed it out of the there so fast I didn't wait to listen to rhyme or reason. This was a summer thing I signed up for, what the hell right did I have abandoning her at the lake like some jealous pussy?

"Sorry. Guess I had my ego kicked in a notch." First honest thought I've shared with her so far. It feels like a crack in the armor, and now, every feeling I've ever had wants to come streaming out.

Her eyes fill with tears. "He asked if I was pissed, and, when I said yes, he pointed the mike at me."

Shit. I should have figured. "Warren always was creative." My chest loosens. It feels like a five-karat weight has been lifted off, and, for the first time in an hour, I can breathe again. It still doesn't make Reese mine, but at least she's not Warren's.

"And tonight"—she dips her hand into my shirt and I don't stop her—"I'm hoping you'll show me how creative *you* are."

"You sure you want to do this?" My Adam's apple rises and falls. Reese bears into me with those crystal clear eyes, and I feel like crap knowing she's not really mine.

"Yes, I want to do this." The sky fills with a pink canopy of stars that explode in quick succession. "There's no one on the planet I'd rather do this with than you."

There it is. That's pretty damn close to exactly what I wanted to hear. Unless of course she's just trying to get in my pants and I laugh a little at that one. The truth is, I'd never deny her a damn thing—for sure not my body.

I pick her up just as the grand finale sets in, but Reese never takes her eyes off mine.

For a second I think about running us over to the falls and tossing us both in the water to cool us off, but my legs move to the tent instead.

"Last chance," I say, setting her down just shy of the orange structure.

She shakes her head, pulling me forward by the tip of my fingers. "There's no way in hell I'm changing my mind." Reese leads us into the tent and lands over the foam bedding I've laid out. "Comfy." She shakes out her hair before pulling me down next to her.

"You sure you don't want to wait for your wedding night?" I'm only half-teasing. If I'm going to try to sober her out of the idea, now's the time to do it. "By the looks of things, it might be on the horizon."

"Nice try." She pulls off my shirt, and I hold back a smile. "Besides"—she leans in and takes a soft bite out of my ear—"I now declare us husband and wife. There"—she purrs—"welcome to your wedding night, Ace Waterman."

"I would have pegged you for a big ceremony with lots of people to witness the event."

"I told you I was a simple girl, and I meant it. Besides, all the important people are here—you and me." Reese lands her lips over mine as if she were sealing a covenant. She tugs and yanks at her dress until it's stuck around her shoulders.

"Let me help you with that." I pull it off the rest of the way, and her hair rumples, sexy as hell. She bites down on her lip in her black lace bra, and my dick springs to life. Reese tugs off the rest of my clothes until I'm splitting the distance between us with nothing but a serious boner.

"Let me help *you* with that." Reese tries to dive down over me, but I gently pull her back. I'm about ready to explode, and I want to bury myself inside her before I do.

My hand glides back and unhooks her bra, pulling it off achingly slow, my eyes never leaving hers. Reese dips her thumbs into her panties and slides them off in one easy move.

"Lay down." I kiss her lips a moment. "Tonight is all about you." I trail my lips down her neck, stopping to appreciate each one of her nipples on the way to her belly. I land my mouth over her stomach and listen as she gasps as if this were the pinnacle of the entire evening. I move my kissing efforts south until my mouth falls into the moist slick I've fantasized over for the entire last decade. The truth is, I've dreamed of doing everything with Reese for as long as I can remember and, tonight, in a small tent next to the falls, I will.

Reese pants heavily, clawing at my shoulder, writhing under my tongue as if the entire world were about to detonate with her.

"Ace." She pulls out of my grasp, and I glance up at her with her lids partially closed, her lips parted just enough. "I want to do this with you." She slips down next me, her hot breath searing over my chest.

I reach into my bag to pluck out a condom, but they're all still safely sealed in the box. I had Gavin run into the general store this morning and buy a shitload of love gloves because I couldn't figure out the math. He asked if I was stocking up for a sexual apocalypse, so I let him in on my weeklong love making plans with Reese. He said it sounded like heaven, and I assured him it would be. I would have bought them myself but the last thing I wanted to do was plunk them on the counter while Neva rang up the register.

"Can I see?" Reese gets up on one shoulder and watches as I roll it on. Her eyes drift up to mine as a wicked grin struggles to break free on my lips. This is it. The train has left the station—one last stop—Reese.

I dive down and land my lips over hers. Reese moans into my mouth—her legs already parting for me.

I'm going to love you Reese, I moan into the thought but I don't say it. I already love her. I think it's about damn time I admitted it to myself—and, if I get the balls, hopefully her.

Reese reaches down and guides me to her, a move I'm guessing she's regretting since Gavin opted for the heavily lubed variety, which judging by how wet Reese is, we didn't really need.

I run my cock over her warm slick nice and slow, teasing the both of us in the process.

Reese lets out a heated cry, and I'm about to lose it. I push in just enough and try to take it slow, but my dick is about to win this battle, and I hope to God I don't hurt Reese in the process. I thrust in hard without meaning to then try to glide out slow as if that might make things better.

Fuck, she's so tight.

"You okay?" I dive a kiss over her ear, and her breathing matches mine breath for heated breath. The way we're panting you'd think we ran out of a burning building, but it's the invisible flames that are making us breathless, years of pent up passion, on my part anyway.

"Ace," she moans, pushing me in by the small of my back and I go with it, settling myself deep inside her. She clenches her body over my dick and I groan.

"I'll take that as a yes." I thrust into her again and again and lose myself in the bliss that is making love to Reese Westfield.

The words I love you beg to stream from my lips, but I don't give them. I don't dare ruin the moment.

This is heaven. Right here with Reese—the two of us together.

I'd like to think it was meant to be like this.

It is.

9

Head Over Heels

Reese

A groan strains from my vocal cords as Ace pants over me, quick and so beautifully dirty. His lids are partially closed as he glances at me. His lips widen into the idea of a smile.

"Reese." He lands his hot mouth over mine as he continues to thrust himself inside me.

My body trembles with pleasure. Every part of me feels far more alive than I ever have before. I can't imagine sharing this with anyone else—I wouldn't want to. I thought this would finally satisfy my ache for Ace, but it only makes me want him more. It feels so natural to want to say those magical words that can change everything. But we're far from I love you. My vocal cords beg to whisper something just as meaningful, but I put a clamp over my throat and refuse my heart the privilege. I have a feeling there's no quicker way to end our prospective weeklong party than for a sober confessional in the middle of outrageous sex.

Ace reaches down and touches me right where his mouth was moments before and all of my wanting, my aches—every desire I've ever had for him pushes from me in a spasm so explosively beautiful I want the moment to last forever.

Ace trembles over my body right along with me, and it feels as if we're expending ourselves, breaking down our bodies in one glorious fit—wringing our pleasure out from the inside without another inch to offer.

He collapses over me, his skin dewy with sweat as we try to catch our breath.

"Reese." He washes my face in kisses, pausing at my lips while a soft laugh bubbles from me. "You're fucking amazing." He dives his tongue into my mouth, and delivers an achingly sweet kiss that make me dizzy all over again.

"*You're* amazing." I peck a kiss over the tip of his nose and take him in with his dark hair, his five o'clock shadow prickling over his cheeks. "So when can we do it again?"

Ace gurgles out a laugh. He rolls next to me and scoops me into his arms until my bottom is tucked into his stomach.

"Let's catch our breath," he whispers, pressing his lips over my ear, making my back arch with pleasure.

His fingers lock over mine, and I nuzzle into him still high off the charge from our heated exchange.

"Was that good for you?" I glance back, turning slightly to see his gorgeous dimples siren on and off.

"Hell yes that was *great*. Did you like it?"

"Nope." I peck his lips with a kiss and his features melt. "I *loved* it."

"Good." A smile ticks on his lips. "You scared me for a second."

"I want to do things you haven't done before." I stroke his rough cheek with the back of my hand like petting a cat. "Is that possible?"

Ace glances out of the tent for a moment as if he was considering this, and I give a dark laugh.

"I didn't think so." It kills me to think that Ace has been with other girls—that he will be again one day.

"You'll make everything better—everything already feels new." He melts a kiss off my lips. "Plus, I've never done it in a tent before."

"How about at the falls?" I'll die if he says yes. I want to be the only one to ever share this with Ace.

"Nope, never at or in the falls."

"Good. I call the falls."

"Oh, you do, huh?" He tweaks my ribs a second.

"So you've done everything." I glance down a moment. "I feel like a newborn, like a kitten."

"A kitten?" He drizzles his lips over my neck. "How about I give you a couple of balls to play with to keep you busy." He growls into my ear.

"I bet you will." I wrap my arms around him until we're facing one another. "Do you feel different about me?" Crap. What the hell is he supposed to say? You had me at that last orgasm? "I mean"—I'm not entirely sure what it is I mean—"do you think we can still be friends without all the weirdness we've just created?" Nice. Equate making love to him as *weirdness*. That'll go over well.

Crap.

"No, you're still weird to me." He bumps his nose to mine, and, strangely, he still very much feels like regular old Ace. "I thought maybe one good roll in the tent would cure it but, nope."

"Be quiet." I swat him over the shoulder. "You're still you."

"And, you're still you. Only now I know what the inside of you feels like."

"What does it feel like?" The smile glides off my face in hopes he'll say something profound that I could squeeze the fantasy that he might love me out of.

"It feels like home." His chest vibrates over mine when he says it, and I melt in a puddle of everything I wish we could be. "Like I was made to be there." His dark eyes drift over mine as if he were sad to say it. "I think this summer fling was the most brilliant idea you've ever had."

Summer fling. Brilliant or tragic—only fall will tell. Speaking of fall, it's coming all too soon.

"Hey"—I tap his bare ass, and a smile spikes on his face—"you ready for round two?"

ജ‍ഇ

I'm not sure whose bright idea it was that we don't bother with clothes as we streak over to the falls, but I can't stop giggling as we climb down the boulders disguised as shadows in this post-midnight world.

Ace takes my hand and guides me carefully down the jagged embankment. It's not until we land at the base do I notice the metallic square in his mouth.

"I see you're making every effort to try to protect me. I bite the metallic wrapper from his mouth and snap it between my fingers. "You're always one step ahead. Thank you."

"You're welcome. And, trust me, I'd rather not use it, but I doubt you want to carry my child so soon in life."

"*Aww,*" I tug at his chin a moment. "I'd love to populate the world with a million baby boys that look just like you."

"And what if they were girls?"

"They'd better have your dimples—and your navy eyes. I'd let them get away with murder." A hard protrusion grazes against my thigh. "Let's get in the water before you get arrested, wielding that snake around like a weapon."

"You think you're funny, don't you?" He scoops me in his arms and walks us to the ledge of the granite base where I used to dive in as a child. Come to think of it, the last time I swam here was with my mother.

"Three," he says, sailing us off into the air. Gravity wraps her arms around us and sinks us into the cold mouth of the water as it swallows us whole. I pop up for air with a scream locked in my throat.

"You!" I splash a wall of water in his face, but he turns and deflects my efforts. "I'm going to get you."

"I'm going to *let* you."

He pulls me in by way of my cheeks, landing his fire-hot mouth over mine. Ace pulls back a moment, washing his gaze over my features.

"God, you're so beautiful, Reese." It streams from him as if it were the greatest tragedy.

"Thank you," I say it dull, unsure of what the right answer might be. All I know is, right about now, my insides are throbbing to have him again. I hold up the condom in my hand, still wrapped in its shiny packaging. "You think this works underwater?" Not that I'd care. I'd have his babies if he let me, starting tonight. I'm on an Ace Waterman high and both the future and my uterus be damned.

"It'd better." He takes it from me and swims us over to the rocks while biting the wrapper open.

"Here, let me." I take it from him and secure it over his tip, carefully pressing down until it covers him like a slimy water balloon. "It barely fits. I think next time you should opt for the next size up."

"There is no size up." He lands in the water next to me while floating us directly under the soft flowing falls. "Reese"—he runs his heated kisses all over my face—"I want you to remember this always." He pulls me up until my legs are wrapped around his waist.

I touch my forehead to his. "I promise you that every day I live, I'll replay our time here at the falls."

The sky explodes in a lime green ball of powder, followed by a barrage of errant fireworks that light up the night like demonic stars.

"Since this is your first time, having a girl at the falls"—I say it playfully—"I want to make sure *you* remember it." I bite down on a smile as I guide him in. "Don't let me hurt you."

His chest thumps. "What if I want you to hurt me?" His dimples go off. The moon shines over him like a blessing, and my stomach singes just looking at him.

"Ask and you shall receive." I fan my nails over his back like wings, and he takes in a breath through his teeth.

"Oh my, God! Did I hurt you?" I spike up in the water, effectively evicting him from my body in the process. Not only am I a novice, trying to pull some serious sadistic moves, but I'm lucky I didn't pluck his penis off in the process.

Ace pulls his lips into a line. "You'll have to try harder. But, first, I want you to reach down, and put it back in."

"Yes, sir," I say never taking my eyes from his.

Ace flutters his lids as I gently sink myself over him.

"Nice." He moves us closer to the falls stealing molten kisses off my lips as we cut through the water. His fingers tighten over my waist and he thrusts himself in and out. I ride over his hips while the water sprays over my shoulders like a baptismal rite. I arch my head into the violent stream as my body jostles in rhythm to his.

Ace and I are making new memories, making moments I'm hoping we'll both never forget. And if he tries, I might just have to lure him right back to the falls and remind him of the magic we once had—that we can have, forever.

He thrusts into me hard, and each time it feels as if his body is saying I love you straight into mine.

He loves me, again, and again, and again.

‡

Our weeklong adventure bumps by in breaths, in the tug and pull of limbs, in kisses that spell out forever and eternity, with the poetry we write with our hearts.

Ace makes eggs and bacon for us each morning, well, late afternoon when we finally rouse from our delicious slumber— not that there's been a whole lot of sleeping going on.

I made it a point to leave my phone in the car so I wouldn't have to hear the annoying beep from the barrage of texts I'm most likely receiving. For the most part I trust Kennedy to do a good job of staving off my father and anyone else who might care to know where I'm at.

"Where does your family think you went?" I comb his hair back with my fingers. I could have said his dad, but I wanted to include Neva in the mix without saying her name. I'm sure just verbalizing it would conjure her up like a demon. God knows she's doing her best impersonation in every other way.

He lets out a breath as he stares up at the tent. "I told them I was going to screw Reese Westfield in the woods for a week."

"Right."

"No I did, but they didn't believe me because what are the odds?"

"Very funny." I swat him with a pillow.

"Gavin knows." His expression sobers up and my heart thumps at the thought of anyone knowing outside of the people I told.

"That's okay." It makes it real. My chest pounds at the idea of Ace and I having something real.

"You don't look okay." His dark brows narrow in on me and I trace my finger over them, content to be here doing just this.

"I was thinking maybe everyone should know." I give a little wink to defuse the idea.

"Every cell in my body knows," he teases, rolling me on top of him.

"Oh, yeah?" I laugh into his mouth as he grazes his teeth over mine. "What if I said that wasn't enough?"

"All of me isn't enough?" His dimples dig in, and I have a tiny orgasm by proxy. "Thanks a lot for insulting the hell out of me."

"Very funny. That's not what I meant."

"I think you just want to show off to the other girls at Yeats—make them feel bad that they haven't seen my mattress moves."

"I would never do that because for one, you'd have a line around the block, and secondly, I need you to save all of your mattress moves just for me."

"Come here." He rolls me onto my back. "I've got a new move for you."

"Are you ready to make love to your sweet innocent bride once again?" I love calling myself his bride. I'd die for it to be true.

"Nope. I'm going to fuck you." He slaps my bottom playfully. "Get on your knees."

"Oh, sounds kinky," I say, complying with his wishes.

"It will be." His dimples twitch as he fiddles with his never-ending condom supply. It's safe to say, Ace estimated just the right amount of prophylactics to bring along for the ride. "Bend over." He gives a wicked grin.

I do as I'm told, landing on all fours.

"On your elbows." He taps my thigh until I've lowered my body. "Open for me."

I part my knees and brace myself, readying for anything he's about to offer. Ace rubs his fingers over me and my head arches back in a fit of pleasure. He plunges a finger into me, and a groan wrenches from my gut. Ace said there wasn't anything he hadn't done, well, he didn't argue when I asked, so I can only assume he's done this with some other girl and a flood of jealousy washes over me. I wish I were his first like he were mine, but, right now, I'm just feeling lucky to be his anything. Ace pulls his hand away and plunges into me with himself a little slower, guided and careful.

"Don't let me hurt you," he strains it out as if he were trying to control his breathing. "Does this feel good?" He moves in and out, and I choke out a yes. "Good." His warm hands land over my back creating heated circles as he throbs into me over and over. His fingers drift down until he's rubbing over my bottom and my eyes spring wide open. Ace dives his finger in slowly, and I try to protest the idea but it comes out far too unintelligible. "You like that, don't you." He gives it in a heated whisper. He wraps around with his other hand and touches me right at that tender spot and I start to lose it. "Wait for me." He presses into me with his body at a quickened pace, his hands matching his rhythm and my body flexes in uncontrollable spams without my permission. Ace grabs ahold of my waist and bears down over me until a wild groan rips from his throat.

He lands over me softly and holds me like that.

"Damn"—he peppers me from behind with his soft kisses—"you're hotter than a firecracker."

"*You're* hotter than a firecracker and a little dirty, too." I bite down on a smile.

"You're the dirty one because you liked it."

"I did like it." I spin into his damp chest. "I like anything you're willing to give me, Ace."

Our eyes lock, and the world stills for a moment.

"One day I'm going to give you everything." He presses a sad kiss to my lips and doesn't move.

"I thought you've already given me everything." I reach down and rake my fingers over his soft curls. A part of me wants to hear him offer me the one thing that I long for.

"Not everything." He collapses his arms around me again. "There's only one thing left to give." He doesn't say anything else just starts to fall asleep with his head tucked against my shoulder.

I hope to God the next thing he wants to give me is his heart.

He already has mine.

Ace

The days and nights blur into one beautiful oblivion as Reese and I eventually lose track of them. We've dwindled down the food supply I lugged up here by the fourth day, and, after that, I've made frequent trips to the vending machine.

"I've got another Snicker's bar to my name, but, after that, I think we should declare a carbohydrate ceasefire and spearfish in the stream," I tease as she gets back in the tent with her hair slicked from the shower. Reese smells like paradise, vanilla and spring flowers. I probably smell like a sack of shit because instead of heading to the showers I opted to take a quick nap.

"The Snicker's is perfect." She lies down, using my stomach as a pillow "It's Tuesday by the way," she says it dejected. "For the second time."

"Shit." I get up on my elbows to get a better look at her. "That means we've been gone eleven days."

"Best damn honeymoon ever." Her hand wiggles between my legs like a fish.

"I couldn't agree more." I pull her up next to me. "Do you think your dad has a bounty out on me yet?"

"Maybe." She leans in and bites down over my lip. "But I don't want to go home. I'd rather be here, doing this with you." She grabs ahold of my dick and rubs the tip with her thumb. "Nothing back home compares to this."

"I agree." I pull my lips across her cheek in one slow line. "I really do, but I'd better get you back to the castle before the king has my balls on a spit."

"There's no hurry, Kennedy is covering for me."

"I promise you, Kennedy is not that good a liar."

"Crap." Her eyes widen a moment. "You're right."

She tries to sit up, but I reel her in by the waist. "Where you off to so quick?" I hold back the grin waiting to erupt and graze my fingers over her chest before taking off her T-shirt. "I think we should at least give this place a proper goodbye."

Her hair spills over her chest like a waterfall at midnight, and her nipples peer out like twin pink pearls.

"Where are my manners?" She lies back and slips off her shorts in one svelte move.

"Who says you'll be lying down?" I pull her up until she's seated over my hips. I pull on a rubber in record time, and she laughs as I graze up behind her. "Get up here, girl." Reese rises before sinking over my cock—purposefully slow—watching me with those glowing eyes as I penetrate her, inch by inch. My head knocks back, and a groan rips from me. "Just like that." I take in a quick breath as her knees lock tight around me. "I'm going to rock your world, literally."

Reese pulls me in by the back of the neck and drowns me with sugared kisses. Her tongue lashes mine as we rock back and forth, her body falling softly over me in rhythm. Reese and I linger, we hold each other and make it last, before picking up our tempo again. It's been hardly two short weeks and already we know the nuances of each other's bodies, the ways to touch, to tease, to bring each other to life in our own unique ways.

I reach down to make sure she's with me, right where she needs to be before I release inside her. Reese arches her head back, and I bow into her with a kiss over her chest. It takes all my strength not to say I love you—because damn it all to hell, I do love Reese.

After a long while of holding one another, getting lost in the rhythm of our breathing, of our hearts, we pack up and fill the trunk of the Cougar with all the crap I managed to lug up here. Unfortunately, my bruised ego caused Reese to miss the ride and now she has to drive back in her own car.

"Ace." She gives a hard sniff in my arms, and I pull back to find tears streaming down her face.

"What's going on?" I brush her tears away with my thumb and tighten my grip around her.

Shit. I did this. I never should have taken advantage of her.

"Nothing." She gives a soft hiccup. "I'm just happy."

"You always cry when you're happy?" More like unhappy. I bet she's sorry about everything that's happened. Knew it. I never should have agreed to anything, and if it were anyone else I would have run in the other direction. This is more than some one-night stand. This took our friendship to a whole new level and turned it into a bona fide relationship whether we want to admit it or not.

Reese doesn't answer. She just rains hot tears over my shoulder, and I hold back the urge to cry right along with her.

"It's going to be okay," I whisper.

And for the first time ever, I think I just lied to Reese.

‎‎❧❧❧

Reese follows me back down toward Loveless, and I can't help steeling glances at her in the rearview mirror. After days of fusing my body to hers, my boys are already going through some serious withdrawals. I take a turn toward Wilson Bridge just as the sun is getting ready to set and catch a glimpse of the lake bathed in pinks and golds. If the landscape could describe what went down between Reese and me in that tent, that would be it—beauty beyond words that only God could accurately depict.

My body aches, every muscle is crying out for Reese.

"I need her," I whisper as I head into the bridge.

I drive into the protective covering of that old rundown scaffolding and park the Cougar before hoping out. Reese does the same.

"You forget your way to Loveless?" She runs at me a million miles an hour, jumps up and wraps her legs around my waist.

"Nope. Just wanted to do this one more time." I bring her in by the back of the neck and kiss her hard. I sit her on the hood of the Cougar, and we break our record for longest lip-lock these past two weeks. Reese's kisses have the power to thrill me, kill me—same difference. They make me want to do insane things like tell her I love her right here, right now.

"Reese." I pull back and take in her beauty—her pale shining eyes that smile just for me. "What had you so upset back there?" Maybe if she goes there first—if she even hints at it, I'll take it and run with it.

"I don't know." Her voice dips down and marinates in grief. "I think—um...you make me happy." Her lips tremble as she says it.

"I think you make me happy, too." This is good. We're definitely headed in the right direction.

"Really?" Her entire body relaxes as she breaks out into an easy smile.

"Hell, yes. You're amazing, Reese. I wish we never had to leave." My heart thumps hard against my chest because I just laid it out on the line. "What we shared was beautiful."

Her gaze dips to my waist. "We can still steal moments." She reaches into my shorts and gently holds me in her hand until I'm growing again. "In fact, we can steal a moment, right now."

"I like where you're going," I say, lifting her skirt past her hips and finding that sweet, dark triangle staring back at me. "You seem to be lacking in the undergarment department." I bury a smile in my cheek.

"Are you complaining?" She pulls me in by the shirt as I dig for the lone condom I stuffed in my pocket.

"Nope. Not me. Just pointing it out in the event you weren't aware."

"It's all your fault." She lowers her lids, drawing me closer. "Besides, you have a way of disintegrating my panties with just one look."

"Is that right?" I graze my teeth over her cheek before holding up the small foil wrapper. "Last one."

"Really?" She snatches it from me and tears it open with her teeth. "I'd hate for it to feel neglected." She rolls it over me, her eyes never leaving mine. Reese has gone from virginal to a seasoned seductress in less than two weeks. She reaches down and runs her fingers over my balls until I groan.

"All right." I push in nice and slow. "Now you're asking for it."

"I am asking for it. Fuck me, Ace," she laughs as she says it, and her voice echoes across the bridge.

"Only because you asked so politely." I pull her in by the face and kiss her sweetly, rocking into her, loving her with everything I can.

Reese and I make that Cougar bounce as she pants her way to oblivion.

"Ace," she cries out and her voice replays itself, refining its passion inside Wilson Bridge like a boomerang.

"Someone's going to hear you." I'm only half-teasing. We're not that far from Loveless, and any moment now I expect a car to come whipping through.

"I want them to hear me." She bubbles the words out. I reach down and touch her scalding hot flesh until she's screaming my name out at the top of her lungs.

Maybe Reese is ready to take this relationship to the next level. Maybe before the summer is through we'll go from the best kept secret to the best new relationship.

Reese collapses over my shoulders and hangs on for dear life as I throb into her. She breathes hard in my ear, her body still seizing and trembling. Her arms are locked over me, and there's no way in hell I'm letting go first.

The sun sets, turning the sky that magical shade of lavender that only twilight can bring. Loveless—the world outside this covered bridge—it all looks different now that Reese and I have crossed that threshold. We had walked so easily into an alternate realm that we failed to realize we'd have to walk through a fire to get ourselves out. Not that I want out, but fall is just around the corner and that's when summer flings tend to come crashing to an end.

"Do we really have to go back?" she whispers.

"There's no reason not to."

"There's every reason not to."

And for the first time, it feels like I'm Reese Westfield's dirty little secret.

10

Platonic Delusions

Reese

In the morning, there's an abrupt knock over my door as Beverly demands I get the hell downstairs before Dad leaves for his meeting.

I throw my body in the shower and wrap myself in my favorite waffle-knit robe before heading to the dining room. I would have jumped down the stairwell for my mother, but a part of me wanted to teach Bev a lesson for talking to me like I was thirteen, or more the point like she really cared.

"You're in deep shit," Kennedy hisses, passing me on the way.

I saw my phone last night for the first time since I left and there were at least a half dozen threats letting me know she was done covering for my ass—that I had everyone on the planet worried, including her.

"Reese." Dad comes at me from the kitchen and nearly drops his coffee as he lunges into an embrace. "Dear God, I was so frightened." His voice breaks, and I hold my breath a second. I haven't seen my father cry since Mom died, and, now, here I was, bringing him a new brand of grief.

"I'm fine." I back up, trying to brush it off. "You guys hungry? I'll make pancakes," I offer. I'd rather go out and ground the wheat myself than stay here and see the sorrow I've etched into my father's face.

"Pancakes? Who could eat?" Beverly's voice hits its upper register. "You had us worried sick." She takes a step into me. "I drove your father to the ER last Thursday because he was having chest pains at the thought of you lying in a ditch." She shakes her finger in my face as a genuine fury brews in her.

I glance to my father. "Did you have a heart attack?" My hand rises to my throat.

In one of her texts, Kennedy mentioned I should get back quick—that there was some kind of family emergency. Of course, I only saw that a few hours ago, but, had I seen it at the falls, I would have assumed she was lying.

"No." Dad shoots Bev a look that suggests he'd rather not go there.

"It was a cardiac episode," she says it stern, glaring at his effort to downplay the event. Bev reverts to me with her pent up anger. "You may be over eighteen but you are not anywhere near the stage in your life where you can pick up for two weeks without explanation." Her crimson lipstick bleeds into the cracks around her mouth. It looks like a fire feathering from her face, and judging by her temper, it may as well be.

"She's right." Dad acquiesces. "I was worried sick, and, quite frankly, if it happens again I'm positive both my heart and my mind will give out." He pulls me in and holds me in his arms as if I had just been rescued from a burning building. I pat his shoulders trying to calm him. He feels frail in comparison to Ace, and for the first time I see my father as a mortal. "I'm pleading with you, Reese, don't be so heartless as to cut us off like that." He picks up my hand, his eyes still aching with worry. "Kennedy said these were friends of yours from school, that were passing through. Did you get lost? Were you hungry?"

Oh crap. On top of everything else, I have to look my father in the eye and lie to him.

"No. I swear I was never lost. I was never hungry. Not once. I was totally safe. We just lost track of time. That's all."

Dad glances down at his watch. "Speaking of losing track of time, I've got to make tracks myself or I'm going to miss this meeting. Try to be here when I get home." Dad squeezes me in a tragic embrace. I can feel the sorrow pouring from him like oil. "There are only a few weeks left before you need to get back to school, and I want to spend all the time with my baby girl I can." He presses a kiss over my forehead. "Both my girls." He points over at Kennedy before whisking himself out the door.

Beverly steps square in front of me with her arms folded tight, her lips pinched as she readies to release some tension.

"I'm sorry." I shake my head. "I swear these girls I was with—"

"You can cut the bull. I know you were with that Waterman boy. Kennedy told me the entire thing." Her murky green eyes narrow in on me, the exact shade of algae-riddled rocks. "You realize your father thinks you're engaged and has leveraged a portion of his business to purchase you a home." Her voice softens with that last bit. "I think at your age, a girl is easily confused. Obviously, you were out having a good time with this Waterman kid, but now you need to focus. You need to revert your attention to the well-educated man who declared his love for you in front of every important person your father and I know. You need to get back to the business of being a Westfield—and a part of that business is stepping up and linking arms with Warren, the man you're destined to marry." She cups my cheek with her hand and tilts into me with a false sense of sorrow. "Don't you worry your pretty little head, there's nothing wrong with keeping company on the side with the ranch hand, the handy man—the woodcutter. My own mother did it."

"Grandma?" Kennedy gasps.

"But"—Beverly holds up a finger to cap Kennedy's reaction—"until you make it legal with Warren, I'd be weary of rocking the boat. Your father's heart—his *life* is on the line. He wants this for you as much as I do. We only want the best for you, Reese." Beverly picks up her tennis racket and marches out the door.

"Do you believe that?" I ask as Kennedy and I stare vacantly at the entry. "Do you think they only want the best for me?"

"I'd like to think so," she pants, still shell shocked from the familial blow Beverly dealt. "But, knowing my mother, I seriously doubt it." She sweeps her fingers through my damp hair. "Do you want what's best for you?"

I startle back to life.

"What the hell kind of question is that?"

"The truthful kind. Do you want Warren in any way, shape, or form? And, if not, why the hell are you keeping Ace from everybody like some big bad secret? Get in or get out, Reese. But you can't have your cake and eat it, too."

Kennedy heads off toward the kitchen and leaves me swirling in the wake of her words.

I don't want Warren.

And I do want Ace.

I love Ace. But how does love fit in a perfectly platonic relationship? In the world of corporate greed my father built?

It doesn't.

ॐ

Late in the afternoon I go for a walk along the shoreline and watch as Warren and Ace glide across the water, easy and lithe as garden snakes skimming the surface.

Brylee has planted herself on a bright pink towel down by the shore that actually hurts to look at, so I flip on my sunglasses and plop down next to her.

"Well look who finally crawled out of her love shack?" She shades her eyes with her hand as she takes me in. "You look thinner—happier."

"I am happier and it has nothing to do with the shape of my body."

"So how was it?" She spins into me and hugs her knees. "Is he worth his weight in the bedroom, or, should I say, the red tent of love?"

"He's amazing. He left me breathless." I shake my head a moment as all those heated memories sear past me like an erotic tornado. I'm afraid I'll get too caught up in the memory and beg him to take me right here on the sand. "We're still friends." I shrug, looking out at him as he narrowly holds his own over Warren in what's panning out to be the race of the century. "I was thinking about talking to him. You know, to see if he was interested in anything more."

"Yes!" Her face brightens ten shades of pink. "Oh my God!" Brylee practically howls it across the lake. "*Please*, talk to him. You guys are so perfect for each other. He's sweet and so are you. Not to mention the fact you've already shared something so intimate and special."

"I know, but"—I shake out my hair and let the wind sweep it behind me—"he was pretty clear about us just staying friends. If I lower the boom, he might think I was trying to trap him into a relationship all along, or worse, he'll think I'm some kind of stalker who cleverly found a way to bed her victim. Of course, both theories are true, but I'd only admit it to you." I kick her gently in the shin. "Besides, if I leave things alone, we'll still be friends. I'll still have Ace in my life and some semblance of normalcy."

"Is that what you want?" She pierces me with those sky blue eyes. "You want things to go back to the way they were?"

Warren and Ace crop up in my peripheral vision as if they were campaigning for my attention all along.

"Being with Warren would make my father and Beverly happy," I start. "But, I would rather gouge my eyes out with a rusty pocket knife than leash myself to him for the rest of my days. And, being with Ace would be a longtime dream fulfilling itself. It would be living out my heart's desire in real time. It would be incredible if he wanted that, too."

"Well"—she nudges me with her knee—"what kind of vibes does he give you? Do you think he's feeling it?"

"I don't know. One minute I think he does and the next he's affirming our friendship status. It's like we're both walking the line, trying not to ruin our friendship, only maybe he really does want to stay friends."

Brylee shakes her head, incensed. "I thought for sure when you guys finally did it you'd wind up on the same page. Who sleeps with someone they're in love with and doesn't bother to say those three little words?" She rages as she looks over her shoulder at Ace.

"I thought the same thing," I whisper. "I'm the worst kind of coward."

"Yeah, well"—she makes a face as Ace and Warren speed over—"you may not be the only coward I know."

Boy, wouldn't that be nice.

Warren cuts Ace off and knocks his canoe over as he glides up in front of us. I watch as Ace rights himself and paddles forward with the water beading off his smile.

"What the fuck?" Warren pants his way over as he falls into the sand next to me.

Ace pauses before taking up his boat and walking toward his house.

"Waterman!" Brylee calls for him and my adrenaline picks up. "Get over here. Dude, where've you been? I haven't seen you in like a week."

Shit. Brylee is such a fucking troublemaker.

Ace tilts his head at her a moment before dropping his boat and heading on over.

Perfect. I'm sure Brylee would want nothing more than front row seats when I finally pour my heart out to Ace. But Warren is here, and, in the event she hadn't noticed, we have a faux engagement I'm still pretty ticked over.

"And what about you?" Warren kicks my foot as he gets up on his elbows. "Ken said you were with Whitney Summers and those airheads she hangs out with. You guys have fun?" Warren's face is clean-shaven, his hair trimmed close to his head on the sides. He looks like a poster child for prep schools everywhere, and Ace sports the perfect five o'clock shadow, his wet hair is almost down to the base of his neck.

I cut a quick glance up to Ace. "Yeah, we had fun." Shit. It's not that I want to lie to Warren but I'm pretty sure he'd slit Ace's throat if I told him the real story—that a faux honeymoon was involved—that nonstop love making ensued for the last eleven days. My insides throb with grief at the thought of not having Ace on command.

"Are you sure you were with Whitney?" Brylee winks into the sun as she studies me with that shit-eating grin locked on her face. "I mean, I thought I saw her last week in Collingsworth, but I could be confusing her with someone else."

Crap.

"Yes, I'm sure." I give her a hard stare. "I was there. I would know who I was with."

Ace turns his head a moment before getting up. "It was nice seeing you guys. Gavin's hauling me out to Medford. There's an entire forest of Redwoods with my name on it."

Warren glares at him. "Season that shit right this year would you? I'm tired of listening to my parent's bitch about it. Tell Gavin he's about to lose the entire lake if his ass doesn't shape up."

"Will do." Ace holds my gaze a moment before taking off down the shore. There he goes, drifting further away from me, his body turning into a fierce shadow.

"*Wait*." I jump up and run after him. "Medford is far," I pant while my heart tries to pummel its way out of my chest. I glance back at Warren and Brylee as they chat in the sand. "And I'm sorry what I said about Whitney." I press my lips together to stave off tears. "I wanted to say it was you."

Ace shakes his head just barely. "Why would you say it was me?" His sad eyes pull toward his cabin, and he starts heading that way again.

"I go back to school on the fourth." I match him stride for stride. "Kennedy wants to get settled, so we we're going back a week early."

"Got it." His eyes widen as he nods into the idea. "You want to pencil in a few more trips to the boathouse—no problem."

"No." My heart drops at what I might have implied. "It's not that."

"No?" He arches a brow, still making his way down the lake, and I follow. "I must have not impressed you."

"Believe me—you impressed the hell out of me," I pant, struggling to keep up with him. "When you come back, do you think we can get together?"

"Yeah, sure." He lifts his canoe up over his head and hikes toward the narrow trail that leads to the main road. "See you around."

"Ace?" I call to him but he's already in the thick of the holly bushes that line the walk.

See you around. That's what you say to a friend.

And my heart breaks.

Ace

Gavin is at the house by the time I get there, and I try not to start beating up the furniture and smashing the windows the way I want. Instead, I toss the canoe into the bushes and stick my face under the garden hose for a solid minute.

"You ready?"

"Not yet." I turn off the hose and glance back at the north side of the lake where I see three small dots in the same place I left them.

"So how'd it go? She everything your wet dreams promised she'd be?"

"That and then some." I lean on the Cougar a moment as I set my gaze in her direction.

"So what happened?" Gavin says it measured as if he knows.

"She's ashamed of him." Neva's voice surprises me from the porch. Shit. I didn't notice her lounging on the bench, and now I'm sorry I ever came home.

"We're just friends," I say. "Get it straight."

"I don't think you're just friends." She sits up and leans over the railing. "I think you're nothing but her little bitch."

"Fuck you." I tuck the canoe under the house and kick the shit out of the tail for sticking out.

"My"—Neva muses—"temper, temper." She purrs like a cat. "What do you think Warren would do if he ever found out?"

"He's not finding out because there's nothing to find out." I glare at her a moment. "We're just friends, Neva. Get it through your skull and forget the rest."

"Let's get out of here." Gavin jumps in his truck and revs the engine.

"It's not right what she's doing to you." The whites of her eyes magnify. "Warren has the right to know his girlfriend is a cheat."

"They're not together." I shake my head because a part of me is starting to think they might be.

"Bullshit," Neva seethes. "Warren says they are."

"Warren is lost in his own delusions."

Neva belts out a laugh. "I guess that makes him a lot like you." She heads into the house and slams the screen.

I guess that would make Warren a lot like me.

I hop in Gavin's truck, and we take off. I watch as Loveless rises in a plume of dust in our wake. I can't help but wonder if that's what Reese and I will have reduced our friendship to in less than two weeks.

Dust.

𞤐𞤐

Gavin keeps us locked inside the redwood forest longer than expected. We don't get back into Loveless until late Sunday. Reese sent three texts.

I miss you.

My body misses your body.

And, **Can we talk? Please call me when you get home. I don't care how late it is.**

Gavin glances over my shoulder. "Nice."

"I guess." I text her back. **Just got these. On my way home. See you tonight?**

I'd be lying if I said I didn't miss her, that my dick hasn't been crying out for her these past few days, that I didn't desperately want to talk to her and let her know how I really feel.

"You going to tell her?" Gavin nods into the road as if he already knows.

"I want to. I'm just not sure it's worth losing a friend over." Deep down inside I feel like I could never lose Reese, never live without her for that matter either.

"You won't lose her." He digs his palm into his eye to wipe out the fatigue. "Tell her everything. In the least, tell her you're going to Yeats. For as much as she's willing to hide, you're no saint yourself."

"Never said I was one."

Loveless comes up over the horizon, and I glance to my left at Reese's house. The waterfront is lit up, there's a makeshift stage, and I can hear the bass from a live band pulsating through the window.

"Looks like there's a big party tonight." Gavin twitches his brows. "We'd better hit the shower and get over there. Looks like someone's getting laid tonight." He offers up a knuckle bump. "That would be me by the way." He scans a group of girls in barely-there skirts as they cross the street. "Sweet God up in heaven." He groans as one of them licks her lips in his direction. "Maybe I'll skip the shower and jump in the lake. You think one of those girls is in the mood for a skinny dip?"

A silent laugh strums from me. That's how it all started for Reese and me.

"If I were you, I'd avoid skinny dipping. It could lead to places that really don't suit you." Like a borderline commitment, but I leave that last part out. Besides, it suits me just fine. In fact, I'd die to have a commitment with Reese—the real deal.

"Skinny dipping always leads to places I like"—he corrects—"unbelievably tight places that especially please my dick."

"Nice," I say as he pulls up to the cabin, and I jump out of the truck. "See you down there. Try not to be such a troll."

"You're the troll. I'm the pervert. Keep it straight."

I salute him with my middle finger as he kicks up the dust in my face with his tires.

Skinny dipping. I wonder if I'd do it all over again. Those hot memories of Reese writhing in my arms come back like a flash fire, and I shake my head.

Hell, yes, I'd do it again.

Every. Single. Time.

ಬಿಂಬ

After a quick shower, and an even quicker bite, I head down to the north side of the lake as the party rages on into the night. I spot Kennedy with Keith, and Neva hanging out by herself, but no sign of Reese, or worse, Warren.

A pair of cool hands glide over my eyes momentarily. "Boo!" A cute female voice perks in my ear, and I turn to find Brylee with a crooked smile.

"Boo, yourself." I flat line, panning the crowd once again. "What's new?"

"You mean, what's new with *Reese*." She jumps in front of me and hops up and down to the music. "You ever plan on having that talk with her?"

"Yup." Not really, but I know for a fact it'll get Brylee off my back.

"Great." Her eyes widen. "You should do it tonight. You know, there's no time like the present. The present is a gift and all that crap."

"She's leaving soon." I cut a glance up to her balcony, her side yard, the McCarthy's home, but there's no sign of Reese or Warren.

"So are you."

"Things might get awkward if I try to turn this into some emotional battle zone. Sorry but I'm not ruining her summer." Or mine for that matter.

The band takes a quick break but my eardrums continue to throb in rhythm to their last disaster. A group of girls belt out a simultaneous laugh. I turn in their direction and spot Reese.

The world stops as her eyes latch onto mine. My adrenaline skyrockets, and my heart starts kicking the shit out of me from the inside.

A smile rises on her face as she bolts over.

"Do yourself a favor and tell her tonight." Brylee ducks into the crowd behind us and disappears from sight.

An older couple crosses my path.

"Excuse me." The man with greying hair pulls in his wife as they make their way past me, and it's only then I recognize him as Reese's dad.

"Ace Waterman?" His wife pulls back a moment and glares into me.

Shit.

"That would be me." I nod politely at the two of them.

"I didn't recognize you." Her father lifts his chin, examining me. "How's your dad doing? I see him tooling around the lake now and again."

Tooling around the lake? Funny. Dad refers to it as work.

"He's doing good. Keeping busy."

He presses out a quick grimace. "Tell him, Chuck Westfield says hello, would you?" He pauses, looking over my shoulder at the cabin. "In fact, tell him I wouldn't mind hitting a bucket of balls with him sometime. My treat."

"What's going on?" Reese lands beside me, resting her arm over my shoulder as she pants out of breath.

"We're heading in, sweetie." He drops a kiss on her forehead. "I'll have your envelope on your pillow by the time you get upstairs."

Reese's eyes glisten with tears as she nods.

Her stepmother leans into her. "Warren is looking for you, love. Rumor has it he has a dozen long stem roses with your name on them." She gives a quick wink. "Enjoy the night." They take off for the house, and Reese continues to glare at her stepmother long after she's gone.

Roses. A girl like Reese deserves roses all year long.

"What are the roses for?" I'm already sorry I asked. It's probably a housewarming gift and she'll slap me for even looking in her direction.

She glances down, and I note the silver tiara on her head.

"It's my birthday."

Oh shit.

"God, it's your birthday?" I ask as if she's contracted some fatal disease before wrapping my arms around her waist to comfort her. My chest pounds wild over hers, and I'm panting because it feels as if Reese were lost, and I found her again.

"Yes." She looks up from under her lashes and gives a sad smile. "And I was so afraid I wouldn't see you." Her eyes drift down to my arms latched around her, and I can feel her body go rigid.

"Sorry." I drop my arms to my sides. "I got carried away."

"No, don't be." She pulls my hands back around her waist, low to her hips right where I want them to be. "You had it right the first time."

"Reese." A tiny smile floats to my lips. It's her birthday. I'm sure every person here has offered her a hug. I'm sure if she had to she could play it off, but a small part of me wants to believe she has me holding her for an entirely different purpose.

A shadow darkens the overhead light, and I glance up at Warren before doing a double take.

"Enjoying the party?" He jumps down from the retaining wall.

Neither Reese nor I say anything, neither one of us moves.

"I asked if you were enjoying the fucking party?" He slams into my shoulder and knocks me back a good three feet. The band starts up again, and my head starts to throb.

"Warren, stop!"

"I'm not stopping." He charges at me again. "Was this shit fucking *touching* you?"

"Relax." Reese lays her hand over his stomach. "He was just wishing me a happy birthday. Cool it will you?"

Warren takes another step in, and I'm ready to bury my fist in his chest—give him a fucking heart-stopper right here as a gift to Reese and myself.

Reese glances from Warren to me as if she were at a crossroad.

"Here, let's dance." She pulls him by the fingers and they disappear into the tangle of bodies.

The crowd moves between us like a busy New York sidewalk, and all memory of the brief exchange with Reese—with Warren—melts away like an illusion.

I glance back at the crowd and find my sister staring at me, so I head over.

"Where's your boy toy?" I gruff. I'm ready to kick some ass and A.J. is as good a place to start as any.

"Where's your girl toy?" she counters. "Oh, wait. She's dancing with her *boyfriend*. How does it feel to be second rate?"

"I wouldn't know."

I head back to cabin because God knows I do know.

And it feels like shit.

11

Loving You, Loving Me

Reese

Some birthday.

Warren slobbers over my neck as the song we're dancing to throbs to an end.

"So I got a gift for you." Warren picks his head up as the song comes to a close.

Warren. I scoff at him a second. I would never have even pulled him onto the dance floor if it weren't for the fact he was about to rip Ace a new one—and that was for sure not the way I wanted to tell Ace I'm in love with him, not with Warren in the front row with his fist at the ready. I made a vow to myself that I'd share my feelings with Ace today even if I had to do it via text message, but he's back from his trip, and I get to tell him in person. My entire body lights up like a Christmas tree at the prospect.

"A gift?" I feign interest while I scan the crowd for Ace.

"Yeah, I'll let you sit on me tonight." He grabs his crotch and shakes it. "I'll make sure all your birthday wishes come true."

"No thanks." I give his shoulder a quick swat as I turn to leave.

"I get it." He steps in front of me. "You're still pissed."

"Yes, I'm still pissed. And, by the way, we have to sit our parents down and tell them we're not really engaged. In fact, I'm hoping to tell my dad tomorrow. They're leaving for a trip oversees—"

"I know, Japan." His jaw clenches. "I work at the office, remember? Look, wait until after the trip. They've got a long flight, and they've got enough bullshit to deal with. Trust me, they don't need you adding any drama to it."

"We can't wait. They get back on the fifth. We'll be back at Yeats by then."

"We'll do it over the fucking phone." He shrugs as if it were no big deal. "Besides, that'll give you another solid week to figure out you're wrong about this whole thing." He spots someone off in the crowd and nods over to them. Warren mock shoots me as he steps in their direction. "We're still engaged. You know you want it. It's going to be me and you in the end—Westfield and McCarthy just the way it's supposed to be." He melts into the crowd, and I shake my head disbelieving. Warren is proving harder to get rid of than head lice.

I pluck out my phone to text Ace, and Neva pops up with her hair teased in a beehive, dark rings circled around her eyes but strangely enough she's still pretty. It would figure that Neva could pull off the night of the living dead look. She's always been stunning.

"My brother wanted me to give you a message," she growls as she pans the crowd behind me. "He said meet him at the boathouse in an hour."

My mouth opens, but not a word flies out.

"His phone died." She shrugs before turning to take off.

"*Wait.*" I pull her back by the elbow, and she's quick to yank free. "Thank you—for relaying the message."

"You're welcome. So I guess, happy birthday. You turned into the happy little slut I always knew you could be." Neva dives back into the crowd without missing a beat.

I pump a dry smile. The truth is, I miss her. I miss her voice, her hugs—the smell of her perfume. Maybe I'll add Neva to the queue of people to have a talk with right after Ace, Warren, and Dad. Hopefully each one of them will understand what I have to say.

A body bumps into mine, and I jolt forward.

"Let's do this, Westfield!" Brylee hooks her arm in mine and starts spinning us in a circle. Her boobs try their hardest to spring free from those eye patches she has them harnessed in.

"Easy." I glide us to a stop. "I've got a date in an hour, and, unlike you, it's not with the bottom of the toilet."

"I'm not tanked." She tries to hold up a finger, and it flails in front of her.

"You will be."

"So you're collecting on the big gift in an hour huh?" She grinds her hips into mine.

"It's more than that. I'm telling him how I feel tonight."

"*Aww!*" Brylee clutches onto my neck like we're slow dancing. "Everything is going to be so much better after that. Just wait and see." She flops into my chest. "But I was sort of hoping he'd tell you first." Her fingers fly to her lips.

"Yeah, well. I'm past the dreaming stage and on to reality. Besides, telling him is sort of my birthday gift to myself. I swore no matter what, I'd let him know that my feelings are so much deeper than just friends." I hike a smile into my cheek because I just sort of verbalized it in front of dozens of people, and it felt damn good. "I love Ace Waterman." I say it just loud enough for my own ears to hear. I glance around, and no one seems worse for wear. The world is still spinning, and I bet my dad is alive and healthy despite my lovesick proclamation.

"Say it again with some feeling." Brylee places her hand over my shoulder as we stare out at the crowd.

"I love, Ace Waterman!" It rips from my vocal cords so loud I can practically hear the echo off the water—but not a living soul even blinks in my direction. And, yet, I feel like a Mac truck has been lifted off my chest.

The fact that I love Ace Waterman makes me feel better than I have in years.

I'm ready to own it. And I hope he'll want to own it, too.

ᏮᎾᏣ

It's cooler out by the water, quiet and dark away from the party. I hug the shoreline as I make my way to the other side of the lake—the boathouse to be precise. I'll have to send Gavin a thank you for letting us turn his storage facility into our own private love shack.

I wonder why Ace didn't come get me himself? And sending *Neva* of all people? Maybe she offered. I bet it's her twisted version of an olive branch. She can be weird like that.

Plus, it's my birthday. I bet Ace wanted to do up the boathouse in balloons and rose petals. He's thoughtful to a fault. My stomach melts just thinking about how thoughtful he is, especially between the sheets—not that there were any sheets in that tiny tent of ours. My insides burn with the memory of his hands raking over my body, his tongue tracking over the most intimate part of me.

Hot damn. Ace Waterman has the power to dissolve me to a puddle, and he's not even in the vicinity.

I take the dirt path past the dogwoods and see there's already a light on in the boathouse. Looks like he *is* in the vicinity. I trot up and catch him with his back to the window, his head bowed down. He lets out an audible groan, and it's only then I see a pair of hands strapped to his thighs, a brunette moving her head back and forth over his crotch, loving him in that way that I thought only I was allowed to do.

A sharp sting ignites over me all at once as I stumble from the porch.

"Holy shit," I hiss.

This can't be true.

The ground rises to meet me as I run up the dirt hill, past the wandering evergreen forest with its dense thicket. My heart thumps like a series of detonations, my lungs sting from the sharp intake of cool night air as I slip and struggle my way up an embankment. A pair of headlights come over the ridge, and I bump hard into a cold, steel fender.

I fall backward down the hill, no worse for wear.

"Reese?"

A car door slams just as I try to get up.

"Shit!" Ace hisses, scooping me up. "You okay?" He brushes the hair from my eyes, his face rife with worry.

"Did you just get here?" I look over at the Cougar parked right where I stumbled into it.

"Yes. I just killed the engine, and you came at me." The muscles in his jaw pop with worry. "Don't do that." He peppers my face with kisses. "Next time the car might win."

"If you're here, then who's—" I glance back at the boathouse.

"Is someone there?" Ace takes up my hand and leads us over to the window.

Their bodies have shifted just enough to expose the girl—and it's none other than Neva. Her head moves in slow, long tracks. The guy's khakis thankfully block the rest of the show.

"Neva?" Ace storms through the door as Neva and the guy she's working part ways. He scoops up his shirt off the bed just in time for Ace to clock him in the face.

Shit. What the hell was she thinking? Why the hell would she be here if Ace was supposed to meet me?

I burst into the boathouse to get a good look at the guy that Ace is busy beating the crap out of.

That carpet of blond waves, those squinted eyes, that square jaw—I know this asshole all too well.

"Warren?" My voice echoes off the walls. I look to Neva, confused. If she wanted to hurt me, she picked a lousy way to do it.

Ace hustles him outside and tosses him down the steps. "Don't show your fucking face around here again." He slams the door shut and turns to glare at his sister. "Why?" he roars.

Neva tries to take a step around him, but he blocks her path.

"Tell me right now, why him?" He demands. "Why here, tonight?"

Neva glares over me, her eyes moistening with tears.

"It's not like it was a one-time thing." She takes a stiff step in my direction, the look of hatred ripe on her face. "We've been at this for *years*." Her lips curve with slight satisfaction. "How does it feel, Reese? Knowing the person you're with thinks you're nothing but trash?"

"Warren doesn't think I'm trash." I cut a glance out the blackened window before reverting to her venomous stare. "He thinks *you* are." I couldn't help it. A part of me wants to hurt both Warren and Neva, and I don't really understand why.

I bolt past the two of them and into the cool of night.

"Reese, wait." Ace jumps down the steps and grabs ahold of my elbow.

The lake shivers in the background. The music is still at it, full tilt, across the way.

"Look"—my voice shakes as I break free from his hold—"I don't know what the heck is going on but that was one hell of a birthday gift."

"What?" He glances back at the boathouse as confused as I am.

"And your sister?" I say incredulous. "Why in the hell would you pull your sister into this? That's just sick." I take off running toward the lake and he's quick to catch me.

"Reese, I swear I had nothing to do with what went on in there."

I pause just shy of the boulders blocking our path.

"Then why did you ask me to meet you here?" I pant as I glance across the water at my birthday bash still raging away without me.

"I didn't ask you to meet me here." Ace grabs ahold of my waist, and I warm to his touch. "I have no clue what's going on, and the last thing I would do is put Neva in that position with anybody. What made you think I told you to meet me here?" His breath plumes out in vapors.

"Neva." I nod over at the boathouse. "She said your phone was dead, so she was relaying the message. When I got here I thought it was you and someone else." I choke on that last half. "I didn't see Neva." I drop my head into his chest and let loose. I sob for what feels like weeks while Ace holds me under a violet-colored sky. I pull back and touch the long black streaks on his shirt left from my mascara.

"Sorry," I whisper.

"Don't be." He strokes my cheek as he draws me in. Ace tucks his finger under my chin and gently lifts me to look at him. "I would never hurt you. I swear to God, I had nothing to do with Neva or Warren being here tonight. Reese"—he studies my features with a patina of hurt in his eyes, but there's something deeper in them that makes my heart race— "I haven't been honest with you all summer, and I think there's something you should know." He swallows hard. A smile curls in the corner of his lips. "I know that the intentions of what went on between us was platonic, but that's not how I feel." He pauses and the night clots up with silence as if all of creation had bent its ear in this direction to hear what he might have to say. "I love you, Reese Westfield—with all my heart I do. There's nobody on this planet for me but you."

My mouth opens and closes. The noise from across the lake, the horror of witnessing Neva on her knees for Warren, it was all plaguing me, and, now, Ace has said something and I think I've misconstrued the words.

"I'm sorry." I move in so close I can feel his warm breath on my lips. "What did you say?"

His grin widens as he takes me in under the angel wing moon.

"I said I love you." He presses into me with those deep knowing eyes. "I would never in a million years hurt you, and"—he pauses to land a soft kiss over my lips—"there's nobody for me but you."

Tears glide down my cheeks in long, hot tracks.

The sound of glass exploding rocks us out of our love struck stupor.

"Shit." Ace pulls me along as we race up the dirt trail to find Neva sobbing on the porch after what looks to be a self-induced tantrum. The glass from the boathouse window has been reduced to shards. "Let's get her home."

Neva shoots a look to us, and her eyes burn wild with fire. "I'm not going anywhere with that bitch."

"You know"—I take a step back—"I think I'll head to the party for a while." I lean up on my tiptoes and press a kiss just shy of Ace's ear. "Come to my room when you're through."

His dimples go off and my entire body dissolves under the leadership of his smile.

He lays his lips over mine, and I greedily take him into my mouth, kissing him as if it were the first time our lips ever met.

Brylee was right. Everything is going to be so much better now.

∞‰

I float back to the party. I'm not sure my feet ever hit the ground. The only downfall is that I never had the chance to tell Ace how I feel. And I damn well plan on rectifying that in just a little while. I scan the blooming crowd for Brylee, but there's no sign.

A pair of arms circle around my waist, and I spin with a smile.

"That was fast," I say, and my smile glides off when I see Warren's bruised face. "Shit!" I jump a little at the sight.

He tightens his grip over me. His lids hood low with a snarl locked on his lips as the stench of vodka washes over me.

"What were you doing at the boathouse tonight?" His demeanor hardens as his fingers dig into my waist. "Neva says you're fucking him. Is that true?"

"You're drunk. Let go." I squirm out of his arms, and Warren reels me right back.

"Tell me right *now*," he roars it over my face, making my skin vibrate in rhythm to his disdain for me. The veins on either side of his neck extend, thick as cables.

"I'll tell you anything you want to know in the morning, when I know for a fact you'll remember it."

I break free and run all the way home—right up into my bedroom to wait for Ace.

ೞೞ

My father's cologne swims through the air as a seam of moonlight bisects my room, exposing a small white rectangle lying on my pillow. I close the door and head over without bothering with the lights. My fingers glide across the cool envelope as my mother's familiar handwriting greets me.

Happy 21st birthday, Reese!

I pet the soft skin of the paper and pretend it's my mother's hair. She wore it long, and when I played with it, I pretended I was combing through silk.

The seal parts for me all the way across without a single nick to the envelope. I slip the letter out and float it between my fingers. In just a little while, Ace will be here. He said he'd gladly read them with me. How much better will it be to read this while nestled safe in his arms? I slip the letter back into the envelope and tuck it under my mattress for safekeeping, right along with the "special recipes" I'm more than ready to read.

The curtains to my room billow like ghosts as the night breeze sails in. I can't wait for Ace to arrive. And the fact I get to share my mother with him on my birthday is the icing on the cake, quite literally.

Kennedy was wrong. I can have my cake and eat it, too. After all, it is my birthday.

I lie down and drift to sleep to the sound of people laughing, and shouting, music blaring in my honor from the lake.

Ace will be here soon. And it's a dream within a dream.

Time passes as I writhe over my sheets lost with Ace in my nocturnal wanderings. I can practically feel his hot lips racing up my neck, his heated hands tracking down my hips then melting lower still.

"Ace," I whisper as my lids flutter. The hands, the body pressed over mine is real.

The strong scent of hard liquor pulls me out of my slumber, and I struggle to get my bearings on reality. He yanks at my dress and tears off my underwear.

"Ace?" I pull back in a panic and knock into the headboard.

"Try again. It's the other man of your dreams." Warren plunges his tongue down my throat, and I twist my head away.

"Get off." I push him up enough for the moonlight to gloss over his skin.

Warren's shirt is off, and I don't see any shorts on him either—he's naked, and proud, and judging by the liquor store he ingested, totally wasted.

He lands over me like a stone and gathers my wrists high above my head.

"You think I'm just going to let you turn me down while you whore around with Waterman?" He says his name like it's a joke. "I fucking hung around for you."

"Get the hell off or I'll scream." I struggle to break free from his grip. "My dad is going to burn you alive if he finds you in here."

Warren clamps his hand over my mouth and works my dress up over my hips.

"You want to scream?" He works my legs apart with his just as my phone buzzes from the dresser.

"Ace," I moan through his fingers.

"What'd you say?" His voice rises in agitation.

I can feel his hard-on grazing over my thigh and my entire body palpitates with fear. Warren tightens his hand over my mouth until he's covering my nose, and I can't breathe.

Shit.

The sound of my name being called softly from outside startles him, and he pauses from his moronic efforts.

I shake my head free from his grip.

"Ace!" My voice shrills through the room, and I hope to God someone, anyone other than Warren heard.

"You fucking little bitch." His mouth slides over mine in a sloppy kiss, and I squirm until my torso falls off the bed. I yank my legs from underneath him and the rest of me sails to the floor.

"Shit." He lands next to me as I crawl away on all fours. "Damn bitch." He catches me by the waist as I let another cry rip from my lungs.

I knock the end table onto his back as I make a break for the window.

"Ace!" I scan the darkened patio below as I fumble with the screen.

Warren yanks me away, and I tear the screen right off the window as he slams me against the wall. I press my hands into his chest as he crushes against my body—his eyes alive with his demented lust.

"I thought you were waiting for me," he grunts, pressing into me with all his strength. "You said you weren't *ready.*" He hoists up my thighs around his waist, and my head slams against the wall. I can feel his hard-on graze against the most intimate part of me, and I let out a cry as a wave of nausea cycles through me. "Well I'm ready for you, bitch." He crashes his mouth to mine, and I turn my face.

"Don't do this." It rips from me, broken and childlike. "You're drunk. You're not this person, Warren."

He tries plunging himself into me and spears up my stomach instead.

The door bursts open.

"Reese?" Ace bolts over.

He plucks Warren off me, and I crash to the floor.

"Thank God." I stumble to my feet.

Warren and Ace wrestle and throw punches in the dark, kicking and grunting until Warren slams Ace into the wall. Ace flips him over, and they both sail right out the window.

Crap.

Ace

We plummet through the air, and the look of horror on Warren's face lets me know this is going to hurt. And, being the nice guy I am, it looks as if I'm about to break his fall.

My back slams into something soft and smooth, and I glide down a three-foot awning and onto an opened umbrella that carefully rolls me to the deck.

"Shit." I marvel as I land on my feet.

Warren slams face first into the railing next to me and flips backward onto the concrete driveway below. I glance over the rail to see him lying with his arms and legs in the running man position like some cartoon line art of a dead man.

"Fuck," I hiss as a crowd begins to gather. I hop over the railing and lower myself down to the concrete next to him.

"Ace!" Reese runs out of the house with her father and stepmother in tow, the two of them cinching their matching robes.

"Reese." I catch her in my arms and squeeze tight. "Did he hurt you?" My lips land over her ear.

"No." She swallows hard looking over at the crowd in the driveway.

Warren sits up with a blanket pulled tight around his body as Reese's stepmother tends to the scrapes on his face.

"What happened?" Her father pulls her from my grasp. "Did those two get in a fight? Do I need to call the police?" He glares at me as he says it.

"Yes, you need to call the police," she pants. "Warren broke into my room and attacked me."

"What?" Her father repels, clearly stunned as if it couldn't be true. "Warren was just probably trying to get you back to the party. He would never hurt you."

"He did. And he's naked in the event you haven't noticed." Reese clings to me even harder. "Trust me, he wanted to hurt me. And if it wasn't for Ace, he would have succeeded."

"What was Ace doing in your room?" His eyes widen with disbelief.

"He heard me screaming. Warren was trying to force himself on me. Do I have to spell it out?"

Her father darts his suspicions from me to Reese.

The McCarthy's waddle over in their slippers. Great. Here we go. Something tells me I'll be needing bail and an attorney of my own before morning.

"Look"—Reese steps into her dad—"if you don't call the police, I will. I'm not putting up with anymore of Warren's bullshit."

"*Reese.*" Her father grits it out like a threat.

"I'm going to get my things." She leans into my chest a moment. "I'll be staying with Ace. He's the one I care about, not Warren. It was never Warren." She looks up at me with tenderness locked in her eyes. "I'm in love with Ace Waterman, and I always have been."

Her stepmother crops up just in time to hear Reese's declaration, and her face bleaches out. I'm sorry if it's not the news she wanted, but in truth, it's exactly what I needed to hear and it feels damn good.

I follow Reese up to her bedroom as she throws a few things in her backpack. She kneels at the foot of her bed and slips her hand into the mattresses, retrieving a small stack of letters.

"They're from my mom." She bows her head a moment before stuffing them into the bag. She gets up and lands her arms around my waist. A sad smile pulls on her lips. "Um, I guess I sort of invited myself, but can I stay with you tonight? If not I can find Bry—"

I touch my finger to her lips. "Tonight and forever." I land a gentle kiss over her cheek and we leave the Westfield house through the back, away from the noise, the accusations and one seriously jacked up Warren McCarthy.

I'm taking Reese home, and I never want her to leave.

❧

The lights are all on at the cabin despite the fact it's well past two in the morning. As soon as Reese and I walk through the door, Neva wastes no time in scowling at us before barreling down the hall to her room.

"What the hell?" Dad stomps out in his boxers with his BB gun at the ready.

Shit.

I fill him in on what happened, and he heads toward the door and cranes his neck out at the lake.

"I'd better get out there to see if you killed anyone tonight." He shoves the BB gun in my chest with a wry smile. "How many times have I told you to keep your nose clean? But"—he looks to Reese and his features soften—"I'm glad you're okay, Reese. I don't want anyone forcing themselves on you. Excuse me while I throw on some clothes." He heads back down the hall at a quickened pace.

"Come here." I press a kiss over her head and lead her to my bedroom. I snap on the tiny desk lamp next to my bed in hopes she won't see that my closet has vomited out into the four corners of the room. "You can take the bed. I'll sleep on the floor."

"No way." She rubs her hands up over my back and settles her eyes on me with the look of genuine affection. "If you don't mind I'd like to jump in the shower—wash Warren off—but when I get out, I want to find you warming the sheets for me."

"For you? I'd set myself on fire to keep you warm." I wrap my arms back around her waist and gaze down at her with a pinch of grief. "Tell me what he did to you."

"Nothing." Her lips press together, white as plaster. "He tried to kiss me, and I artfully deflected his efforts." She glances away a moment. "Then he tried to, you know—and he couldn't."

"Shit." An instant rage pumps through me. "If I didn't kill him, I'll have to rectify that tomorrow." I'm not fucking kidding.

"Please don't." Her lips curve up one side, and her tiny dimple goes off like a comma. "I don't want you in prison because then we can't do this." She leans up on her tiptoes and lands a careful kiss over my lips. "God—Ace." Her lids flutter a moment. "You saved me." She tightens her grip around my waist and gives a hard sniff. "I'd better hop in the shower." She wipes the tears from her eyes. "I want to scrape him off my body."

"Take your time." I land another kiss on her lips, and this time we linger.

"I love you, Ace Waterman." She blinks up at me with those expectant blue eyes.

"I love you, too, Reese Westfield."

She takes off for the bathroom, and I flop down on my bed. My back is still broken from hacking down a forest, not to mention rolling out a window.

A gentle knock erupts at my door before Neva pokes her head in. She glances around for signs of Reese, and I nod toward the bathroom.

"Did he hurt her?" Her eyes glisten with tears. She's wearing a Winnie the Pooh oversized T-shirt, and her hair is combed back. Neva looks all of twelve, and a part of me is relieved she has the ability to morph back anytime she wants.

"Yes—almost," I say, pulling up on my elbows. "I want you to stay away from him. He's gutter trash."

Neva averts her eyes as if she knows better.

"I know," I grunt as I pick up my laptop. "He probably said the same thing about me."

"He didn't." She looks nervously over at my bathroom. "He said he liked you. He said he liked Reese, that he *loved* her. He thought she was his—like he owned her or something. Look, Warren is a really nice guy once you get to know him."

"He attacked her. He broke into her room and tried to force himself on her—*in* her. He's not a nice guy. And I know him pretty damn well, Neva—so does Reese."

"He was just wasted."

"*Neva.*"

The water turns off, and any second now Reese is going to find me pelting my sister with a pillow to knock some sense into her. "He tried to fuck her without her permission." I stare her down, confused as hell as to why she would stick up for his sorry ass. "You're into him, aren't you?" There's no way I'll even hint at the fact she might be in love with Warren. A thought comes to me, and I'm blindsided with rage. Warren said he was boning someone on the side, someone who was an expert at exactly what she was doing to him earlier. "Shit," I seethe. "He's using you, Neva."

"You wish." Her voice shakes. "Look, he had his reasons to overreact tonight. I filled him in on the fact she was whoring around behind his back with *you* of all people."

"What the hell is that suppose to mean?" I get up and charge at the door.

"It means she's using you. She thinks *you're* gutter trash. That's all we've ever been to her. And you can forget your fantasy that Warren is using me. What we have is special." She rushes out of the room and slams the door in my face.

Reese comes out just in time to cool my temper. Her hair is slicked back, and she's wearing nothing but a towel. I lock the door to avert another Neva inspired disaster tonight.

Reese glides on my bed and pats a spot next to her so I comply.

"It's my birthday." She lays her head on my chest, and I pull her into my lap.

"I would have bought you a thousand gifts if I knew. Some best friend I am." I bring her hand to my lips and kiss it.

"You're all the gift I need." She glances down and interlaces our fingers. "I have something to confess."

"What's that?"

"That night we went skinny dipping, and I asked you to be my fling?" She lowers her lids a moment.

"Yes." My heart thumps against my chest like a caged gorilla.

"I think maybe I misled you." Her eyes needle into mine, and she doesn't let up her gaze.

Oh shit. I hope this goes in the right direction, but if not, I'll love Reese no matter what. I'm just glad she's safe.

"I wasn't totally honest with you that night." She gives my hand a squeeze as a smile plays on her lips. "You see, for as long as I can remember I've been madly, achingly, desperately in love with you, Ace Waterman."

I blow out a breath I didn't even know I was holding. Every muscle in my body relaxes.

"I'm in love with you too, Reese. From the moment my hormones kicked into gear, I have been." I brush my lips over her neck. "All that time, all this summer it's been killing me not to tell you. I wanted to. Hell, I started to, but I would have bet my life this was a friends only deal, and I didn't want to ruin anything for you. I would die if I lost you as a friend, Reese." I stroke my fingers through her wet hair. "And I'm glad I didn't."

"I want to be with you, Ace." She blinks back tears. "Out loud, in public, at home and at school. I want everyone to know that I'm with you and nobody else." She tucks a smile into her cheek. "Is that taking things too far?"

"Not at all." A dull laugh beats over my chest. "In fact, it's not enough because I want the world"—I dot her cheek with a kiss—"the water, the forest, the fucking sky to know that we're together. I want every person on the planet to know how much I love you, Reese." My voice breaks with that last part, and I bite down hard on my lip.

"Really?" She shakes her head in disbelief, her eyes glossed with tears.

"Really." I land my mouth over hers and indulge in an achingly sweet exchange. Her tongue touches mine, and I lose it. Reese and I lounge this way for what feels like hours. I dot kisses all the way to her ear. "This is real. What we have is something special."

"Something special, for sure." Reese presses out a mile-wide smile. "I want to share something with you. I hope it doesn't freak you out." She reaches down to her bag and pulls out a stack of envelopes.

"Did you get your letter?" A spike of adrenaline courses through my veins, and I'm happy for Reese more than I would be if it were me.

"Yup." She plucks one out from the pile and waves it in the air. "My dad left it on my pillow before I went to bed. I saved it. I wanted to read it with you—safe in your arms."

I tighten my grip around her, and my throat locks up with a knot the size of a fist.

Reese pulls the letter out and smooths over it with her hand.

"*Dear Reese,*" her voice breaks as she starts, and I rock her into me.

"*Another year is under your wing and you're already so much wiser. I'm sure with your father's guidance, you're shaping up to be the woman I always knew you were destined to be, strong, independent—knowing yourself so well you'd follow your heart to the ends of the earth if you thought it was the right thing to do. Sometimes in life we're asked to make hard choices, sometimes that means not agreeing with what everyone else thinks and going out on your own to do the things you need to do, to be with the people you need to be with. A long time ago, I had two great loves. I followed my heart and chose one over the other because I knew he was the one I was truly meant to be with. I broke the other boy's heart. He accused me of not loving him because he didn't have the nice things your father did, but that wasn't true. At the end of the day, your father's warm heart and kind smile won out over the dark-haired boy who was a little rough around the edges. Some days it felt as if he liked the bottle more than he liked me. The reason I'm telling you this is because you might find yourself between a tender hearted boy and someone else, and I won't be there to tell you to follow your heart and do the right thing—to pick the boy with the kind smile because he will always love you best. Never compromise who you give your heart to. Once you give it away it's hard to get it back. Give your heart away once and to the right person—to the one who loves you more than himself and lets you know how amazing you are each day, because if I can't be there to say those very things then it's my wish for you to find someone who will.*

Be strong.

Be brave in all you do.

Put school first. Prepare yourself to be the success I know you will be. I'll be watching over you, until we meet again.

I love you with my whole heart baby girl,

Love,

Mommy"

Reese breaks down and sobs into my chest, and I cry silent tears right along with her. I pull up the sheets, holding her all night like that, the letter folded in her hand as if it were a part of her mother herself.

જ્ઞદ્ય

A light knock vibrates over the door, and I rouse to find Reese in my arms, the early morning sun spraying over her beautiful face.

"Ace?" Dad's voice thumps from the other side. "Mr. Westfield is here to see her."

"Got it," I moan, sealing a kiss over Reese's temple. Her towel dislodged in the night, and she's lying naked in my arms like a work of art. My boner tries to pop up to greet her just as she blinks into me. "Your dad's here."

"Crap." She scrambles out of bed and throws on her dress from the night before. She rakes my comb through her hair and steps into her shoes.

I hop up, and we hit the living room together.

Dad and Mr. Westfield are standing awkwardly in front of the TV. Neva's already at the kitchen table primed and ready to watch the show.

"Daddy!" Reese speeds over to him. "You're going to be late for your trip."

"Don't you worry about it. I've canceled. You're much more important to me than some business meeting." He takes up Reese in his arms, and for the first time I can see the resemblance in their eyes. "I talked to the police last night and they said anytime you want to stop by today you're welcome to press charges."

"What will happen if I do?" Reese glances over at me for a second.

"He'll most likely turn around and press charges against Ace." He gives an apologetic nod. "Warren's father will bail him out—your friend may not be so lucky." He gives a bleak smile to Dad. "But I'd do it. In fact, if you want, I'll throw the book at Warren. I'm sick at the thought of him trying to force himself on you."

"He was drunk!" Neva belts it out at the top of her lungs.

"That doesn't excuse him. And neither should you." Mr. Westfield doesn't hesitate in reprimanding my sister. It makes me like him more. "Being a drunk gets you nowhere and most certainly doesn't give you the right to put your hands on anyone." He shakes his head. "Nevertheless, the McCarthy's and I aren't seeing eye to eye on the matter, but they say they'll respect whatever we decide."

"Go ahead and throw the book at him." Reese sags into his chest. "Even if his dad does make sure he doesn't spend an hour behind bars, at least he'll learn not to mess with me or anyone else for that matter."

"Can I make a suggestion?" Dad interjects and Reese gives a nod. "In addition to whatever you've got planned, make him take an anger management course—put him in a sober living home to detox. Life will be a whole lot easier for him if he breaks down his demons right now." He glances out the window a moment. "The more you wait, the more you lose."

"That sounds good." Reese offers her dad another hug and pulls back with a solemn expression. "I read my birthday card."

"Oh, yeah?" He gives a soft smile down at her. "Any words of wisdom you'd like to share?"

"She said, be careful who you give your heart to."

"I'll have to approve of anyone you even *think* of giving your heart to." He taps her on the nose with his finger.

"It's too late." Reese comes over and wraps her arms around my waist. "I already gave it away."

"Ace Waterman, huh?" Mr. Westfield looks from Dad to me and breaks out in a gentle grin. "You're lucky I approve."

Reese bubbles with a laugh before turning to me and landing a kiss over my lips.

Mr. Westfield says his goodbyes, and Reese follows him out.

I nod over at Dad, perturbed. "What's with the send him off to rehab routine?" Not that I'm opposed to Warren getting help, it just seems like a strange recommendation from my father of all people.

"I'd a been a better man for it." He pulls a cigarette off the table and lights up. "I fucked up a long time ago, but you can be glad, or else neither you or Reese would be here today."

I glance out the window at Reese, and her mother's letter comes back to me.

"You were into her mom?"

"Into? I was the shit. She was into *me*." He takes an arrogant puff, and the smoke billows through the room. "All right. I was whooped and she wisely didn't choose me in the end. Damn near killed me. And, when she died, I almost died with her."

A brick settles in my throat. I couldn't handle losing Reese. I can't imagine what he went through.

"Is that why you and Mom split up?"

"Nope. Loved her, too. She couldn't stand me. Found someone who treated her better." He says that last part in air-quotes and the ashes from his cigarette spray over my bare foot. "Look, be good to your lady, or she'll find someone else. It's that easy." He points to Neva. "And you don't settle for shit." He grabs his patrol jacket off the hook. "I'm going to work. Keep out of trouble." He storms out the door, and I follow him outside to where Reese is standing alone, staring at the lake.

I run a string of kisses up over her face. "You want to go camping for the day?"

"Just one day?" She turns and her laughter ripples from her chest to mine. "I've got at least four before I have to get back to school." Reese tilts her head and the light shines over her hair, illuminating each strand with the fire from the morning sun.

Neva pokes her head out the screen and scowls at the two of us before pulling her lips back into something just this side of a smile. I don't blame her for not expanding. Her face might crack from the effort.

"I just want to say I'm sorry," she gives it just above a whisper as she looks to Reese. "And, if you want to go for coffee sometime, I'm okay with that."

"I'd love that." Reese takes in a hard breath as if she were fighting tears.

Neva bolts back into the house—probably to crawl back into her casket for the day.

I toss the tent in the back of the Cougar and get the cooler together before Reese and I take off for the falls.

We get up to the top and Reese throws the tent up in the air and laughs as it pops into shape, landing with a whisper over the dirt. I embed us in a clearing under the pines and scoop Reese into my arms as I take us inside our little orange love shack.

"I'm going to love you forever, Reese."

"I'm going to love you twice that long."

I land a kiss over her lips, hot as a firebrand.

Reese pulls me down over her, and I make love to her sweetly until long after the sun goes down.

12

Catching Ecstasy

Reese
One week later

The brick walkways at Yeats University are filled with bicycles and skateboards rushing by at this late hour in the afternoon. The eucalyptus trees create a wall of greenery that leads out to the expansive lawns where girls sit in clusters while boys throw a football back and forth. Classes start in a week, and I've already situated myself. I have no idea why I let Kennedy talk me into joining her when I could have spent a few more blissful days with Ace. But he mentioned he had a trip planned with Gavin so we wouldn't be together anyway. The distance is already killing me, and it's been less than twenty-four hours.

Thank God I have Brylee. She bops alongside me like a child at an amusement park, gawking at all the boys zipping by while they openly flirt with the two of us.

"This year is going to be masterfully insane." She grips my arm. Her blonde hair billows in the breeze like pale feathers. "I'm going to have orgasms by the dozen just walking to class in the morning."

"Eww, and remind me to walk in another direction." I lead us over to the giant falls that cascade over the English building into a narrow reflecting pool that runs down the center of campus. "This sort of reminds me of the Forbidden Falls." It was a special place to my mother and me, and now Ace and I will always have those amazing memories there.

We take a seat on the edge of the retaining wall, and I pluck out the envelope marked *Special Recipes*.

"You ready?" She pulls her knees to her chest, looking intently at me.

"As ready as I'll ever be."

I knew Brylee would be the best person to have by my side while I read this. Kennedy might have balked at my mother's whimsical advice. And I would have done it with Ace but a part of me is afraid she'll say something that might make me cringe in front of him.

I pull out the letter and hold it in my hand a moment. It's soft and supple as my mother's flannel nightgown. The letter unfolds with the breeze, and I'm startled to see so few words.

Brylee leans in and wraps her arm around me.

Dear Reese,

If you're reading this you have already found love. I'll pepper my birthday letters to you with advice, but here I'll give you just the bare bones. I could say, make sure he loves you, treats you right, make sure he's gentle, and has a livable sense of humor. Make sure he's kind, cooks, and cleans up after himself. Make sure he shares the remote, but I won't say any of those things. I trust you to know them. But I will say this:

Does he make you happy? Then you've caught your ecstasy.

You already know the true recipe for love. It's been buried in your heart all along—trust it.

Love you forever,

Mommy

A single tear runs from my cheek, staining the page right over the word ecstasy and makes it bleed out, stretching its inky tendrils across the parchment. That would be just like my mother, demanding I let the ecstasy take over. She had a zest for life especially in those last few weeks. She called it instant perspective. She said life liked to throw us a curve ball sometimes until we got it right. My curve ball came last year when I had to spend it away from Loveless—away from Ace. But, now, a magical summer has passed and he's mine, and yet, I still ache for him as much as I did before, if not more. For now, it looks like I'll have to catch my ecstasy on the weekends with him.

I curl in and hug the letter as if it were my mother.

Brylee is busy texting away on her phone.

"Geez, sorry I bored you," I whisper.

She looks up, her eyes stained with crimson lines. Tears roll down her face as she shakes her head. "You killed me." She lunges over and gives me a hard squeeze. "I have to run, but do me a favor—don't move. I have a surprise for you." She wipes her tears with the back of her hand. Brylee leans in and gives me a sweet kiss on the cheek. "I hope I'm as lucky as you someday." She hops up and skips off toward the bookstore.

I sink myself back into my mother's letter and touch her pretty handwriting, laying my fingers where hers once were. It's magic like this with her, my hand over hers just like in those final hours. The breeze picks up, it whistles and howls, and I hear her whisper my name clear and high like a knife over crystal.

A body sinks next to me, and a familiar cologne filters through the air. I'm afraid to glance over, afraid to break the delusion.

"Heads, we play Monopoly. Tails, we skinny dip."

I suck in a breath and look up.

"Ace!" I fall over him with a hug until I nearly knock us backward into the water.

"Let's preserve this." He helps me put my mother's letter back into the envelope.

"You drove all the way down to see me? This is why I love you." I dot his face with kisses, his eyelids, each deep well in his cheeks—I never want to stop.

"I love you, too. But actually I drove down here to ask where Beueller Hall is?" He flattens a paper that looks an awful lot like an admittance letter.

"Beueller Hall? That's my dorm." I hold his gaze hoping he'll say what I desperately want to hear.

"Good because that's my dorm, too." His dimples dig in as he holds that killer grin back just enough.

I pull him up and leap onto him with my legs tight around his waist. Ace spins me, and I lean my head back feeling dizzy and light—head over heels in love.

"I'm on the team." He melts a kiss off my neck. "Practice starts tomorrow."

"You're on the team!" I take a soft bite out of his ear. "I'm so proud of you. I always knew you had it in you."

"Thanks." He closes his eyes a moment before digging something out of his pocket. "You never answered my question." He tosses a quarter into the air and it reflects the orange sunset like a salmon swimming upstream. I catch the coin midair and hold it close to my chest like catching ecstasy.

"Now we'll never know if we were destined to take off our clothes or barter for plastic real estate." His dimples go off and seduce me without even trying.

"We are definitely destined to take off our clothes," I assure him.

"Is that so?"

"It's a promise."

"I'm glad you think so because I've got a surprise for you." His dark hair shines in the ever-dimming light. His eyes beam like blue velvet.

"Another one?" Ace was all the surprise I needed.

"I got your roommate to switch with me for the week."

"Just one week?" Elation blooms in me at the thought of all the things I can do to him in that tiny box of a room.

"It might have been a semester."

"You're a master manipulator." I tighten my legs over his hips.

"I have you, don't I?"

"You didn't manipulate a darn thing to get me. I was yours from the day you told me to stay the hell away from your marbles."

He gives a little wince. "I may have done a little manipulating."

"Like?"

"Like that day at lake. I was going to make sure it was tails no matter what. There's no way I was going miss skinny dipping with Reese Westfield."

I bounce in his arms.

"That's because you, Ace, are a brilliant man." I land a kiss over his lips. "You ready for another fake honeymoon?" I bite my lip and nod toward Beueller Hall.

"About that. I think maybe we should have a real one. You know, tear it up over in married housing—show those other newlyweds how it's done through those paper thin walls."

"Really?" A breath gets caught in my throat. The world spins in one giant kaleidoscope of color as his words swirl through my mind.

"Yes, really. Would you do me the honor of marrying me, Reese Westfield?"

"There's not another living soul I'd rather spend my life with. Yes, I'll marry you, Ace Waterman."

Ace and I seal the moment with a kiss that redefines every other kiss we've ever shared. His hungry mouth lapses into soft, sweet, soulful kisses as his tongue aches for mine to have it.

I pull back and take him in through tears.

"You make me happy," I whisper right into his lips.

"You make me insanely happy."

In a small way, my mother played a part in our love story by spurring me on to create this amazing adventure to begin with.

Our special summer was a perfect ending to the old Reese and Ace, and a perfect beginning for the new Mr. and Mrs. Waterman.

I crash my lips into his as Ace and I finally catch our ecstasy.

Thank you for reading, **Beautiful Oblivion.** If you enjoyed this book, please consider leaving a review at your point of purchase. Look for **Beautiful Illusions** (Beautiful Oblivion Book 2).

The following is a brief preview of **Beautiful Illusions**!

Beautiful Illusions

(BEAUTIFUL OBLIVION 2)

ADDISON MOORE

Edited by: Sarah Freese
Cover Design and Photograph by: Regina Wamba of
www.MaeIDesign.com
Interior Design and Formatting by: Gaffey Media

Prologue

Demi

The Past

Death is a peculiar kind of tragedy. After its wake you're either robed in immortality or plunged into eternal darkness. The living never quite know how deeply to mourn. The speculation is ours but the judgment is not. By the tender age of fifteen, I had mastered death's destruction and racked up a body count. I had killed the only two people who ever truly loved me—my mother and my father.

Years ago, when my parents married, they built their home from the ground up. They unleashed their wildest imaginations and created a legacy for our family so magnificent in girth and stature it dwarfed the other embarrassingly large homes that surrounded us. They had grand plans of filling it with children, four girls, four boys. My parents dreamed big and lived bigger. They christened our home *Winter Haven* because in the hard Connecticut winters it was just that. The icicles bled off the eaves like a fairytale, and the woodland creatures flocked to the many feeders my mother laid out. But any ideas of mass procreation that my parents harbored were cut short once I was born—their only child, a girl. I slashed my way into this world, barreling in with a curse on my back that left my mother clinging to life less than five minutes after I arrived. She didn't make it.

Growing up it was just my father and me. He focused his white-hot attention over my every move, and it was nirvana. I knew no other existence. The sun rarely shined over Winter Haven. The sky held a perennial cloud cover, thick as grief. It pressed over our home like a bruise. Later, my stepmother, Nora, and her son, Josh, slid into our lives swift as demons, after all, that's what they proved to be.

We lived in a world of shadows. My father said my mother took the sun with her and that I was his little bit of sunshine. That was his pet name for me right up until the day I killed him.

Then came a season of darkness, of haunted echoes, wild cries, of howls and aches—the knife of my parents' deaths plunging into my broken heart night after night. Nora and Josh had taken the throne at Winter Haven. I was nothing more than her battering post, his shiny new plaything.

Josh has a few years on me. He's gorgeous and buff, every cheerleader's dream. He has flocks of wealthy friends and no shortage of beautiful girls that linger at the house well into the night. But when all is said and done, the party is over, and all of his drunk cohorts speed off in their expensive Italian sports cars, it's my bed he crawls into. I didn't ask for it. I didn't stop it either.

"I just want to talk." His voice is raspy, unrecognizable. He's panting. His eyes are glossed over in an animalistic manner. "I get it. I get how much you hurt, Demi. My own father abandoned me."

The knife twists just enough with his words. My father did abandon me. I was so eager to buy the lie.

Josh slips into the bed beside me until his body is pressed close to mine. My heart thumps into my throat, steady as a jackhammer. I'm quivering, scared, excited. I can't remember the last time I was this close to another person. A part of me craves to touch him, to have him touch me. And he does. Josh slithers his viper-like arms around me, and soon I'm enveloped in the cloud of vodka spewing from his lungs. I memorize the way it feels to have someone hold me again as I take in a deep lungful of his toxic breath. The truth is I had died right alongside my father, and now I'm finally breathing again. Maybe Josh is the one who would resuscitate my corpse.

Holding me led to his lips finding mine. Before I knew it, his fingers were between my legs. Eventually, Josh pried me open and thrust his way into my life. Night after night, I was his dirty little secret. He wouldn't say two words to me at school, after all, he was a senior and I was a lowly freshman. But late at night, while the world slept, he became a regular visitor to my bedroom. At fifteen I didn't know what to think, or how to react. All I knew was this gorgeous boy, who the entire school worshiped, who the girls stabbed each other in the back for, was interested in me. He wanted me. Once again I was the object of someone's white-hot attention. No, there wasn't any love. I was simply trying to fill the gaping hole in my heart my father left. But none of those nightly visits were ever enough to fill it.

I missed my father, and strangely enough, my mother, too. All I had left of them was Winter Haven, an empty shell of who we once were—who we could have been. They made it powerful and beautiful, but they died, took their beauty and power with them and left me alone with a woman who openly wished I were buried too. Nora played on my grief. She assigned me a psychiatrist. I had more labels thrown at me than the canned food aisle at the supermarket, more pills to swallow than sand on the shore.

As I grew older, I joined the august body of Mitchell University, but things had already hit a boiling point at home. Nora wasn't about to let me too far off the leash. The idea of living on campus set her greedy teeth on edge. The more I pushed, the more she smothered me with narcotics. Nora's nickname for me was garbage. She threw a Bible at my head, and I read that sacred tome from cover to cover. Then I prayed. I prayed God would strike dead both Nora and Josh and free me from this insolent hell. I prayed He'd change them—do the unthinkable and change *me* to accept them—send outside help to free me from the prison that my home had become. Her increasing cruelty grew like a weed and choked out of me any glimmer of hope that she would ever change, that I would ever survive her tyranny. An open grave waited for me if I stayed at Winter Haven. And with each passing day, Nora became more eager to push me in it.

God wasn't answering my prayers.

I was down to one alternative, answering them myself.

So I did the only thing I could.
Run.

1

Lost in Loveless

Demi

Three and a half years later...

"Can I help you?" He's dripping wet, straight from the shower with a towel draped low on his waist, and I gasp because he has the face of a god, the body of a demon, and the eyes of the bluest sky. He's built like a linebacker, and he's way too young to ever fit into the stereotypical johns I'm forever hearing Eva complain about.

His lips twitch. His eyes give an amused smile as if confirming the fact he knows exactly how wickedly gorgeous he is. My body ignites like a flare. My neck heats, brightening with color the way it does when I'm having a visceral response.

"The door was unlocked, so I let myself in." My voice wobbles, and I cringe. My fingers shake as I clutch at the oversized feather duster in my hand. I'm not used to feeling out of control. I'm usually abhorrent to anything that makes me feel that way, but something in me refuses to hate him over something so petty.

I snatch the edge of my skirt and give a little curtsey in the ridiculous French maid costume I've donned. It isn't the cheap kind that reeks of polyester and Halloween. It's the real deal with a corset that shows off my assets, a thick, layered tulle skirt that stands erect like cardboard just past my hips. If anything, this getup makes its naughty intentions crystal clear. Reeva, my so-called boss, provides nothing but the best—her clients expect nothing less.

My legs shake so hard I lean against the bedframe in an effort to anchor myself from jittering across the room. It's not every day my nerves are shot to hell. Then again it's not every day I'm turning tricks for a dollar.

He gives a wry smile. My insides pinch at how alarmingly attractive he is. I'm not one to chase after gorgeous men. I'm more the get drunk, fuck 'em, and leave 'em type before I ever really get a good idea of what they look like. How they look is never all that important. It's the end game that counts—the part where they make me feel alive if just for a second. But that was before, when I was still giving it away for free. This is different. Tonight I cross a line that I can never recover from.

"It's pretty bad out there. I'm glad you're inside." His cut features make it hard to look away. Something about those hypnotic, glowing eyes magnetize me, and I'm sure every other woman, to him. "But you don't look too prepared for what's being billed as the snowstorm of the century." He leans in, inspecting me from head to toe and his sizzling gaze feels as if it's tearing a fire line up my body. He's not the type of man I'm usually paired with, but then, this is the first time I'm advancing to a bodily exchange for cash. Up until today, Reeva kept me as a "casual" which entailed little more than putting on a nice dress and showing up for charity functions with wealthy perverts. It wasn't big bucks, but it was enough to keep a roof over my head at Reeva's house of depravity, at least it was up until now. She made it clear there was no more room at the inn for casual girls. If I wanted to maintain a toasty home for the winter, I needed to pull my weight, and somewhere between my desperation and her smooth talk, I agreed to sell my body and soul to the devil herself.

"Look"—he nods past me, and his jaw tightens making him that much more alarmingly attractive—"I've got a pair of jeans and a T-shirt lying on the bed. If you want to toss them over, I'd more than appreciate it."

I eye them as if they were snakes. What the hell does he want his clothes for?

I spot my bag lying right over them, wrinkling them into oblivion. They're probably expensive couture jeans that, if sold on eBay, could feed an entire starving village in some third world country. If that's the case I've just demoted Hot Towel Guy to douchebag. Personally, I'm allergic to wealthy assholes even though my own father had enough billions to stack to the moon. My father was a saint—too bad he didn't raise one.

My fingers shake as I get straight to the task of folding them but note they're just Levis, dirty at that. His T-shirt reads, Jackson Lumber, *We hack it and stack it.*

"You don't need to do that." He steps forward, and, instinctually, I pull my shoulders back. My stomach quivers until it feels as if I'm going to be sick. Truthfully, if he weren't half as handsome, if he didn't have that gentle look in his eyes, if this were some fifty-year-old sleazebag waiting to ravage me with his greasy intent, I would have vomited minutes ago. The worse thing I ever did was agree to advance my standing in Reeva's twisted harem. I should have said no. I should have happily frozen to death in my Honda rather than die of some self-imposed STD. Although Reeva swears up and down her clients are clean, yet somehow I'm still disbelieving. God knows anything that comes from Reeva's mouth is far from gospel. Not that this one looks disease-riddled. In fact, he looks anything but.

"Did Ace put you up to this?" He picks up his shirt and slips it on. The fabric catches on his serrated muscles, and he kneads it down with his hands. His voice is smooth and mellow as a butter cream sky. I could fall asleep just from the sound. It reminds me of my father's, and my heart warms at the idea. My dad didn't have a care in the world. But that was back when we had each other, and now, all he has is a casket, and I have a hole in my heart the size of my daddy.

"Is Ace coming, too?" It wouldn't surprise me too much if this turns into some frat house spectacle. God, I'm going to kill Eva for saying hello to me in that greasy diner all those years ago—but something about her charmed me, and she's been my best friend ever since.

"Somehow I doubt that." He shakes his head with a laugh buried in his chest. "Ace likes to pull one over on me every now and again. And I'm long overdue, so I'm not too surprised. I'm just sorry you got dragged into this."

Perfect. This is nothing more than a prank, and I'm the butt of the joke. Figures. A guy like this probably has them lined up around the block. The only thing he ever has to pay for is dinner.

"I don't know anything about Ace. All I know is Reeva said this was the place to be."

He arches his brow while taking back his jeans, and my insides tighten because he's so gorgeous that I'm about to beg him to have me regardless. Those abs, those pecs, those full lips—my mouth is already demanding a taste. I don't see why not. Reeva always takes payment from the clients upfront, so someone out there might as well get their money's worth.

What am I saying? I should grab my things and run like hell. I'm about to demote myself from part time slut to fulltime prostitute. I bet my father is looking down and thanking God he's cold in a grave so he doesn't have to hear of this. But, then again, his death is the reason I'm here to begin with.

I glance out the window as the snow continues to pile up on the road like bolts of cotton batting. Chains or no chains, there's no way my twenty-three-year-old Honda Civic will ever make it down that hill. I'll probably have to sleep in the car tonight. Looks like the universe hasn't taken freezing to death off the table just yet.

"I don't know what the hell Ace is thinking." He makes his way into the bathroom and leaves the door open. I try not to look, but as soon as I hear the soft thud of his towel hit the floor, I peer over and catch him jumping into his jeans, pulling them up over his perfect bare ass, and my adrenaline skyrockets because I'm fairly certain I've just seen far more than he was willing to show.

I glance around at the tiny cabin. It's smaller than a thumbtack. Reeva said it was a boathouse, so I fully expected a stack of canoes or at least a rusted out aluminum vessel. For the entire drive up the mountain, I envisioned myself being paddled with the fat end of an oar. I'm not jaded. I don't expect any one of Reeva's triple X clients to *make love* to me, which would be a joke to begin with because true love is for fairytales, and, for damn sure, I don't live in one of those. Hooker, prostitute, call it what you want—at the end of the day I'm shaping up to be quite the whore. My stepbrother, Josh, was right, he nailed it just like he nailed me for the hell of it. Our parents married when we were teenagers, and as much as I protested the idea of him sneaking into my bed, in a sick way, I wanted it. Josh had every girl in a fifty-mile radius panting. I thought it was a dream, the quarterback from school, with his dark hair and deep dimples—interested in me, of all people. He quickly made it a habit to slip into my room at night, and one disaster led to designer boots—to purses that cost more than my entire wardrobe, to scarves imported from Paris, and I thought that's what love was. That it could be bought and sold as a commodity. I took his gifts because I thought I was his girlfriend, but he set me straight pretty quick. I was stupid then, just like I'm being now.

The Towel God emerges with his caramel hair combed neatly back, his skin still ruddy from the shower and motions for me to have a seat on the bed while he pulls out a chair for himself at the tiny table, hardly big enough for two.

I'm his for the night if he wants me, but something tells me he won't. This is just one of those cruel tricks life plays. I can practically hear Josh laughing. *See what you can't have, Demi? You can never have a man like this. It's nothing but a joke to think he'd ever want you in his bed.*

I take a seat on the edge of the mattress, slightly pissed because now all I want to do is run into the blizzard that's reeking havoc outside the door.

"What's your name?" His voice is tender. His features soften as if he's sorry for me, and it only seems to enrage me. I like the rage, the way it warms me from the inside. Oddly, it's been the rage in my life that feels most stable since I lost my father.

"De—" Crap. I almost broke Reeva's number one rule, no real names. But something in me doesn't want to lie to him. Instead, I want to fall to my knees and sob out my entire life story and hope he'll somehow make things better—bring my father back from the dead and reverse the nightmare that caused my world to unravel. I smirk at the idea of myself as a damsel in distress. The thought disgusts me. I hate how weak he's rendered me without even trying. I gave up on people and relationships right after I left Winter Haven for good. The world is full of people like Nora and Josh, and I, for sure, want nothing to do with them. Except for Eva—for whatever reason I gave her a pass. "It's Emmy," I say with a renewed confidence. "My name is Emmy."

"Gavin." He leans forward and offers his hand. His fingers are thick and rough as if they've seen more of Mother Earth than they have the monetary exchange. His hand clasps mine, strong and tight—powerful, the way I imagine it feels closing your fingers over an exposed electrical wire. I couldn't let go if I wanted.

"Did you say, Gavin?" Something in me rattles. "You mean *Warren*?"

"No, I'm pretty sure it's Gavin."

Shit. I pull the feather duster to my chest in an effort to hide my overexposed cleavage.

"Sorry, I must have gotten lost." God, it all makes sense now. "I was supposed to meet someone else." I jump to my feet and riffle for my keys.

"Warren McCarthy?"

"Yes." My body jolts as if I were mildly electrocuted. Crap. Rule number two: Never tell anyone your client's name. But then I was never big on rules. "Is this his boathouse?"

His features harden. The warm smile he held a minute ago dims. "It's the next one over." He runs those clear summer sky eyes over my body, up and down, judging me as if the pieces had come together, and now he understands that I wasn't impersonating some wayward hussy. I was the real deal.

"I guess I'd better get going." I cinch my bag in one hand, my feathered friend in the other. "And to think, I almost dusted the wrong chandelier." He doesn't laugh at my lame attempt to add levity to the situation. I stride past him as if I were in a hurry, but it takes every ounce of willpower for me to open that door. The hard bite of winter blasts its way in and licks me in places that winter and its icy tongue should never venture.

Gavin springs up between me and the barbaric weather conditions, effectively blocking the wind from having its way with me.

He glances down at the feather duster in my hand. "You won't find a chandelier next door, Emmy," he says it far more somber than it ever is sarcastic. His eyes plead with mine in a strange way that I've never seen before, as if I've intentionally hurt him, as if he's hurting for *me* as much as it is I'm hurting on the inside. "But something tells me you're not going to get a lot of cleaning done."

And there it is—his judgment falling over me like an anvil.

The last thing my stepmother said to me the morning I left was *you're the worst of all sinners, a whore who seduces innocent young men and leads them astray. That red painted mouth of yours is nothing but an open grave. You look cheap, Demi.* Those didn't even make the shortlist of hurtful things my stepmother has told me over the years but that last one stuck out. What I really heard was *you're cheap, Demi.* And I used it as a battle cry the last three years to justify all of my piss-poor decisions. Desperation only gets you so far. You need a catalyst to ride before you demote yourself to becoming something less than human, and, for me, that came on the coattails of years of listening to Josh and my stepmother, Nora. After all, I was the reason my father was no longer living. I think I died right along with him in that car—at least I wish I did.

Gavin pumps a dry smile and steps over to the tiny kitchenette before returning with a sponge and dishtowel.

"You might need this." He bears into me with those intense mournful eyes because, for whatever reason, he's decided to play along. "I have a broom you could borrow. It could double as a weapon." His brow arches, slightly amused, but there's a layer of sadness just beneath. "Knowing Warren, you'll need it."

A car barrels down the street, and I step onto the frozen porch to see a gleaming, black Mercedes take the turn before it disappears just past the evergreens and out of sight for good.

"Warren *Senior*?" Gavin steps in behind me, and the heat radiates from his body, warming me. The scent of fresh soap and spice emanates from him, and it takes all of my willpower not to lean in.

"If he's older than fifty, he meets the profile." I touch my hand to my forehead and cringe at the things Reeva is going to do when she finds out I screwed this one up. She made it a point to let me know she pawned me off as a virgin—that he paid *twice* as much as he did the last time he used the service. And now I've put a dent in her reputation. The last girl that dinged her questionable social standing was Lenora Woods. She went out on a call one night, and we never saw her again. I asked Reeva about her, but she simply shrugged and said girls take off all the time. It was the furthest thing from the truth, and we both knew it, but I played along, and now here I am on the verge of some black hole that Reeva arranges for girls to get sucked into. These were dangerous people, and this was a dangerous game.

A spurt of desperation bursts from me. "I have to get in touch with him." I turn and land my arms over his chest, stealing the warmth from his body. "Can you tell me where he went?" My voice quivers, my body shakes, and it has nothing to do with the fact I'm subjecting myself to subzero temperatures in this ridiculous state of undress.

"*Whoa.*" He gently pulls the curtain of hair from my eyes and hitches it behind my ear. Something about that tender act endears me to him even more than before. "There's a big Christmas party tonight, sort of a community-wide event. He'll be there." His cheek rises, but Gavin is slow with his sad smile. "I'll take you under one condition."

"Anything."

"You'll be my date."

Gavin

The snow comes down in drifts like sheets pulled violently from some oversized bed in the sky. I help Emmy up the Westfield walkway to the festively decorated doors with their golden wreathes and miles of fresh garland, but Emmy outshines any opulence the Westfield house might have to offer tonight or any other night. She's dressed to the nines and looks gorgeous as hell. I let her borrow one of Zoey's dresses. My sister still has half her closet at the cabin, and, every now and again, she threatens to pick it up. She's due back in Loveless at some point during her winter break. Zoey is a freshman at a private university where she managed to score a full ride, and I'm damn proud of her. I cover most of her food and housing. It's not easy, but I'd die trying to give her the best education possible. I know my parents wouldn't have wanted it any other way.

"You sure no one will mind?" Emmy is shaking twice as bad as she was back at the boathouse.

I thought I was dreaming when I stepped out of the shower to find the most beautiful woman I've ever laid eyes on waiting for me, dressed to impress with her feather duster poised to touch me in all the right places—only it wasn't me she was looking to touch. Her hair is spun gold, and her eyes shine crimson and fire, mostly because she seems angry with the world, but I'd be lying my way into hell if I didn't say it made me want her that much more. I'm used to girls playing nice around me. They make it real easy for me to land them horizontal with their overtly flirtatious giggles, their sweet-as-frosting adulation. There's usually not a thing I can do wrong, but, with Emmy, it feels as if there's not a thing I can do right. Maybe it's the challenge she brings to the table that caught my attention. Who am I kidding? Everything about her has brought me to the table. I predict by the end of the night, I'll be on my knees begging for crumbs.

"I promise, no one will mind." I press my hand into the small of her back and take in her sweet scent. Emmy might have an icy air about her, but she holds the scent of warm vanilla. It's taking everything in me not to bury my face in her hair. "Besides, this is a community event. And if Loveless is anything, it's about fostering togetherness." The deep pockets around here like any excuse for a chance to network. There's a smattering of tourists from the local chalet. The Loveless Christmas party is as much a marketing ploy as it is an attempt to make the residents feel good about being trapped on this overgrown rock.

Her dark eyes widen, brown and red, the color of glossy mahogany. I make a mental note to mix that exact shade for my next stain. There's a bear I've been working on, carving my heart out trying to bring it to life, for the last three months. It's just about finished and ready for a good coat. I can't wait to bless it with the color of Emmy's eyes.

"Loveless sounds like a great place." Her lips curl down at the sides. "Anyway, I should probably just get in there and speak to him." She nods toward the door as if it were Warren Senior himself. Damn pervert. Just the thought of him touching her—*looking* at her—makes me want to bash his skull through a window. His son was just arraigned on assault charges, not that it amounted to much. They put him under house arrest for a few months, and he's already out on the prowl again. He lost his spot on the rowing team back at Yeats because the university didn't want any part in the controversy or his sorry ass. But, nevertheless, he and the old man look like they share the same loose moral code. I guess the apple doesn't fall far from the perverted tree.

"How about we grab a bite first?" I lead her in, and the sound of Christmas carols lights up the air. The smell of roast beef sings a love song right to my stomach, and if I pace myself just right, I'll be hitting up the buffet more than once this evening. But the last thing I want to happen tonight is for Emmy to get dragged into some dark corner to satisfy Warren McCarthy's middle aged, very much married, "needs."

Acknowledgments

BIG thank you to my awesome readers who have been so kind and supportive. I cannot tell you enough that you are like family to me.

Thank you to Christina Kendler you really do save me time and time again! Hugs and kisses for that. I think it warrants an extra gift at Christmas. Rachel Tsoumbakos, your proofreading superpowers astound me. You are word ninja that demands honor. Sarah Freese, where to even begin? I love that you push me to go further and fix scenes that need adjustment (read murderous hacking sprees). And in the event I never tell you, I think you're always right. No, really, I do.

To my family, I'm just glad that most of you remember what I look like. Also, thank you for letting me use the dining room table as my office. It makes it totally reasonable for me to snack All. Day. Long.

And finally, to Him who sits on the throne; worthy is the Lamb. Your word is manna for my hungry soul. I owe you everything.

About the Author

Addison Moore is a *New York Times, USA Today*, and *Wall Street Journal* bestselling author who writes contemporary and paranormal romance. Her work has been featured in *Cosmopolitan* Magazine. Previously she worked as a therapist on a locked psychiatric unit for nearly a decade. She resides on the West Coast with her husband, four wonderful children, and two dogs where she eats too much chocolate and stays up way too late. When she's not writing, she's reading.

Feel free to visit her at:

http://addisonmoorewrites.blogspot.com
Facebook: Addison Moore Author
Twitter: @AddisonMoore
Instagram: @authorAddisonMoore

CPSIA information can be obtained at www.ICGtesting.com
Printed in the USA
LVOW11s1529300616

494763LV00006B/603/P